Copyright © 2016 by Robert A. Curedale

Second edition January 2016

Published by Design Community College Inc.
https://dcc-online.selz.com

Design Community College Inc.
PO Box 1153
Topanga CA 90290 USA

info@curedale.com
Designed and illustrated by Robert Curedale

ISBN-10: 1-940805-20-1
ISBN-13: 978-1-940805-20-7

DESIGN THINKING
PROCESS & METHODS GUIDE
2ND EDITION

Robert Curedale

PUBLISHED BY DESIGN COMMUNITY COLLEGE LOS ANGELES
https://dcc-online.selz.com

"

Design Thinking is all about creating intelligent change

INTRODUCTION

Over the last decade design has moved from being a tool of marketing towards being an imperative for intelligent change. It has become less about making people want things through advertising and marketing and more about making things people want through good design that answers human need. This is Design Thinking and it is a better way of thinking. It is less about ego, fame and desire and more about collaboration and human need. It is a honest approach to designing things the world needs.

In 2008 I established a number of social networks for working designers. These groups have grown to over one million members and may now constitute the largest global network of working designers. I have been spreading the word about the value of Design Thinking through this huge network, presenting on-line classes and publishing books about Design Thinking. This book incorporates the evolution of ideas that has happened in the field over the years since I published the first book "Design Thinking Process and Methods Manual"

There has been a rapidly growing interest in Design Thinking. Recently large corporations including Pepsi and IBM announced major initiatives to train their staff and adopt Design Thinking. Design Thinking is an approach to designing products, services, architecture, spaces and experiences as well as complex systems of these things that is being quickly adopted by designers. The list of world's leading brands that are using it has grown considerably from the introduction in my first book and now includes such as GE, Pepsico, Target, Deloitte Innovation, SAP, Singapore And Australian Governments, Procter And Gamble, Whirlpool, Bayer, BMW, DHL, Daimler, Deutsche Bank, Philips Electronics, Infosys, AirBnB, Autodesk, Bank Of America, Mayo Clinic, Steelcase, Black & Decker, Mattel, Microsoft, Miele, Airbus, Panasonic, Shell Innovation Research, Glaxosmithkline, Nike, Cisco, Jetblue, Kaiser Permanent, Unilever, Electrolux Arup, IDEO and Intuit. It is being taught at leading universities including Stanford, Yale and Harvard.

Design Thinking creates practical and innovative solutions to problems. It drives repeatable innovation and business value. Design Thinking can be used to develop a wide range of products, services, experiences as well as design and business strategy. It is an approach that can be applied by anyone. Design Thinking can also be fun. I hope that you will find this third book useful.

"

Design Thinking is about changing from:

Making people want things [through advertising and marketing] to making things people want

PIETER BAERT
Service consultant

CONTENTS

Introduction

Contents

17 **Design Thinking case studies**
18   Some organizations learning and applying Design Thinking
20   Public service organizations using design thinking
22   Pepsi
        AirBnB
23   Ericsson
        Singapore Government
24   Proctor & Gamble
        Intuit
25   Pulse
        IBM
26   infosys
        Siemens ct china
27   GE healthcare
        Embrace
28   IBM

31 **The history of Design Thinking**
33   Introduction
34   Related Design Movements
35   Design thinking time line

45 **Principles of Design Thinking**
47   Design Thinking process
48   What is Design Thinking?
        Who invented Design Thinking?
        Evidence supporting the value of Design Thinking
        Why use Design Thinking?
49   Who can use Design Thinking
        20 ways Design Thinking is being used
        Characteristics of design thinkers
        Evolution of Design Thinking
        Attributes of Design Thinking
        The ten faces of innovation

49 Design Thinking process
50 Why Design Thinking should be at the core of your design
51 and Business strategies
Design Thinking is gathering traction in business
52 The design ladder
54 20 ways Design Thinking can be used
55 Characteristics of Design Thinkers
56 Evolution of Design Thinking
57 Attributes of Design Thinking
59 Ten faces of innovation
60 Design Thinking process
61 Some benefits of Design Thinking
62 Ideas for using Post-it-notes
65 Design Thinking Process
67 Process Models
70 Where can design methods be used?
75 Empathy
78 Shoshin: the beginner's mind
81 Diversity
83 Design Thinking spaces
84 Context
Fresh eyes
Cross pollination
Balanced design
85 Cross disciplinary collaboration
Collective intelligence
Culture of prototyping
86 Unrecognized and unmet needs
Curiosity
87 Feedback from stakeholders at each stage
88 Human-centered
Optimism
89 Storytelling
Actions speak loader than words
Build iterations
90 Be visual
Continuous learning
Inexpensive mistakes

92   Toolbox
          Evidence based design
93   Wicked Problems
          Analogous Situations
          Evidence based design
          Re framing the problem
          Future oriented
94   Everyone can contribute
95   Focus on people
          Get physical
          Take considered risks
          Use the tools
          Learn to see and hear
96   Team collaboration
          Repeatable innovation
          Combine analytical and creative thinking
          Design Thinking is a balanced approach

100   **Thinking styles**
          Abductive thinking
          Deductive thinking
          Inductive thinking
          Critical thinking
          Design Thinking
          Analytical thinking
          Creative or intuitive thinking
          Integrative thinking
          How to use integrative thinking
104   Divergent thinking
          Convergent thinking

107   **Warming up**
108   Innovation diagnostic
109   Innovation diagnostic test
111   How well did you score?

112   **Warming up methods**
       Action Plan
114   Warming up exercises introduction
115   Common ground
116   Desert Island
117   Diversity
118   Expectations
119   Hopes and Hurdles
120   Interviewing warming up exercise
121   Jumpstart storytelling
122   Milestones

125   **Discovery frameworks**
       Ethnographic frameworks Introduction
128   AEIOU
129   LATCH
130   Spool
132   Nine Dimensions
133   POSTA

135   **Research Empathize Discover**
137   Assemble your team
       Define your target audience
138   Team building exercises
       Share what you know
       Identify what you need to know
       Uncover needs
139   Define the goals
       Uncover peoples stories

Discovery Methods
141   Affinity diagram
142   How to create an affinity diagram
144   Anthropump
147   Behavioral map
149   Benchmarking

150   Cultural inventory
151   Cultural probes
152   Camera Journal
153   Day in the life
154   Diary study
155   Design workshops
156   Design charrette
157   Creative toolkits
158   Empathy probes
160   Empathy tools
161   Eyetracking
163   Five Whys
164   Fly-on-the-wall
165   Focus groups
166   **Interviewing**
167   Interview guide
169   Contextual inquiry
171   Contextual laddering
172   Conversation cards
173   Emotion cards
174   E-mail
175   Extreme user
176   Group
177   Guided storytelling
178   Man in the street
179   Naturalistic group
180   Octogon
182   One-on-one
183   Photo elicitation
184   Structured
185   Unstructured
186   Telephone
187   Magic thing
188   Method bank
189   Mobile diary study
190   **Observation**
191   Covert
192   Direct

193   Indirect
194   Non participant
195   Participant
197   Overt
198   Structured
199   Unstructured
200   Personas
202   Personal inventory
203   Shadowing
204   Stakeholder map
206   Through other eyes
207   WWWWWH
208   Some WWWWWH questions

209   **Visualization tools**
212   Bar chart
214   Linking diagram
217   Onion map
219   Process diagram
220   Radar chart
222   Venn diagram

225   **Synthesis**
     Actionable insights
     User need statement
     Point of view statement

229   **Synthesis Methods**
     Assumption surfacing
231   Backcasting
232   Benefits map
235   Blue Ocean Strategy
236   C-Box
238   Context map
240   Decision rings
243   Emotional Journey Map
244   Empathy Maps
246   How to create an empathy Map

248 Experience maps
251 Fishbone diagram
252 Force field analysis
254 Future wheel
256 Maslow's Hierarchy of Needs
258 Mind maps
260 Perceptual map
262 Service blueprints
264 Sustainability map

267 **Design Brief and Point of View**
269 BHAG
270 Boundary examination
271 Checklist for environmentally responsible design
272 Goal grid
274 Reframing the problem
275 Reframing Matrix
277 Premortem
279 SWOT
281 Sample SWOT Questions

283 **Ideation**
284 User Stories scenarios and cases

286 **Ideation methods**
10 x 10 sketch method
288 Dot voting
289 Scenarios
292 **Brainstorming**
Refreshments
Facilitating
Rules for brainstorming
Post-it voting
Group review
Preparing for brainstorming
Create a strategy
Choosing a technique
The environment

Methods of arranging ideas

Brainstorming Methods

295	101 method
296	635 method
298	Aoki Method
299	Bodystorming
300	Boundary shifting
301	Brainwriting
303	Disney method
305	Dot voting
307	Heuristic ideation
308	Idea advocate
309	KJ method
310	Lotus Method
312	Out of the box
313	NHK Method
314	Nominal group method
315	Nyaka
316	Objectstorming
318	Personal
319	Personas brainstorming
320	Pin cards
321	Related context
322	Resources
323	Rolestorming
324	SCAMPER
325	SCAMPER questions
326	Scenarios
327	Sensorial method
329	Word lists
331	Semantic intuition
332	STP method
333	Six thinking hats
334	Synectics

337   **Prototype**

Reality check
Identify stakeholders for feedback
Review questions
Seek feedback
Create low fidelity prototypes
Low fidelity prototype kit

Prototype Methods

339   Appearance prototype
341   Dark horse prototype
343   Generative prototyping
345   Low fidelity prototyping
346   Low Fidelity prototype kit
347   Pictives
349   Role playing
351   Storyboards
353   Video prototyping
355   Wire-framing

357   **Test**

Do a reality check
Identify stakeholders for feedback
Obtain feedback
Design review questions
Test
Refine and test again

Testing methods

359   Heuristic evaluation
360   Make a video
361   Think out loud
363   Wizard of Oz

365   **Iterate**

369 **Implement & Deliver**
370   Test and evaluate
             Finalize your production design
             Build external partnerships
             Sign off from stakeholders
             Make your production samples
             Authorize vendors
             Launch
             Pre-launch
             Mid-launch
             Post-launch
371   Deliver
             Did you meet it's goals?
             Measure success
             Ways to measure success:
             What could be improved?
             Define next vision

373 **Exercises**
374   Design Thinking resources
375   Low fidelity prototype kit
376   Warming up
377   Interviews
378   Identify key stakeholders
379   Research questions
380   Synthesis questions
381   Your answers
382   SWOT
383   Point of view questions
384   Ideation instructions
385   Prototype
386   Test questions
387   Iteration questions

389 **Templates**
390   Personas
391   Storyboards
392   635 brainstorm

393   Context map
394   Competitor matrix
395   Evaluation matrix
396   Perceptual map
397   Spider diagram
398   Influence map
399   Design thinking rubric

400 **On-line programs**

402 **Other titles**

406 **Index**

414 **About the author**

DESIGN THINKING CASE STUDIES

SOME ORGANIZATIONS LEARNING AND APPLYING DESIGN THINKING

3M
Accenture
AdaptAir
Adobe
Ahold
AirBnB
Airbus
Amway
ANZ Bank
Center for Entrepreneurial Leadership at African Leadership Academy
Apple
Arup
Australian Taxation Office
AutoDesk
Bank of America: Keep the Change
Bayer
Bayteq
BBVA Bancomer
Bertelsmann
BMW
Bristol Maids
Celfinet
CERN IdeaLab
Charité Berlin, BCRT/BSRT, Biothinking Program
Charité: Onkolizer
Chick-fil-a
Cincinnati Children's Hospital Medical Center
Cisco
Citrix
Clorox Company
Condair: JS Humidifiers
Creuznacher

D.Light
Daimler
Datascope Analytics
Deloitte digital
Deloitte Innovation
Derdack
Deutsche Bahn
Deutsche Bank
DHL
D-Lab: Charcoal
D-Rev: ReMotions's JaipurKnee
EBS Business School
Electrolux: Design Lab
Embrace Infant Incubator
Everest
Flad Architects
Fraport
Future Balloons
FutureGov
GE
GE: GE Adventure Series
GE: Healthcare
Georgia Tech
GlaxoSmithKline
Godrej: Chotu Kool
Google: Google Ventures
GoPro
IBM
IKB Innsbrucker Kommunal Betriebe
IKEA + IDEO
Infosys
Intuit Inc.
Israel Palestine Center for Research
Janssen-Cilag
JetBlue
JLL-Jones Lang LaSalle

Juntos Finanzas
Kaiser Permanente
Kickstart
Lambeth Council
Mappy
Marriot 4 Seasons
Mattel: Platypus
Mayo Clinics
Metro AG
Metropolitan Group
MeYouHealth
Microsoft
Miele
Miraclefeet Brace
Nasdaq
Naval Undersea Warfare Center
(NUWC) Newport
Nestle?
New York Times
NIKE
Novabase
Onclaude
P&G
P&G früher)/ Blackberry
P&G: Consumer Products: Swiffer
Panasonic: Oxyride
PepsiCo
Pfizer: Nicorette
Philips Electronics (PHG)
Pillpack
Ploom
Pulse
Pulse
PwC Australia
RadBoud REshape
Ravel
San Francisco's Department of

Emergency Management
SAP
SAP CSR + Sankara eye care
Schröder und Partner
Sennheiser
Sense Consulting Ltd. Croatia
Shell Innovation Research
Shimano
Siemens
St. Joseph Health
Stanley Works: Black & Decker
Steelcase
Sternin Positive Deviance Initiative
SunCorp
Swisscom
Telekom
THALES
The Australian Center for Social
Innovation
The Good Kitchen
Three Twins Organic Ice Cream
Toyota
Unilever
University of Pittsburgh Medical
Center
US - Presidential Innovation
Fellows Program
VF Corporation
VisioSpring
Vlisco
VW
Whirlpool
WikiMedia
Xing
ZOO Hannover

SOME PUBLIC SERVICE ORGANIZATIONS USING DESIGN THINKING

AMERICAS
BRAZIL
Brazilian Innovation Agency,
www.finep.gov

CANADA
MaRS Discovery District,
www.marsdd.com/

MEXICO
Laboratorio para la Ciudad,
http://labplc

PANAMA
Autoridad Nacional para la
Innovación Guber

(AIG), www.innovacion.gob.pa/

USA
Code for America,
http://codeforamerica.org/

Launch, www.launch.org/

Public Policy Lab,
http://publicpolicylab.org/

ASIA-PACIFIC
AUSTRALIA
Australian Government Public
Sector Innovation,
https://innovation.govspace.gov.au/

DesignGov,
http://design.gov.au/

HONG KONG, CHINA
Efficiency Unit,
www.eu.gov.hk/eindex.html

INDIA
National Innovation Council,
www.innovationcouncil.gov.in/

SOUTH KOREA
Korean Institute of Design
Promotion,
www.kidp.or.kr/kmain/

THAILAND

Future Innovative Thailand
Institute, http://fit.or.th/

National Innovation Agency,
www.nia.or.th/en/

Thailand Creative & Design
Center, www.tcdc.or.th/about/

SINGAPORE
Human Experience Lab

EUROPE
DENMARK
MindLab Denmark,
www.mind-lab.dk/en

FRANCE

Region 27,
http://la27eregion.fr/

FINLAND

Helsinki Design Lab,
http://helsinkidesignlab.org/

Sitra, www.sitra.fi/en/
Tekes, www.tekes.fi/

NORWAY

Innovation Norway, www.
innovasjonnorge.no/

SWEDEN

VINNOVA, www.vinnova.se/en/

UNITED KINGDOM

Design Council, www.
designcouncil.org.uk/

The Innovation Unit, www.
innovationunit.org/

Nesta, www.nesta.org.uk/

Technology Strategy Board,
www.innovateuk.org/

Policy Lab, https://twitter.com/
PolicyLabUK

Northern Ireland Innovation
Laboratory (announced)

Source: Design Thinking for Public Service Excellence. Global Center for Public Service Excellence. Singapore

CASE STUDIES

PEPSI

PepsiCo is the latest company to come out in support of "Design Thinking" and to make a case for investment in design. In the September 2015 issue of the Harvard Business Review, PepsiCo CEO Indra Nooyi describes using Design Thinking to "rethink the entire experience, from conception to what's on the shelf to the post-product experience." Nooyi describes that, although early days, she believes her approach has "delivered great shareholder value while strengthening the company for the long term."

"First, I gave each of my direct reports an empty photo album and a camera. I asked them to take pictures of anything they thought represented good design. After six weeks, only a few people returned the albums. Some had their wives take pictures. Many did nothing at all. They didn't know what design was"

For companies like PepsiCo, encouraging, and even mandating, a perspective that insists on customer experience and empathy can lead to richer insights, more on-point products and clearer strategies to deliver them by helping brands connect to what customers find compelling.

Source: brandchannel.com

AIRBNB

In 2009, Airbnb was close to going bust. Like so many startups, they had launched but barely anyone noticed. The company's revenue was flatlined at $200 per week. Split between three young founders living in San Francisco, this meant near indefinite losses on zero growth.

The two founders who had design backgrounds decided to reinvent the company using Design Thinking. A little over a year later the company had a billion dollar turnover.

AirBnB's Head of User Research (2012-2014)
""having designer founders and being design-centered from day one makes you [as an organization] pay attention to those details. ... A lot of Design Thinking is about being creative [but it is also] about looking at what we know and triangulating information that we have and having that inspire creativity.""

"There are engineers who care about their engineering problems and maybe the users are less relevant. We just don't hire these kind of engineers here. Every engineer cares about the user and has a respect for design"

ERICSSON

Ericsson apply Design Thinking process and methods through Innova, a startup incubator within the company to assess existing ideas and turn them into marketable concepts.

"It was one unit introducing Design Thinking in their organizational structure and it became an innovation practice. A practice that they now share with the whole company."

Innova aims to support an entrepreneurial spirit amongst Ericsson's employees. After its third year, the Innova platform had 6.000 users. More than 4.000 ideas were submitted to the platform, with more than 450 ideas receiving first round funding and 45 receiving second round funding.

Source : thisisdesignthinking.net

SINGAPORE GOVERNMENT

The Ministry of Manpower's Work Pass Division used Design Thinking to develop better ways to support foreigners who choose Singapore as a destination to live, work and set up businesses.

Design Thinking methods were applied. Work Pass Division began to consider services through the eyes of their users the employers, employment agencies and foreign workers.

Between 2005 and 2009, the EPOL was redesigned to increase the information flow to users of the system. This has helped to shift the perception of WPD from a high-handed regulator to a responsive and transparent facilitator of employment.

PROCTOR & GAMBLE

Clay Street Project @ Procter
& GambleIn 2004, Procter &
Gamble (P&G) established an
internal innovation pro-gram, which
incorporated Design Thinking. In
the program teams from multiple
disciplines and units within P&G
gather for a period of 10 to 12
weeks to develop user-centered
solutions. Since Clay Street
produced numerous internal
success stories P&G decided to
provide their setup as a service
for other business partners. The
oferings range from one-day
workshops to project support over
a period of several weeks. The
Clay Street initiative and a Design
Thinking Network now serve as
a foundation to spread Design
Thinking in the organization.

http://www.theclaystreetproject.com

INTUIT

Design for Delight (D4D) Design
Thinking program was established
in 2007. Its mandate is to foster
more entrepreneurial behavior
throughout the whole organization.
So far, over 200 innovation
catalysts have been trained and
support teams from multiple
disciplines in the design of financial
service experiences for Intuit's
customers. They are allowed
to dedicate a minimum of ten
percent of their working time to
training and helping others in their
projects. Catalysts were enabled
by a massive internal change
program, which integrated a
redefinition of the company's core
values and major changes into the
spatial working environments.

http://intuitlabs.com

PULSE

Ankit and Akshay develop Pulse with Design Thinking and empathy. They took a 10 week class called launchpad course at the d school at Stanford where rule number one is start with empathy. Students must start a business and have customers by week 5. Students must talk to customers from day one.

Ankit had a software company in india before coming to the United States. He says that we never talked to a customer and as a result we never had a customer. To develop the class project they set up shop in a coffee shop in Palo Alto for ten hours a day for several weeks. They are not allowed back there.

They see everyone reading a newspaper so decide to do a news aggregator for iPad.At first they used post it notes because they had no software.First week everyone did not like it by week 3 everyone asking whether it shipped with the iPad. They made 100 changes a day based on customer feedback.

At Ian iPad developers conference Steve jobs showed an iPad with their software. Pulse had soon developed 20 million users and Linkedin bought their company for 90 million dollars

INFOSYS

30,000 Infosys staff to be trained on Design Thinking

MUMBAI: Infosys has already signed up 22 customers on its Design Thinking offering and will train 30,000 of its employees on Design Thinking by the end of the year to further boost growth in that consultancy service, chief executive officer Vishal Sikka said. Sikka has been pushing Design Thinking as the cornerstone of his plan to help the company grow. The company has also trained 250 of its top executives and its sales teams on Design Thinking.

""With Design Thinking, we should be able to identify problems and not just solve them for customers that are pointed out to us. No one is doing this sort of consultancy in a big way," Sikka said

Design Thinking is also a way for the company to win deals focused on new digital technologies, that are likely to help the company in the rebid market, he said.

Source: Times of India

SIEMENS CT CHINA

Siemens has developed the program "Industrial Design Thinking in China (i.DT)" to train the creativity of Research & Development teams through real projects for need driven innovation with disruptive potential. The i.DT lab ran in the spring of 2015, with large workshop room, several dedicated project rooms, and an advanced machine shop with 3D printer, Computerized Numerical Control (CNC) and laser cutter to take the low resolution prototypes to the next professional level.

The process of i.DT, which can last for several months and include a number of workshops, starts from the definition of the innovation target and ends with a sales pitch. It uses extreme users and low resolution prototypes as stimuli, to satisfy unmet needs by integrating multiple technologies or businesses through fast iterations of needfinding, brainstorming, prototyping, and testing. The method has been successfully used in China for the past three years, in more than 20 development projects to date. Now i.DT is also coming to Germany to support business.

Source: Siemens Press release 2015

GE HEALTHCARE

The challenge was how to create a more child friendly CT, X-Ray and MRI scanning experience.

Diagnostic imaging procedures are an unpleasant experience for patients. Doug Dietz is an industrial designer, working for GE healthcare since more than 20 years. He saw a little girl who was crying on her way to a scanner that was designed by him. Doug Dietz tried to find inspiration for this project through Design Thinking. "I started to imagine how powerful this tool could be if I brought it back and got cross-functional teams to work together." He started by observing and gaining empathy for young children at a day care center. Next, he created the first prototype of what would become the "Adventure Series" scanner and was able to get it installed as a pilot program in the children's hospital at the University of Pittsburgh Medical Center."

The patient satisfaction scores went up 90 percent. Children do not suffer of anxiety anymore. Instead some of them even ask their parents if they can come back tomorrow.

EMBRACE

Students at the Stanford d. school were challenged to design a less expensive incubator for babies born prematurely in Nepal. The students traveled to Nepal to meet with families and doctors and see the problem for themselves.

Based on the data collected, the design team reframes the design problem.

They used pictures, videos and storytelling of their experiences to brainstorm solutions. The students who undertook this project didn't stop with a prototype. They formed a company called Embrace and started manufacturing the product, which sells for $25. Embrace now has programs in 11 different countries and has helped over 50,000 premature and low birth weight infants. And all it started with the Design Thinking process. It has estimated that the product has saved 20,000 lives.

It has been so successful that the product is being purchased by US health providers where the cost of incubation using traditional methods in hospitals may be more than $100,000 per child.

Source: http://blog.triode.ca/

IBM

"Mr. Gilbert and his team talk a lot about "iteration cycles," "lateral thinking," "user journeys" and "empathy maps." To the uninitiated, the canons of Design Thinking can sound mushy and self-evident. But across corporate America, there is a rising enthusiasm for Design Thinking not only to develop products but also to guide strategy and shape decisions of all kinds. The September cover article of the Harvard Business Review was "The Evolution of Design Thinking." Venture capital firms are hiring design experts, and so are companies in many industries.

The computing giant has discovered "Design Thinking," the product-development technique that puts customers first on the way to creating goods and services. Lohr writes that IBM plans to hire 1,100 designers across the company by year-end, on a path to employing 1,500. The goal is to have their methods infuse every aspect of how IBM does business

Asked what she tells anxious large shareholders, Ms. Rometty replied that "the key message" is that IBM is the only technology company that is more than a century old because it has reinvented itself repeatedly in the past, and it is doing so again today.."

Soruce New York times November

14 2015
Design thinking is now in wide use at IBM.

* 70+ software projects
* 68+ project teams have participated in Designcamp
* 500 leaders have participated in two leadership summits in 2014.

IBM Design Thinking has four steps, plus three practices that help to execute those steps effectively.

The four steps are:

1. Understand
2. Explore
3. Prototype
4. Evaluate

IBM Design Thinking model includes three core principles and practices that differentiate their design and development competency from those of other companies

Hills
This practice focuses projects "on big problems and outcomes for users, not just a list of feature requests."

Sponsor users
This practice helps teams to "design experiences for real target users," rather than trying to satisfy

the imagined needs of abstract personas. Sponsor users are "a set of real users recruited to join the product team for a period and do participatory design."

Playbacks

This practice aligns teams, stakeholders, and clients around the user value they want to deliver as a team rather than project line items. In a playback, the team plays back "the user experience for a defined scenario" to stakeholders to foster collaboration, encourage feedback, and achieve alignment. "All conversation and alignment is around the user value that the team will deliver." IBM has "a culture of showing versus telling," during playbacks. To leverage visual communication, they might create pictures, but more often they prefer to create prototypes.

Designcamps

IBM Design created and deliver what they call Designcamps to educate and activate teams by teaching them how to deliver great experiences together.

IBM has, at this point, held over 100 Designcamps for product teams, product managers, IBM executives, new-hires, and more.

IBM's development model focuses on three shared values:

1. Market outcomes for users
2. Continuous learning
3. Radical collaboration

Source Todd Wilkens 2015

"

Design Thinking is about changing from:

Making people want things [through advertising and marketing] to making things people want

PIETER BAERT
Service consultant

HISTORY OF DESIGN THINKING

"

An Industrial Designer can design a better kettle.

A Design Thinker can design a better way of boiling water than a kettle.

HISTORY OF DESIGN THINKING

Design Thinking has evolved over a period of twenty to thirty years and incorporates ideas from a number of design methodologies and movements. The term first emerged in the 1980s with the rise of human-centered design

In the 1960s efforts were made to develop the field that has become known as Design Research to better inform the practice of design. The notion of design as a "way of thinking" was explored by Herbert A. Simon in his 1969 book The Sciences of the Artificial. It was further explored in Robert McKim's 1973 book Experiences in Visual Thinking. Rolf Faste expanded McKim's work in the 80s and 90s in his teaching at Stanford, defining and popularizing the idea of "design thinking"as a way of creative action that was adapted for business purposes by IDEO through his colleague David M. Kelley.

Peter Rowe's 1987 book Design Thinking was the first popular usage of the term "Design Thinking" in the literature on design. The 1992 article by Richard Buchanan titled "Wicked Problems in Design Thinking" expressed a broader view of Design Thinking.

Through the 1980s it was recognized that design needed to focus on understanding the needs and designs of people as well as business. Design Thinking incorporates some ideas from the user centered design movement that developed during this period. By the 1990s David Kelley of IDEO, Larry Leifer and Terry Winograd were amongst the founders of what is now known as the Design Thinking movement.

In 2005, SAP co-founder Hasso Plattner made a personal donation of U.S. $35 million to fund the d.school, which is officially named "Hasso Plattner Institute of Design at Stanford. that has pioneered the teaching of Design Thinking. The approach is now taught at a number of leading business schools such as the Rotman School in Toronto and at Harvard as well as many design schools.

I have listed here some of the important contributions to the field with dates and contributors.

RELATED DESIGN MOVEMENTS

YEAR	DESIGN MOVEMENT	DESIGN APPROACHES	PEOPLE
2010s	Design Thinking	Experience design	David Kelley
		Creative class	Tim Brown
			Roger Martin
			Bruce Nussbaum
			Rolf Faste
2000s	Service Design	Human Centered Design	Lucy Kimbell
1990s	Process Methods	Meta Design	Ezio Manzini
			William Rause
			Richard Buchanan
1980s	Cognitive Reflections	User Centered Design	Don Norman
			Donal Schon
			Nigel Cross
			Peter Rowe
			Bryan Lawson
1970s			Robert McKim
1960s	Design Science	Participatory Design	Horst Rittel
		Design Methods	Herbet Simon
			Bruce Archer
1950s	Creativity Methods	Brainstorming	Alex Osborn

HISTORY OF DESIGN THINKING

380BC

380 BC Plato's Republic contains some of the roots of participatory design.

300BC

Porphry of Tyros develops mind maps.

100BC

Hermagoras of Temnos, Quis, quid, quando, ubi, cur, quem ad modum, quibus adminiculis.(Who, what, when, where, why, in what way, by what means)

1877

Georg von Mayr invents radar charts.

1879

Louis Emile Javal develops eye tracking.

1880

John Venn invents Venn Diagrams

1890S

Credit Agricole pioneer co-creation methods.

1909

E.B. Titchener invented the word empathy in an attempt to translate the German word "Einfühlungsvermögen".

1921

Robert Bruere first uses the terms primary research and secondary research.

1928

Margaret Mead develops ethnographic field studies.

1929

Bonislaw Malinowski develops ethnographic field studies.

1940S

2nd World War from which came operational research methods and management decision-making techniques

1940

Robert Merton develops focus groups.

Harold van Doren published "Industrial Design – A Practical Guide to Product Design and Development",covering design methods and practices.

1942
Gordon Allport, may have been the first to describe diary studies.

1943
Kelly Johnson invents the term Skunkworks.

1944
Alex Bavelas develops Fly on the wall method.

1948
Edward Tolman invents Cognitive Maps.

1950
Herman Kahn Rand develops Scenarios method.

1950S
Development of creativity techniques

1953
Term brainstorming was popularized by Alex Faickney Osborn in the 1953 book Applied Imagination

1957
Walt Disney Corporation develop activity maps method.

1958
Michael Polanyi uses the term Tacit Knowledge.

1960S
Designers explore models for design methodology, and "design research" to better understand and improve design processes and practices This movement marked the beginning of a debate over the process and methodology of design.

1960
Affinity diagram was devised by Jiro Kawakita

Allan Collins, Northwestern University USA develops mind maps.

1961
Gordon The first creativity books start to appear
1962 The First 'Conference on Design Methods,.

1962

Archer, L. Bruce. Systematic Method for Designers.

Ernest Becker Behavioral Maps

1963
Osborn, Alex F. Applied Imagination: Principles and Procedures of Creative Thinking. New York: Scribner,

1964
Alexander The first design methods or methodology books start appearing:

1965
Bruce Archer professor of Design Research at the Royal College of Art is arguably the first author to use the term design thinking in his book "Systematic Method for Designers" London: Council of Industrial Design, H.M.S.O.

Archer, L. Bruce. Systematic Method for Designers. Council of Industrial Design, H.M.S.O.

1965
SWOT Analysis developed by Albert Humphrey Stanford University

1967
Francis J Aguiler develops PEST Analysis.

1968
Kaoru Ishikawa develops fishbone diagram.

Professor Bernd Rohrbach pioneers 635 Brainstorming Method

1969
Herbert A. Simon establishes a "science of design" which would be "a body of intellectually tough, analytic, partly formalizable, partly empirical, teachable doctrine about the design process."

Simon, Herbert (1969). The Sciences of the Artificial. Cambridge: MIT Press.

Bill Gaver Royal College of Art cultural probes

Visual psychologist Rudolf Arnheim publishes his book Visual Thinking, which inspires the teaching of ME101: Visual Thinking, by Robert McKim, in the School of Engineering at Stanford University

1970S

John Chris Jones, "**In the 1970s I reacted against design methods. I dislike the machine language, the behaviorism, the continual attempt to fix the whole of life into a logical framework.**"

1970

Jones, John Christopher. Design Methods. New York: John Wiley & Sons.

John Chris Jones, designer and design thinking theorist, stated: "In the 1970s I reacted against design methods. I dislike the machine language, the behaviorism, the continual attempt to fix the whole of life into a logical framework.

"I've disassociated myself from the field. There is so little in what is called 'design methods' that has anything useful to say about how to design buildings that I never even read the literature anymore. I would say forget it, forget the whole thing."

1973

Robert McKim's publishes

Experiences in Visual Thinking The class McKim creates, "ME101: Visual Thinking,"in the design program at Stanford University.

1979

Bruce Archer "**There exists a designerly way of thinking and communicating that is both different from scientific and scholarly ways of thinking and communicating, and as powerful as scientific and scholarly methods of inquiry when applied to its own kinds of problems**."

1980S

The term first emerged prominently in the with the rise of human-centered design. Rolf Faste building on McKim's work in his teaching at Stanford,

Systemic engineering design methods are developed, particularly in Germany and Japan.

1980s sees the rise of human-centered design and the rise of design-centered business management.

1980

Bryan Lawson, "How Designers Think: The Design Process Demystified" and "How Designers Think about design cognition in the context of architecture and urban planning.["

1981

George Doran develops Smart Goals Method.

Koberg, Don, and Jim Bagnall. The All New Universal Traveller: a Soft-systems Guide To: Creativity, Problem-solving and the Process of Reaching Goals. Los Altos, CA: Kaufmann

The American Society of Mechanical Engineers conference on Design Theory and Methodology. The rise of human-centered design and the rise of design-centered business management.

1982

Cross, Nigel. "Designerly Ways of Knowing." Design Studies 3.4 (1982): 221-27.

1983

Schön, Donald. The Reflective Practitioner: How Professionals Think In Action. New York: Basic Books, 1983.

Lyn Shosack develops service blueprinting method.

1984

Jay Conrad Levinson guerilla ethnography

1985

Edward de Bono Six Thinking Hats.

1986

Six Sigma emerges to streamline the design process for quality control and profit.

1987

Peter Rowe professor at the Harvard Graduate School of Design, book Design Thinking was the first significant usage of the term "Design Thinking" in literature. Rowe, G. Peter (1987). Design Thinking. Cambridge: The MIT Press. ISBN 978-0-262-68067-7.

1988

Rolf Faste, director of the design program at Stanford, publishes

"Ambidextrous Thinking,"

Whiteside, Bennet, and Holtzblatt Contextual Inquiry.

Rolf Faste, director of the design program at Stanford, creates "Ambidextrous Thinking", a required class for graduate product design majors that extends McKim's process of visual thinking to design as a "whole-body way of doing.

1990S
Human-centered design evolves from a technology driven focus to a human one.

1991
Rowe popularized the phrase "design thinking" referring to the ways in which designers approach design problems,

Mood boards first used by Terence Conran. IDEO combines from three industrial design companies. They are one of the first design companies to showcase their design process, which draws heavily on the Stanford University curriculum. IIT Institute of Design establishes the first PhD program in Design in the United States

1992
Richard Buchanan's article "Wicked Problems in Design Thinking," Design Issues, vol. 8, no. 2, Spring 1992. adopts a broader view of Design Thinking

1994
Rolf Faste, "Ambidextrous Thinking", Innovations in Mechanical Engineering Curricula for the 1990s, American Society of Mechanical Engineers, November 1994

Matthew Van Horn invents the term Wireframe the term in New York.

1995
Ikujiro Nonaka expands the ideas of Michael Polanyi on tacit versus explicit knowledge.

1997
David Kelley contributed to the book the article The Designer's Stance through an interview by Bradley Hartfield,
"It might help to pose two caricatures two hypothetical extremes. One is engineering as problem solving; the other is

design as creating. "

"the designer wants to create a solution that fits in a deeper situational or social sense." "design is messy. Engineering ... is not supposed to be messy. The designer can handle the messiness and ambiguity and is willing to trust intuition." " Successful design is done in teams." David Kelley

1999

The term Critical Design was first used in Anthony Dunne's book "Hertzian Tales"

IDEO Design Thinking approach was the featured on ABC's Nightline in 1999 in an episode called "The Deep Dive."

2000S

Debate about the hijacking and exploitation of design thinking by business educators.

2000

Brandt and Grunnet develop Empathy Tools.

The Rotman School of Management develops a new model for business education based on Dean Roger Martin's integrative thinking for solving wicked problems.

2002

Florida, Richard L. The Rise of the Creative Class: and How It's Transforming Work, Leisure, Community and Everyday Life. New York, NY: Basic, 2002.

William McDonough Cradle to Cradle.

2000

Bodystorming Buchenau and Fulton.

2003

Misuse Scenario method developed by Ian Alexander.

2005

The Hasso Plattner Institute of Design or the d.school is established at Stanford. 2005, SAP co-founder Hasso Plattner made a donation of U.S. $35 million to fund the d.school, which is named the "Hasso Plattner Institute of Design" at Stanford."

2006

Lawson, Bryan. "How Designers Think." Oxford UK: Architectural Press Elsevier, 2006

Pink, Daniel H. A Whole New Mind: Why Right-brainers Will Rule the Future. New York: Riverhead, 2006

Jeff Howe uses the term Crowd Sourcing.

2007

Cross, Nigel. Designerly Ways of Knowing. London UK and Boston MA: Birkhauser Verlag AG, 2007.

Hasso Plattner Institute for IT Systems Engineering in Potsdam, Germany establishes a design thinking program

Martin, Roger L. The Opposable Mind: How Successful Leaders Win through Integrative Thinking. Boston, MA: Harvard Business School, 2007.

2008,

HPI at Potsdam and Stanford University launched a joint research program on innovation, which is jointly led by Leifer and Christoph Meinel.

2009

Tim Brown of IDEO, and is the author of Change by Design: How Design Thinking Transforms Organizations and Inspires Innovation

Design Thinking authored by Plattner, Meinel, and Weinberg

Roger Martin, Dean of the Rotman School of Management in Toronto, authors The Design of Business: Why Design Thinking is the Next Competitive Advantage

Brown, Tim. "The Making of a Design Thinker." Metropolis Oct. 2009: 60-62. Pg 60: **"David Kelley... said that every time someone came to ask him about design, he found himself inserting the word thinking to explain what it is that designers do. The term design thinking stuck."**

The MMM Program at Northwestern University is the first MBA program to incorporate design thinking into its core curriculum.

2010

Lockwood, Thomas. Design

Thinking: Integrating Innovation, Customer Experience and Brand Value. New York, NY: Allworth, 2010

2011

Faste, Rolf. "The Human Challenge in Engineering Design." International Journal of Engineering Education, vol 17, 2001.

Dorst discusses how a core element of expert design is framing dealing with the paradoxes that arise from conflicting considerations in order to create value.

A number of schools begin teaching design thinking in classrooms and community projects

Cross, N (2011) Design Thinking: Understanding How Designers Think and Work, Berg, Oxford and New York.

"

Design Thinkers
create for others first

PRINCIPLES OF DESIGN THINKING

"

Good design

Is innovative

Makes a product useful

Is aesthetic

Makes a product understandable

Is unobtrusive

Is honest

Is long-lasting

Is thorough down to the last detail

Is environmentally friendly

Is as little design as possible

DIETER RAMS
Industrial Designer.

UNMET USER NEED

Define the problem

Test learn refine

Understand the user identify unmet needs

DESIGN THINKING PROCESS

Prototype

Create ideas

DESIGN SOLUTION

DESIGN THINKING

WHAT IS DESIGN THINKING?

Design Thinking is or approach to designing that supports innovation and intelligent change. Design Thinking is a human-centered approach which is driven by creative and analytical thinking, customer empathy and iterative learning.

It involves a toolkit of methods that can be applied to different problems by cross disciplinary groups or by individuals. Anyone can use Design Thinking. It can be fun.

WHO INVENTED IT?

The origins of Design Thinking date back to before the 1950s. Design Thinking adopted ideas that came from the creativity methods of the 1950s, the design science and design methods movements of the 1960s, user centered design movement of the 1980s and experience and service design from the 2,000s. In 1987 Peter Rowe, a Professor at the Harvard Graduate School of Design, published "Design Thinking" the first significant usage of the term "Design Thinking" in literature. After 2000 the term became widely used.

WHY USE DESIGN THINKING?

Design Thinking is useful when you have:
1. A poorly defined problem.
2. A lack of information.
3. A changing context or environment
4. It should result in consistently innovative solutions.

Design Thinking seeks a balance of design considerations including:
1. Business.
2. Appropriate application of technology
3. Empathy with people.
4. Environmental consideration.

Design Thinking seeks to balance two modes of thinking:
1. Analytical thinking
2. Creative Thinking

WHAT CAN IT BE APPLIED TO?
1. Products
2. Services
3. Experiences
4. Interactions
5. Systems of the above

DESIGN THINKING PROCESS

Design Thinking has a particular process

1. Define intent
2. Through ethnographic research develop empathy for the point of view of the user.
3. Synthesize the research
4. Frame insights
5. Explore Concepts
6. Synthesize the concepts generated
7. Prototype the favored ideas
8. Test the prototypes with users
9. Incorporate changes
10. Iterate prototype and testing till a workable design is reached
11. Implement
12. Deliver Offering

RESOURCES

Multidisciplinary team of 4 to 12 people
A project space
Post it notes
Dry erase markers
White board
Digital camera
Copy paper
Chairs
Large table

WHO CAN USE DESIGN THINKING?

Design Thinking is a technique for everyone and any problem. Design Thinking process involves many stakeholders in working together to find a balanced design solution. The designer is a member of a type of design orchestra. The customer is involved throughout the design process and works with the design team to communicate their needs and desires and to help generate design solutions that are relevant to them.

The many methods used help anyone to understand the diverse perspectives of the many stakeholders. It takes some courage to listen and recognize the point of view of the stakeholders. Managers, designers, social scientists, engineers marketers, stakeholders customers and others can collaborate creatively to apply Design Thinking to everyone's benefit.

The process is one of co-creation and the designer is a listener and a facilitator. Everyone adds value to the design. Design Thinking is not just for professional designers. Everyone can contribute. Many schools are now teaching Design Thinking to children as an approach that can be applied to life.

Why Design Thinking should be at the core of your design and business strategies

Number of companies surveyed

129 125 86 32 32 20 9

71% — Design Thinking improved our working culture

69% — Design Thinking makes our innovation process more efficient

48% — Design Thinking has led to us integrating our users more frequently

29% — Design Thinking helps us save costs

18% — Design Thinking helps us increase sales

18% — Design Thinking helps us increase profitability

5% — None of the above

Data from 2015 study by Hasso-Plattner-Institut für software/systemtechnik an der Universität Potsdam, September 2015 of 235 German and international companies of all sizes

Design Thinking is quickly gathering traction in industry.
Chart of organizations years of Design Thinking experience [2015]

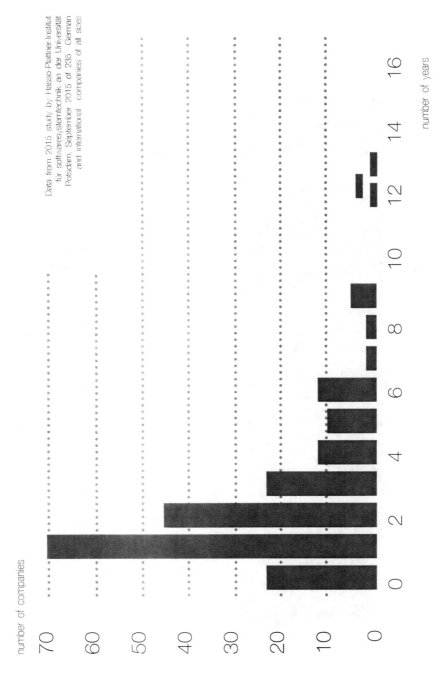

Data from 2015 study by Hasso-Plattner-Institut für softwaresystemtechnik an der Universität Potsdam. September 2015 of 235 German and international companies of all sizes

number of companies

number of years

THE DESIGN LADDER

Companies often start at stage one then progress to higher levels. At the beginning of the 5 year study 36% of 1,000 companies were at stage 1 by the end of the study only 15% of companies remained at stage 1.

Stage 4

Design as Strategy

Design is a key strategic means of supporting innovation. These companies have VPs of Design. Design connected to all business decisions.

Stage 3

Design as Process

Design is integral to the development process. Design is often a sub department of marketing or engineering. Companies may have cross disciplinary teams.

Stage 2

Design as Styling

Design is focuses on appearance and aesthetics. This is the traditional approach to teaching design at many design schools.

Stage 1

No design

Design plays no role in product / service development

Source: Danish Design Center study of 1,000 companies 2003

Average growth in turnover based on study of 1000 companies and their position on the Design Ladder

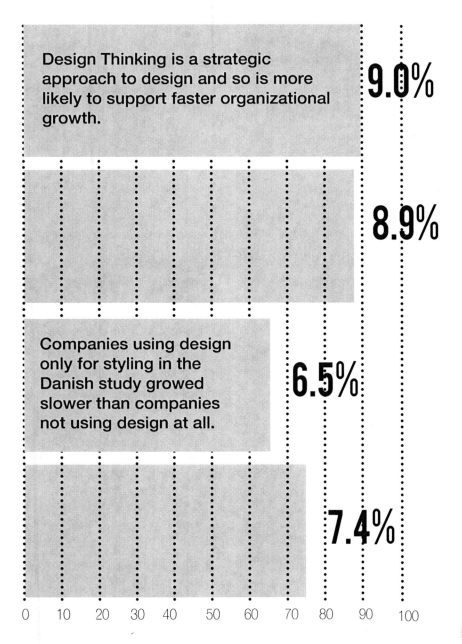

Design Thinking is a strategic approach to design and so is more likely to support faster organizational growth.

9.0%

8.9%

Companies using design only for styling in the Danish study growed slower than companies not using design at all.

6.5%

7.4%

0   10   20   30   40   50   60   70   80   90   100

20 WAYS DESIGN THINKING IS BEING USED

1. Service provision, which is sold to customers for better solution finding or as a program for internal change

2. New product and service development/improvement

3. Better alignment, collaboration and knowledge transfer

4. Empathy for the customer: gaining a better understanding of the customer and user

5. Improving own internal business processes and organizational structures

6. Commercial innovation and more efficient insight-driven marketing campaigns

7. Internal staff training for human/customer-centered mindset.

8. Toolbox. Adapting specific tools and methods to fit an individual purpose

9. Development of better teaching and training formats

10. Increasing creativity in teams

11. Customer engagement and co-creation

12. Public relations and reputation management vehicle

13. Service and experience design improvement

14. Test assumptions and iterate solutions

15. New business models and go-to-market strategies

16. Attractive recruiting tool

17. Means for more efficient meetings and arrangements

18. Generating demand and better customer acquisition via workshops

19. Improving the innovation process

20. Means for improving the style of design outcomes

2015 study by Hasso-Plattner-Institut für softwaresystemtechnik an der Universität Potsdam, September 2015 of 235 German and international companies of all sizes

CHARACTERISTICS OF DESIGN THINKERS

U.SCHOOL BOOTCAMP BOOTLEG (2009)	U.SCHOOL BOOTCAMP BOOTLEG (2010)	TIM BROWN (2008)	BAECK & GREMETT (2011)	COMMENT
Focus on human values	Focus on human values	Empathy	Empathy	"Focus on human values" includes empathy for users and feedback from them.
Create clarity from complexity	Craft clarity	Integrative thinking	Ambiguity Curiosity Holistic Open mindset	All these items refer to styles of thinking. "Clarity" refers to producing a coherent vision out of messy problems. Baeck & Gremett focus on attitudes of the Design Thinker.
		Optimism		Only mentioned by Tim Brown, but seems to be regarded as a universal characteristic of Design Thinkers.
Get experimental and experiential	Embrace experimentation	Experimentalism	Curiosity Open mindset	Experimentation is an integral part of the designer's work.
Collaborate across boundaries	Radical collaboration	Collaboration	Collaborative	Refers to the collaboration between people from different disciplines (having different backgrounds and viewpoints).
Show, do not tell Bias toward action	Show, do not tell Bias toward action			Emphasizes action, for example, by creating meaningful prototypes and confronting potential users with them.
Be mindful of process	Be mindful of process			Emphasizes that Design Thinkers need to keep the overall process (which is regarded as a core element of Design Thinking, in mind with respect to methods and goals.

Source: Gerd Waloszek, SAP AG, SAP User Experience – September 1, 2013

EVOLUTION OF DESIGN THINKING

YEAR	DESIGN MOVEMENT	DESIGN APPROACHES	PEOPLE
2010s	Design Thinking	Experience design	David Kelley
		Creative class	Tim Brown
			Roger Martin
			Rolf Faste
2000s	Service Design	Human Centered Design	Lucy Kimbell
1990s	Process Methods	Meta Design	Ezio Manzini
			William Rause
			Richard Buchanan
1980s	Cognitive Reflections	User Centered Design	Don Norman
			Donal Schon
			Nigel Cross
			Peter Rowe
			Bryan Lawson
1970s			Robert McKim
1960s	Design Science	Participatory Design	Horst Rittel
		Design Methods	Herbet Simon
			Bruce Archer
1950s	Creativity Methods	Brainstorming	Alex Osborn

ATTRIBUTES OF DESIGN THINKING

AMBIGUITY	Being comfortable when things are unclear or when you do not know the answer	Design Thinking addresses wicked ill-defined and tricky problems.
COLLABORATIVE	Working together across disciplines	People design in interdisciplinary teams.
CONSTRUCTIVE	Creating new ideas based on old ideas, which can also be the most successful ideas	Design Thinking is a solution-based approach that looks for an improved future result.
CURIOSITY	Being interested in things you do not understand or perceiving things with fresh eyes	Considerable time and effort is spent on clarifying the requirements. A large part of the problem solving activity, then, consists of problem definition and problem shaping.
EMPATHY	Seeing and understanding things from your customers' point of view	The focus is on user needs (problem context).
HOLISTIC	Looking at the bigger context for the customer	Design Thinking attempts to meet user needs and also drive business success.
ITERATIVE	A cyclical process where improvements are made to a solution or idea regardless of the phase	The Design Thinking process is typically non-sequential and may include feedback loops and cycles (see below).
NON JUDGMENTAL	Creating ideas with no judgment toward the idea creator or the idea	Particularly in the brainstorming phase, there are no early judgments.
OPEN MINDSET	Embracing Design Thinking as an approach for any problem regardless of industry or scope	The method encourages "outside the box thinking" ("wild ideas"); it defies the obvious and embraces a more experimental approach.

Core Attributes of Design Thinking from Baeck & Gremett, 2011

THE TEN FACES OF INNOVATION

ANTHROPOLOGIST	Excels at human observation and research
EXPERIMENTER	Tests ideas through trial and error
CROSS-POLLINATOR	Finds ideas from other industries and cultures
HURDLER	Finds a way around obstacles
COLLABORATOR	Brings groups together
DIRECTOR	Helps select and guide the team
EXPERIENCE ARCHITECT	Considers the experience of the user
SET DESIGNER	Creates an environment for teams to work
CAREGIVER	Knows the customer's needs before they do
STORYTELLER	Communicates within and outside the company

The ten faces of Innovation: David Kelley

DESIGN THINKING PROCESS

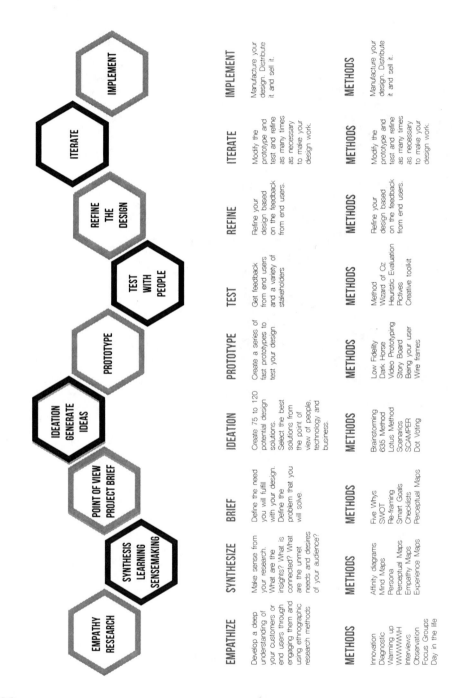

EMPATHIZE — **RESEARCH**

Develop a deep understanding of your customers or end users through engaging them and using ethnographic research methods

METHODS

Innovation Diagnostic
Warming up
WWWWWH
Interviews
Observation
Focus Groups
Day in the life

SYNTHESIZE — **SYNTHESIS LEARNING SENSEMAKING**

Make sense from your research. What are the insights? What is connected? What are the unmet needs and desires of your audience?

METHODS

Affinity diagrams
Mind Maps
Persona
Perceptual Maps
Empathy Maps
Experience Maps

BRIEF — **POINT OF VIEW PROJECT BRIEF**

Define the need you will fulfill with your design. Define the problem that you will solve.

METHODS

Five Whys
SWOT
Re-framing
Smart Goals
Checklists
Perceptual Maps

IDEATION — **IDEATION GENERATE IDEAS**

Create 75 to 120 potential design solutions. Select the best solutions from the point of view of people, technology and business.

METHODS

Brainstorming
635 Method
Lotus Method
Scenarios
SCAMPER
Dot Voting

PROTOTYPE — **PROTOTYPE**

Create a series of fast prototypes to test your design

METHODS

Low Fidelity
Dark Horse
Video Prototyping
Story Board
Being your user
Wire frames

TEST — **TEST WITH PEOPLE**

Get feedback from end users and a variety of stakeholders

METHODS

Method
Wizard of Oz
Heuristic Evaluation
Pictres
Creative toolkit

REFINE — **REFINE THE DESIGN**

Refine your design based on the feedback from end users.

METHODS

Refine your design based on the feedback from end users.

ITERATE — **ITERATE**

Modify the prototype and test and refine as many times as necessary to make your design work.

METHODS

Modify the prototype and test and refine as many times as necessary to make your design work.

IMPLEMENT — **IMPLEMENT**

Manufacture your design. Distribute it and sell it.

METHODS

Manufacture your design. Distribute it and sell it.

SOME BENEFITS OF DESIGN THINKING

1. A people-centred perspective;

2. Reduced risks of partial approaches;

3. A comprehensive, holistic problem perspective;

4. Reduced duplicated efforts, policy inconsistencies or overlaps;

5. Enhanced synergies and better addressed trade-offs;

6. Integrated and better-targeted solutions;

7. Stronger reality-checks at earlier stages;

8. Reduced risks of unintended consequences; and

9. Higher chances to deliver more complete and

10. Resilient solutions.

Source: Design Thinking for Public Service Excellence. Global Center for Public Service Excellence. Singapore

DESIGN THINKING FOR KIDS

"Often schools are teaching kids things they might never need to know again. We're not teaching them how to be creative, or design, or deal with unexpected situations. A lot of people are aware that we really need to change education, but they don't know how. This is one method that could inspire people. It's basically design thinking, adapted for children."

Emer Beamer, Dutch design thinker

IDEAS FOR USING POST-IT-NOTES

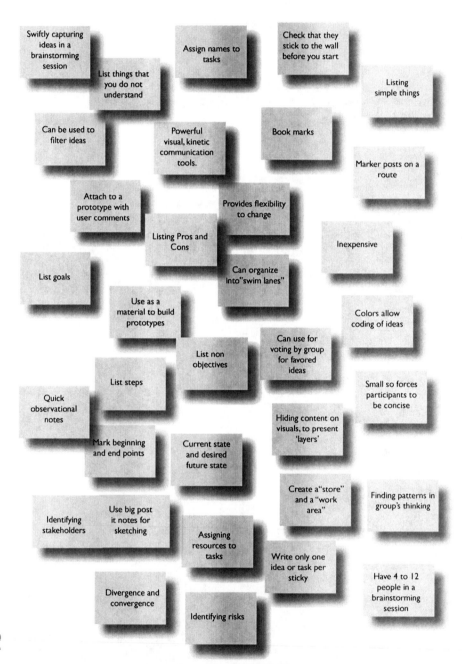

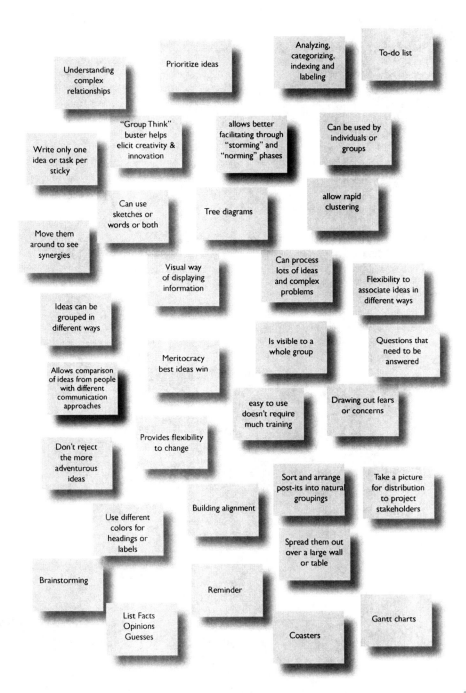

DESIGN THINKING PROCESS

GOALS?
What are we looking for?

1. Meet with key stakeholders to set vision
2. Assemble a diverse team
3. Develop intent and vision
4. Explore scenarios of user experience
5. Document user performance requirements
6. Define the group of people you are designing for. What is their gender, age, and income range. Where do they live. What is their culture?
7. Define your scope and constraints
8. Identify a need that you are addressing. Identify a problem that you are solving.
9. Identify opportunities
10. Meet stakeholders

DISCOVER EMPATHIZE RESEARCH
What else is out there?

1. Identify what you know and what you need to know.
2. Document a research plan
3. Benchmark competitive products
4. Create a budgeting and plan.
5. Create tasks and deliverables
6. Explore the context of use
7. Understand the risks
8. Observe and interview individuals, groups, experts.
9. Develop design strategy
10. Undertake qualitative, quantitative, primary and secondary research.
11. Talk to vendors

SYNTHESIZE
What have we learned?

1. Review the research.
2. Make sense out of the research
3. Develop insights
4. Cluster insights
5. Create a hierarchy

DEVELOP A UNIQUE POINT OF VIEW
What is the design brief?

IDEATE
How is this for starters?

1. Brainstorm
2. Define the most promising ideas
3. Refine the ideas
4. Establish key differentiation of your ideas
5. Investigate existing intellectual property.

PROTOTYPE TEST AND ITERATE
How could we make it better?

1. Make your favored ideas physical.
2. Create low-fidelity prototypes from inexpensive available materials
3. Develop question guides
4. Develop test plan
5. Test prototypes with stakeholders
6. Get feedback from people.
7. Refine the prototypes
8. Test again
9. Build in the feedback
10. Refine again.
11. Continue iteration until design works.
12. Document the process.

13. When you are confident that your idea works make a prototype that looks and works like a production product.

IMPLEMENT AND DELIVER
Let's make it. Let's sell it.

1. Create your proposed production design
2. Test and evaluate
3. Review objectives
4. Manufacture your first samples
5. Review first production samples and refine.
6. Launch
7. Obtain user feedback
8. Conduct field studies
9. Define the vision for the next product or service.

DESIGN THINKING PROCESS MODELS

HAYES 1989	AMABILE 1989	PLATTNER 2009 DESIGN THINKING	KOLKO 2007	IDEO KELLEY 2002	TREFFINGER 1992	ROOZENBURG 1995
	task presentation	understand		understand	mess finding	function
identify the problem	preparation	observe	research	observe	data finding	analysis
problem representation		point of view	synthesis			synthesis
planning the solution	idea generation	ideate	ideation		problem finding	
execute the plan		prototype	refinement	visualize	idea finding	
						simulation
evaluate the plan	idea validation	test		evaluate and refine	solution finding	evaluation

	WIKIPEDIA HERBERT SIMON	IDEO TOOLKIT	TIMBROWN IDEO	D.SCHOOL D-SCHOOL HPI	D.SCHOOL BOOTCAMP BOOTLEG HPIMODES	BAECK & GREMETT 2011	MARK DZIERSK FAST COMPANY
Understand the problem	define	discovery	inspiration	understand	empathize: observe, engage, immerse	define the problem to solve	define the problem
observe users	research			observe		look for inspiration	
interpret the results		interpretation		point of view	define problem statement		
generate ideas	ideation	ideation	ideation	ideate	ideate	ideate	create many options
prototype experiment	prototype	experimentation	implement	prototype	prototype	generate prototypes	refine directions repeat
test, implement, improve	objectives/ choose implement learn	evolution		evolution	test refine and improve solutions	solicit user feedback	pick the winner, execute

Source: this page adapted from Gerd Waloszek, SAP AG, SAP User Experience 2012

WHERE CAN DESIGN METHODS BE USED?

Legend:
- ■ Often Used
- ▨ May be used
- □ Less commonly used

Method	Warming up exercises	Empathy Discover	Synthesis	Point of View	Ideation	Prototype	Test	Iterate	Implement
Common Ground	■	□	□	□	▨	□	□	□	□
Desert Island	■	□	□	□	▨	□	□	□	□
Expectations	■	□	□	□	▨	□	□	□	□
Diversity	■	□	□	□	▨	□	□	□	□
Hopes and hurdles	■	□	□	□	▨	□	□	□	□
Interview Icebreaker	■	□	□	□	▨	□	□	□	□
Jumpstart storytelling	■	□	□	□	▨	□	□	□	□
Milestones	■	□	□	□	▨	□	□	□	□
WWWWWH	▨	■	▨	▨	▨	▨	▨	▨	▨
AEIOU	▨	■	▨	▨	▨	□	□	□	□
9 Dimensions	▨	■	▨	▨	▨	□	□	□	□
POSTA	▨	■	▨	▨	▨	□	□	□	□
Latch	▨	■	▨	▨	▨	□	□	▨	□
Affinity diagram	▨	■	■	■	■	■	■	■	▨
Anthropump	□	■	□	□	□	□	□	□	□
Behavioral map	□	■	▨	□	□	■	■	■	□
Benchmarking	□	■	■	■	□	■	■	□	□
Blueprint	□	■	■	■	■	▨	■	□	▨
Cultural inventory	□	■	■	▨	□	□	□	□	□
Cultural probe	□	■	▨	□	□	□	□	□	□
Customer experience map	□	■	■	■	▨	■	■	■	▨
Camera Journal	□	■	□	□	□	▨	▨	▨	□
Diary Study	□	■	□	□	□	▨	▨	▨	□

Design Phase

Often Used ■
May be used ▦
Less commonly used □

■ Often used

▦ May be used

□ Less often used

Design Phase

Method

Method	Warming up exercises	Empathy	Discover	Synthesis	Point of View	Ideation	Prototype	Test	Iterate	Implement
Design workshops	■	■	■	■	■	■	■	■	■	□
Design charrette	■	■	■	■	■	■	■	■	■	□
Creative toolkits	▦	■	■	■	■	■	■	■	■	□
Dramaturgy	□	□	□	□	□	□	□	□	□	□
Emotional journey map	■	■	■	■	■	□	□	□	□	□
Empathy map	■	■	■	□	■	□	□	□	□	□
Empathy probes	□	■	□	□	□	□	□	□	□	□
Empathy tools	□	■	□	□	▦	■	■	■	□	□
Eyetracking	□	■	■	□	□	■	■	□	□	□
Fly-on-the-wall	□	■	■	□	□	□	□	□	□	□
Innovation diagnostic	■	□	□	□	□	□	□	□	□	□
Day in the life	□	■	■	□	□	□	□	□	□	□
Interview methods	□	■	□	□	□	■	■	■	□	□
Magic thing	□	■	▦	▦	□	■	■	■	□	□
Method bank	■	■	■	■	■	■	■	■	■	■
Mobile diary study	□	■	▦	▦	□	□	□	□	□	□
Observation	□	■	▦	▦	□	□	■	■	□	□
Personas	■	■	■	■	■	■	■	■	■	■
Personal inventory	□	■	▦	▦	▦	□	■	■	□	□
Shadowing	□	■	▦	▦	□	□	■	■	□	□
Stakeholder map	▦	■	▦	▦	□	■	□	■	□	□
Storyboards	□	■	■	■	■	■	■	■	□	□
Through other eyes	□	■	■	■	■	■	■	■	□	□

WHERE CAN DESIGN METHODS BE USED?

Legend:
- Often Used ■
- May be used ▨
- Less commonly used □

Method	Warming up exercises	Empathy Discover	Synthesis	Point of View	Ideation	Prototype	Test	Iterate	Implement
Backcasting	▨	■	■	■	■	▨	▨	▨	□
Banned	□	■	▨	▨	■	□	□	□	□
Benefits map	□	□	■	□	□	□	□	□	□
Think out loud	□	■	▨	▨	▨	■	■	▨	□
Blue ocean strategy	□	▨	■	■	■	▨	▨	▨	■
Context map	□	▨	■	■	▨	▨	▨	▨	□
Fishbone diagram	□	■	■	■	▨	▨	▨	▨	□
Mind map	■	■	■	■	■	▨	▨	▨	▨
Linking diagram	□	■	■	■	▨	▨	▨	▨	□
Process flow diagram	□	■	■	▨	▨	▨	▨	▨	□
Action plan	□	▨	■	■	▨	▨	▨	▨	▨
Appreciative inquiry	□	■	□	□	□	□	□	□	□
Decision rings	□	■	■	■	▨	▨	▨	▨	□
Force field analysis	□	▨	■	■	▨	▨	▨	▨	□
Radar chart	□	■	■	■	▨	▨	▨	▨	▨
Venn diagram	□	■	■	■	▨	▨	▨	▨	□
Perceptual map	□	■	■	■	▨	▨	▨	▨	□
Sustainability map	□	■	■	■	▨	▨	▨	▨	□
SWOT analysis	□	■	■	■	▨	▨	▨	▨	□
Onion map	□	■	■	■	□	□	□	□	□
Mirror	□	■	■	■	□	□	□	□	□
Octagaon	□	■	■	■	□	□	□	□	□
Bar chart	□	■	■	■	▨	▨	▨	▨	▨

Design Phase

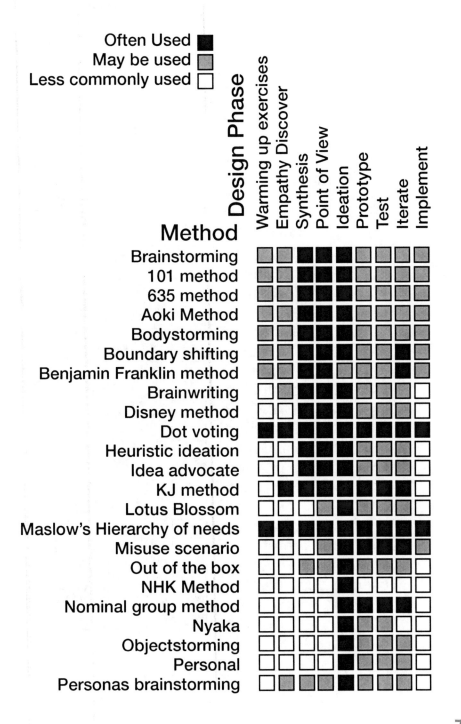

WHERE CAN DESIGN METHODS BE USED?

Often Used ■
May be used ▦
Less commonly used □

Method	Warming up exercises	Empathy Discover	Synthesis	Point of View	Ideation	Prototype	Test	Iterate	Implement
Pin cards	□	□	□	▦	■	▦	▦	▦	□
Related context	□	□	□	▦	■	▦	▦	▦	□
Resources	□	□	□	▦	■	▦	▦	▦	□
Rolestorming	□	■	■	■	■	■	■	■	□
Sensorial method	□	■	■	■	■	■	■	■	□
Scenarios	■	■	■	■	■	■	■	■	□
Word lists	□	□	▦	▦	■	▦	▦	▦	□
Semantic intuition	□	□	▦	▦	■	▦	▦	▦	□
SCAMPER	□	□	▦	▦	■	▦	▦	▦	□
STP method	□	□	□	▦	■	▦	▦	▦	□
Six thinking hats	□	□	■	■	■	▦	▦	▦	□
10 x 10 sketch method	▦	□	□	□	■	▦	▦	▦	□
Synectics	□	□	□	□	■	▦	▦	▦	□
Pictives	□	■	▦	▦	■	■	■	■	□
Appearance prototype	□	□	□	□	▦	■	■	■	□
Dark horse prototypes	□	□	▦	▦	□	■	■	■	□
Low fidelity prototypes	▦	■	■	▦	■	■	■	■	▦
Generative prototyping	■	■	■	■	■	■	■	■	□
Creative toolkits	■	■	■	■	■	■	■	■	□
Wireframe	▦	■	■	■	■	■	■	■	□

EMPATHY

Empathy is sometimes defined as 'standing in someone else's shoes' or 'seeing through someone else's eyes'. It is The ability to identify and understand another's situation, feelings and motives. In design it may be defined as: identifying with others and, adopting their perspective. Empathy is different to sympathy. Empathy does not necessarily imply compassion. Empathy is a respectful understanding of what others are experiencing and their point of view.

E.B. Titchener invented the word in 1909 in an attempt to translate the German word "Einfühlungsvermögen".

WHY HAVE EMPATHY

1. Empathy is a core skill for designers to design successfully for other people.
2. Empathy is needed for business success.
3. Empathy is needed for products and services to be adopted by the people we design for.
4. Empathy builds trust.

HOW TO PRACTICE EMPATHY

1. Put yourself in contact and the context of people who you are designing for.
2. Ask questions and listen to the answers.
3. Read between the lines
4. Observe.
5. Listen
6. Restating what you think you heard.
7. Recognize that people are individuals.
8. Notice body language. Most communication is non verbal
9. Withhold judgment when you hear views different to your own.
10. Take a personal interest in people

ITERATION

Design Thinking follows an iterative process. Iterative design is aimed at refining a design based on learning from user interaction. Iterative design is a cyclic process of prototyping, testing, and refining a product, system service, experience or process. Following testing the most recent iteration of a design with end users, changes and refinements are made. This process is intended to improve the quality and functionality of a design. In iterative design, interaction with the design is used as a form of research for informing and evolving a project, s successive versions, or iterations of a design are created.

Iterative design is the best approach when desiring to design products or systems that are user friendly and functional well.

"

Design Thinking has a wide variety of tools that you can select to work on your design problem. There is usually more than one tool that can be used.

SHOSHIN: THE BEGINNER'S MIND

WHAT IS IT

The phrase shoshin means beginner's mind. It refers to having an attitude of full of openness, enthusiasm, and fresh perspectives in learning something new, eagerness, and lack of preconceptions even at an advanced level, like a child.

Shoshin also means "correct truth" and is used to describe a genuine signature on a work of art. It is use to describe something that is perfectly genuine.

WHERE DID IT ORIGINATE?

1. Shoshin is a term from Zen Buddhism and Japanese martial arts.

HOW TO USE SHOSHIN

1. Withhold judgment. Do not suggest that an idea will not work or that it has negative side-effects. All ideas are potentially good so do not judge them until afterwards.
2. Observe and Listen
3. Ask why
4. Be curious
5. Look for new connections

WHY USE SHOSHIN

1. Sometimes expertise can create closed mindedness.
2. Our assumptions can stand in the way of creating new ideas. A beginner is not aware of biases that can stand in the way of a good new idea.
3. Our experience is an asset but our assumptions may be misconceptions and stereotypes,
4. Innovation often requires looking at a problem in a new way.
5. Beginner's minds can help make breakthroughs
6. Shoshin can transform a routine task into something more enjoyable and less stressful.
7. Observe and engage users without value judgments.
8. Question your assumptions. Ask why?
9. Be curious and explore.
10. Search for patterns and connections no one else has seen.
11. Be open and listen

Source : http://blog.triode.ca

"

Integrative thinking
is critical. You need
to balance business,
people issues,
aesthetics and usability,
application of the
best technologies
and consider the
environmental
consequences

DIVERSITY

DIVERSITY

Diversity means different genders, different ages, be from different cultures, different socioeconomic backgrounds and have different outlooks to be most successful.

WHY HAVE DIVERSITY

1. To attract good people
2. It broadens the customer base in a competitive environment.
3. Diversity brings substantial potential benefits such as better decision making and improved problem solving, greater creativity and innovation, which leads to enhanced product development, and more successful marketing to different types of customers. Diversity provides organizations with the ability to compete in global markets

HOW TO PROMOTE DIVERSITY

1. View employees as individuals.
2. Seek commitment from key participants.
3. Be open-minded. Recognize, and encourage employees to recognize, that one's own experience, background, and culture are not the only ones with value to the organization.
4. Articulate the benefits and motivations for becoming a more diverse organization.
5. Develop a definition of diversity that is linked to organizational mission.
6. Identify other organizations, both locally and nationally, that might serve
7. As models for diversity efforts.
8. Develop a realistic action plan for diversity efforts that takes into account ongoing operations and competing priorities.
9. Develop criteria to measure success. In other words, begin to build an evaluation plan.
10. Create a safe environment for candid and honest participation
11. Set relevant, pragmatic and achievable goals for bringing about organizational diversity.
12. Articulate expected outcomes and measures of change.

"

Design today is no longer about designing objects, visuals or spaces; it is about designing systems, strategies and experiences.

GJOKO MURATOVSKI
Professor in design and innovation
Tongji University, Shanghai

DESIGN THINKING SPACES

1. Lightweight, comfortable, readily movable chairs perhaps on wheels can maximize a relatively small footprint and be arranged in multiple configurations
2. Show your work in progress and let people comment.
3. Surround yourself with the material that your team is working on.
4. Mobile large white boards 6 ft x 4 ft and pin boards.
5. Mobile boards can have a magnetic white board on one side and a pin board on the reverse side.
6. A laptop-sized surface for each attendee
7. Walls can be used for projection, writing, or pinning up information in areas visible to everyone
8. Acoustic privacy should be ensured.
9. Large walls can be used as display spaces.
10. Use work tools that are easily accessible
11. Think of every vertical surface as a potential space for displaying work
12. Use flexible technologies such as wi-fi that allow relocation of services such as internet and power connections.
13. Have a projector and screen
14. Team rooms should offer the flexibility to be arranged to suit the project at hand
15. Seating should allow all participants to see one another and read body language
16. Select furniture with wheels that can be easily moved
17. Small tables can be used for breakouts or grouped into a common surface
18. Ample writing and display areas, as well as surfaces for laying things out, support the need for visual cues and reference materials
19. Provide a large area of vertical displays such as walls white boards, pin boards, foam core boards, projection surfaces, that allow users to actively and flexibly interact with the information
20. Build spaces that support different types of collaboration.
21. Consider physical and virtual collaboration.
22. Spaces should be flexible for unplanned collaboration.
23. Position individual works paces around group spaces for flexibility
24. Provide comfortable group areas for informal interactions and information sharing.
25. The spaces need to be large enough to accommodate all the research materials,
26. visuals, and prototypes in order to keep them visible and accessible all of the time.

Source: Adapted from Haworth recommendations

CONTEXT

Context is external elements that influence a design. These elements are physical and non-physical. Roads, buildings, and land contour are examples for physical elements related to the context of architecture while non-physical elements are weather conditions, local culture, as well as political and economic constraints.

The environmental context relates to the time, the day, the location, the type of place and any other physical aspect that could influence your design.

The user context is about how people are different. It's about what every user likes, and dislikes It's also about the user's state of mind their habits and their state of mobility.

The surrounding context influences the success of a design

FRESH EYES

Outside people have a different perspective that may allow them to contribute new ideas and see problems with existing ideas and directions. Outsiders may have experiences from other industries that can help solve problems

Outside people may be aware of other people who can contribute something valuable. They may ask different questions. They may have relevant experiences that are lacking in your design team. At several points in your design process invite outsiders to review your design and give you feedback.

CROSS POLLINATION

Cross-pollination helps grow ideas. To solve complex problems, designers need to incorporate a wide range of styles, skills, and perspectives,

A team may lack diversity and not understand the perspective of end users.

The more we cross pollinate with other disciplines, the stronger our designs become.

Use cross disciplinary teams. Share ideas and observations with people outside your organization.

Travel can help your design team get exposed to new ways of looking at a problem.

Diversity including race, culture, gender, and income can help cross pollinate your design with different perspectives that may reflect your customer's perspectives.

Read outside your field. Talk to people in different industries

Design Thinking involves understanding your customers' needs, and building your products and services and experiencing life in their context.

BALANCED DESIGN

Design Thinking seeks to find an

optimal balance between four factors.
1. Business needs, including return on investment, growth, price point, competitive advantage cash flow.
2. Technology. Selection of appropriate manufacturing methods and processes, materials and engineering approaches.
3. People's needs and desires. This includes the usability, and aesthetics.
4. Environmental factors. This includes environmental sustainability.

Designers have often in the past oriented designs towards people's needs and desires but been less successful balancing business, environmental and technological factors. Many businesses have oriented their goals towards business factors. Companies that find a sustainable balance between these factors develop a competitive advantage over companies that tend to be oriented towards one factor.

CROSS DISCIPLINARY COLLABORATION
Depending on the design challenge, design teams can engage anthropologists, engineers, educators, doctors, lawyers, scientists, etc. in the innovative problem solving process.

Design Thinking draws on the creative and analytical talents of the design team to reframe the design problem as needed. Design Thinking combines the wisdom and skills of many disciplines working in close and flexible collaboration. Each team member requires disciplinary empathy allowing them to work collaboratively with other discipline members.

COLLECTIVE INTELLIGENCE
Collective intelligence is a type of shared intelligence that emerges from the collaboration of many people and is expressed in consensus decision making

Collective intelligence requires four conditions to exist.
1. Openness Sharing ideas, experiences and perspectives
2. Peering People are free to share and build on each other's ideas freely.
3. Sharing knowledge, experiences ideas.
4. Acting Globally

CULTURE OF PROTOTYPING
Design Thinking involves embodied learning—learning to "think with your hands."

Prototypes can be anything from a storyboard, to a role play, to an actual physical object.

Prototypes of creative ideas are built as early as possible so the design team can learn just enough to generate useful feedback, determine an idea's strengths and weaknesses, and decide what new directions to pursue with more refined prototypes.

The important point is to learn by doing by giving form to an idea, evaluating it against other ideas, and ultimately improving upon it. "Fail early, fail often" is the motto, so prototyping is "quick, cheap, and dirty."

Make simple physical prototypes of your ideas as early as possible. Constantly test your ideas with people. Do not worry about making prototypes beautiful until you are sure that you have a resolved final design. Use the prototypes to guide and improve your design. Do a lot of low cost prototypes to test how your ideas physically work using cardboard, paper, markers, adhesive tape, photocopies, string and popsicle sticks. The idea is to test your idea, not to look like the final product. Expect to change it again. Limit your costs to ten or twenty dollars. Iterate, test and iterate. Do not make the prototype jewelry. It can stand in the way of finding the best design solution. In the minds of some a high fidelity prototype is a finished design solution rather than a tool for improving a design. You should make your idea physical as soon as possible. Be the first to get your hands dirty by making the idea real.

UNRECOGNIZED AND UNMET NEEDS

The methods of Design Thinking are capable of identifying and developing design solutions to meet human needs sometimes even before people know that they have needs. Testing prototypes with real people and observing their interactions and responses can lead designers to innovative solutions that are not yet recognized.

6 key principles that will ensure a design is user centered:
5. The design is based upon an explicit understanding of users, tasks and environments.
6. Users are involved throughout design and development.
7. The design is driven and refined by user-centered evaluation.
8. The process is iterative.
9. The design addresses the whole user experience.
10. The design team includes multidisciplinary skills and perspectives.

Some Questions to ask:
1. Who are the users?
2. What are the users' tasks and goals?
3. What are the users' experience levels?
4. What functions do the users need from the design?
5. What information will be needed by end-users?,
6. In what form do they need it?
7. How do users think the design should work?

CURIOSITY

Curiosity is having an interest in the world. Curiosity is related to exploration, learning and innovation. Curiosity is one of the main driving forces behind human progress such as a caveman experimenting with fire.

High levels of curiosity in adults are connected to greater analytic ability, problem-solving skills and overall intelligence. Creativity is about exploring the unknown and curiosity can be the entry point into this exploration.

Children learn about the world through curiosity. A curious mind dives beneath the surface to understand the process. Curious people look at a challenge from multiple perspectives. Curious people find new paths to solutions.

The more exploration of the unknown, the more likely it will be that you will discover a new and better way of doing something. Curiosity allows a designer to make new connections and find inspiration in new places. The tools of Design Thinking such as observation methods, prototyping and interviewing allow curiosity to be applied in a systematic way. Curiosity helps create new insights which are the starting point for innovation.

FEEDBACK FROM STAKEHOLDERS AT EACH STAGE

Stakeholders include any individuals who are influence by the design. Specifically, the project team, end users, strategic partners, customers, alliances, vendors and senior management are project stakeholders

Possible stakeholders
1. Employees
2. Shareholders
3. Government
4. Customers
5. Suppliers
6. Prospective employees
7. Local communities
8. Global Community
9. Schools
10. Future generations
11. Ex-employees
12. Creditors
13. Professional associations
14. Competitors
15. Investors
16. Prospective customers
17. Communities

Why involve stakeholders? Stakeholder analysis helps to identify:
1. Stakeholder interests
2. Ways to influence other stakeholders
3. Risks
4. Key people to be informed during the project
5. Negative stakeholders as well as their adverse effects on the project

HUMAN-CENTERED

Unlike the traditional approach to design, Design Thinking does not start with the technology or a product or a service. Design Thinking starts with the people who
need the product, process, or service and innovates for them.

Design Thinking identifies and addresses human needs. Design Thinking attempts to balance business requirements, human needs, the application of technologies and environmental sustainability.

Designers research how the end user has adapted their environment with their own designs or workarounds.

Human needs are investigated throughout the design process and the solution is refined through repetitive iterative steps with physical prototypes.

Design Thinking adapts the solution to the end user through understanding the end user.

OPTIMISM

Design Thinking is driven by the optimistic belief that we can create positive change. Creativity requires optimism, believing that all problems have a solution. A willingness to try new things, experiment, prototype, give up on old ideas or ways of doing things. It is a generative activity. The word is derived from the Latin word optimum, meaning "best." Being optimistic, means that you believe that you will discover the best possible solution to a design problem. To create anything new requires a belief that there is a better way. Some people will tell you why your idea will not work.

Some comments that kill optimism and progress:
1. We tried that before.
2. It costs too much
3. Let's get back to reality
4. That's not our problem
5. Now is not the right time.
6. It's impossible.
7. Quit dreaming.
8. We haven't got time for research
9. It's too radical
10. Let's put that one on the back burner for now.
11. We know what our customers want
12. I always follow my secretary's advice on color. She likes green.
13. I do not like the idea.
14. We are the experts
15. That's not my job.
16. We'll be a laughingstock
17. We've always done it this way

STORYTELLING

A powerful story can help ensure the success of a new product, service or experience. Storytelling can be an effective method of presenting a point of view. Research can uncover meaningful stories from end that illustrate needs or desires. These stories can become the basis of new designs or actions and be used to support decisions. Research shows that our attitudes, fears, hopes, and values are strongly influenced by story. Stories can be an effective way of communicating complex ideas and inspiring people to change.

How to tell an effective story

1. Answer in your story: What, why, when, who, where, how?
2. Offer a new vantage point
3. Share emotion
4. Communicate transformations
5. Communicate who you are.
6. Show cause and effect Describe conflicts and resolution.
7. Speak from your experience.
8. Describe how actions created change
9. Omit what is irrelevant.
10. Reveal meaning
11. Share your passion
12. Be honest and real
13. Build trust
14. Show connections
15. Transmits values
16. Share a vision
17. Share knowledge
18. Your story should differentiate you.
19. Use humor
20. Engage the audience
21. Craft the story for your audience.
22. Pose a problem and offer a resolution
23. The audience must be able to act on your story.

ACTIONS SPEAK LOADER THAN WORDS

Many companies today suffer from people who participate in discussion in meetings but do not follow through effectively with actions.

Design Thinking methods are focused on actions and creating real physical progress rather than discussion. Design Thinking is experiential and involved improvisation like a caveman experimenting with fire.

The process is continually hands on and means rolling your sleeves up and getting your hands dirty by trying things, making things and interacting rather than being a spectator.

Design Thinking deliberately takes an action oriented approach. This means that you should initiate physical actions yourself early in the project and continually as the project proceeds.

BE VISUAL

Design Thinking is an effective approach for solving ambiguous, complex and changing problems. The solving of such problems often involves communicating ideas which are hard to describe in words. Visual mapping methods, images and sketches can help make complex ideas easier to understand and share.

You can use visual techniques even if you are not good at drawing. Take pictures of user interactions with your camera or phone. Explore some of the mapping methods described in the Methods chapter of this book. Use Venn diagrams, experience journeys, perceptual maps and radar charts to make information easier to comprehend. These visual methods are good ways of communicating connections and relationships.

CONTINUOUS LEARNING

Design Thinking is an ongoing learning process that seeks to incorporate the lessons learned into a continuous improvement of design. It incorporates ideas drawn from the Japanese management philosophy of Kaisen, Japanese for "improvement", or "change for the better" which focus upon continuous improvement of products and processes

INEXPENSIVE MISTAKES

Design Thinking makes successful designs by making mistakes early in inexpensive prototypes and learning through end user and stakeholder feedback. Prototypes are conceived and constructed in order to learn. We retain the features that are working and discover areas where the design can be improved. A process built around prototyping is an effective way of reaching an effective design solution in the most efficient way.

Designers must be willing to make mistakes in order to reach a successful solution. The environment should not punish exploration and iterative failures. Design Thinkers are searching for validity. They are problem solvers.
The price of failures rises as the project proceeds. It saves cost to fail early.

Abductive thinking which is the style of reasoning most likely to develop new innovative ideas and solutions makes reasonable assumptions based on incomplete information.

With this mode of thinking it is inevitable that some experiments directions will result in unexpected results. These unexpected results may be viewed as mistakes or as part of a learning process to find the best solution.

"

Making products for
your customers is far
more efficient than
finding customers for
your products.

SETH GODIN
Author and entrepreneur

TOOLBOX

Design Thinking process is facilitated by a large number of design methods or tools.
The tools allow a designer to make informed design decisions that are not only about physical things but also about complex interfaces, systems, services and experiences. They will enable you to design products, systems buildings, interfaces and experiences with confidence that you have created the most informed design solutions for real people that is possible. These tools help designers think in four dimensions instead of three. .

The methods contained in this book will help you close the gap between your clients and organizations and the people that you are designing for to help you create more considered, informed, repeatable, innovative, empathetic design solutions that people need but may not yet know that they want. Different design practitioners can select different methods for their toolkit and apply them in different ways. There is no best combination.

EVIDENCE-BASED DESIGN

Design Thinking uses both intuitive and evidence based design. Evidence-Based Design is the process of basing design decisions on credible research to achieve the best possible outcomes. Evidence based design emphasizes the importance of basing decisions on the best possible data for the best possible outcomes

1. Evidence Based Design provides real evidence that improves outcomes and help with the clients bottom line.
2. The design is no longer based just on the designer's opinion
3. Define the problem that you are trying to solve.
4. Start with people. Identify the group of people that the design solution will be useful for.
5. Use an integrated multidisciplinary approach.
6. Use a human centric approach
7. Consider the business case and return on investment.
8. Design to measurable outcomes and to involve end users.
9. Use strategic partnerships to accelerate innovation,
10. Use simulation and testing to understand the end user's perspective
11. Communicate with and involve the stakeholders in the design process.

WICKED PROBLEMS

Design Thinking focuses on solutions to problems, It may be better than traditional design processes at addressing what have been called "Wicked Problems". Wicked problems are ill-defined or tricky problems, not necessarily wicked in the sense of evil. The iterative prototype and testing based approach does not assume a solution from the outset but experiments and tries alternative solutions and proceeds to refine the designs on the basis of successful testing.

Super wicked problems

K. Levin, proposed an additional type of problem called the "super wicked problem."He defined super wicked problems as having the following additional characteristics:
1. There is limited time.
2. No central decision maker.
3. The people who are trying to solve a problem are the same people who are causing the problem.
4. Policies discount the future irrationally.

Rittel and Webber specified ten characteristics of wicked problems in 1973:
1. "There is no definitive formulation of a wicked problem
2. Wicked problems have no stopping rule.
3. Solutions to wicked problems are not true-or-false, but better or worse.
4. There is no immediate and no ultimate test of a solution to a wicked problem.

5. Wicked problems do not have an enumerable set of potential solutions,
6. Every wicked problem is essentially unique.
7. Every wicked problem can be considered to be a symptom of another problem.
8. The existence of a discrepancy representing a wicked problem can be explained in numerous ways. The choice of explanation determines the nature of the problem's resolution.
9. The planner has no right to be wrong
10. Wicked problems have no given alternative solutions."
Source: Rittel and Webber

ANALOGOUS SITUATIONS

"Bring your staff together in a large room and put up a big white board. Create two columns, one for emotions and activities involved in your customer experience and a second one for similar situations which incorporate the same emotions and activities. Once you start filling in the first column, people will naturally start to brainstorm the analogous situations. When those are noted on the white board, people will start adding new emotions and activities to the first column based on their own experiences with the analogous situations. At the end of the process, choose the most vital pain points and use them as the basis of a brainstorming session to look for solutions and methods of improving the overall customer experience.

EVERYONE CAN CONTRIBUTE

Design Thinking process involves many stakeholders in working together to find a balanced design solution. The designer is a member of the orchestra. The customer is involved throughout the design process and works with the design team to communicate their needs and desires and to help generate design solutions that are relevant to them.

The many methods used help the design team to understand the diverse perspectives of the many stakeholders. It takes some courage for a designer to listen and recognize the point of view of the stakeholders. Managers, designers, social scientists, engineers marketers, stakeholders and others collaborate creatively to design.

The process is one of co-creation and the designer is a listener and a facilitator. Everyone adds value to the design. Design Thinking is not just for professional designers. Everyone can contribute. Many schools are now teaching Design Thinking to children as an approach that can be applied to life.

RE FRAMING THE PROBLEM

Reframe to create different perspectives and new ideas.

How to reframe:
1. Define the problem that you would like to address.
2. There is more than one way of looking at a problem. You could also define this problem in another way as."
3. What if a male or female used it?
4. What if it was used in China or Argentina?
5. "The underlying reason for the problem is."
6. "I think that the best solution is."
7. "You could compare this problem to the problem of."
8. "Another, different way of thinking about it is"

FUTURE ORIENTED

Design Thinking is a future oriented approach to designing. Most organizations base their new designs on what exists. Design Thinking allows an organization to change for the better. It allows an organization to move from being a follower to being a leader in the market.

FOCUS ON PEOPLE

Design is about people than it is about things. Stand in those people's shoes, see through their eyes, uncover their stories, share their worlds. Start each design by identifying a problem that real people are experiencing. Use the methods in this book selectively to gain empathy, understanding, and to inform your design. Good process is not a substitute for talented, motivated and skilled people on your design team.

GET PHYSICAL

Make simple physical prototypes of your ideas as early as possible. Constantly test your ideas with people. Do not worry about making prototypes beautiful until you are sure that you have a resolved design direction. Use the prototypes to guide and improve your design. Do several low cost prototypes to test how your Ideas physically work using cardboard, paper, markers, adhesive tape, photocopies, string and popsicle sticks. The idea is to test your idea, not to look like the final product. Expect to change it again. Limit your costs to ten or twenty dollars. Iterate, test and iterate. Do not make the prototype jewelry. It can stand in the way of finding the best design solution. In

TAKE CONSIDERED RISKS

Taking considered risks helps create differentiated design. Many designers and organizations do not have the flexibility or courage to create innovative, differentiated design solutions so they create products and services that are like existing products and services and compete on price.

USE THE TOOLS

To understand the point of view of diverse peoples and cultures a designer needs to connect with those people and their context. The tools in this book will help you see the world through the eyes of those people.

LEARN TO SEE AND HEAR

Reach out to understand people. Interpret what you see and hear. Read between the lines. Make new connections between the things you see and hear.

COMBINE ANALYTICAL AND CREATIVE THINKING

Effective collaboration is part of effective design. Designers work like members of an orchestra. We need to work with managers, engineers, salespeople and other professions. Human diversity and life experience contribute to better design solutions.

LOOK FOR BALANCE

Design Thinking seeks a balance of design factors including:

1. Business.
2. Empathy with people.
3. Application OF technology.
4. Environmental consideration.

TEAM COLLABORATION

Design today is a more complex activity than it was in the past. Business, technology, global cultural issues, environmental considerations, and human considerations all need careful consideration. Design Thinking recognizes the need for designers to be working as members of multidisciplinary multi skilled teams.

REPEATABLE INNOVATION

a 2015 study found that in 69% of companies interviewed considered that applying the Design Thinking process and methods had made their innovation more efficient. This study was the first large scale study of the innovation effect of implementing Design Thinking.

Data from 2015 study by Hasso-Plattner-Institut für softwaresystemtechnik an der Universität Potsdam, September 2015 of 235 German and international companies of all sizes

"

The secret to collaboration is finding a rhythm that alternates between team creativity and individual creativity.

MARTIN NEUMEIER
American author who writes on the topics of brand, design, innovation, and creativity

DESIGN THINKING
LOOK FOR BALANCE

PEOPLE

ENVIRONMENT

BUSINESS

TECHNOLOGY

"

Good design begins
with honesty, asks
tough questions and
comes from collaboration
and from trusting your
intuition

FREEMAN THOMAS
Automotive designer

THINKING STYLES

ABDUCTIVE THINKING

With abductive reasoning, unlike deductive reasoning, the premises do not guarantee the conclusion. Abductive reasoning can be understood as "inference to the best explanation" Abductive reasoning typically begins with an incomplete set of observations and proceeds to the likeliest possible explanation for the set. It's goal is to explore what could possibly be true.

"A person or organization instilled with that discipline is constantly seeking a fruitful balance between reliability and validity, between art and science, between intuition and analytics, and between exploration and exploitation. The design-thinking organization applies the designer's most crucial tool to the problems of business. That tool is abductive reasoning." *Roger Martin*

Charles Sanders Peirce originated the term and argued that no new idea could come from inductive or deductive logic.

DEDUCTIVE THINKING

The process of reasoning from one or more general statements (premises) to reach a logically certain conclusion. Deductive reasoning is one of the two basic forms of valid reasoning. It begins with a general hypothesis or known fact and creates a specific conclusion from that generalization.

Described by Aristotle 384-322bce, Plato 428-347bce, and Pythagoras 582-500 BCE

INDUCTIVE THINKING

Inductive thinking is a kind of reasoning that constructs or evaluates general propositions that are derived from specific examples. Inductive reasoning contrasts with deductive reasoning, in which specific examples are derived from general propositions.

Described by Aristotle 384-322bce,

CRITICAL THINKING

"The process of actively and skillfully conceptualizing, applying, analyzing, synthesizing, and evaluating information to reach an answer or conclusion. disciplined thinking that is clear, rational, open-minded, and informed by evidence, willingness to integrate new or revised perspectives into our ways of thinking and acting"

Critical thinking is an important element of all professional fields and academic disciplines

DESIGN THINKING

Design Thinking is a formal method for practical, creative resolution of problems and creation of solutions, with the intent of an improved future result. In this regard it is a form of solution-based, or solution-focused thinking

Source: Wikipedia

BUSINESS THINKING	DESIGN THINKING	CREATIVE THINKING
Left Brain	Uses whole brain	Right brain
Rational	Both rational and intuitive	Emotional
Structured	Structured and intuitive	Intuitive
Analytical	Analytical and creative	Creative
Likes well defined problems	Works with defined and ill defined problems	Works with ill defined complex problems
Does not tolerate mistakes	Mistakes are inexpensive and a learning opportunity	Tolerates mistakes during exploration
Analyse then decide	Prototype test decide	Ideate then decide
Focuses on parts of a problem	Focuses on parts and on whole iteratively	Holistic diffuse focus
Convergent	Convergent and divergent	Divergent
Vertical	Vertical and Lateral	Lateral
Objective	Objective and subjective	Subjective
Linear	Linear and associative	Associative
Yes but	Yes and yes but	Yes and .....
Verbal and mathematical	Visual, verbal mathematical	Visual
The answer	Explores, tests iterates	One possible answer
Judges	Withholds judgment until tested	Withhold judgment
Probability	Possibility and probability	Possibility
Improve	Improves and innovates	Innovate
Sequential	Sequential and synthesizing	Synthesizing
Analyze and evaluate	Imagines, synthesizes and tests	Imagine
Parts and details	Parts and the whole	Whole and big picture
Observe	Imagines and observes	Imagine
Numeric models	Numeric and experiential	Experiential models
Phases	Phases and dimesions	Dimensions
Sort and separate	Sorts infuses and blends	Infuse and blend
Independent	Independent and interdependent	Interdependent
Successive	Successive and simultaneous	Simultaneous
Safe	takes risk but minimizes the cost of failure	Risk taking
Knows	Believes, tests and knows	Believes

CREATIVE & ANALYTICAL THINKING

CREATIVE THINKING
Right Brain
Traditional training of designers and artists

Explore
Generate ideas
Imagine possibilities
Re-frame
Build ideas
"Yes and what if?
Try different perspectives
Imagine extreme cases
Increase ideas

DIVERGENT THINKING

CONVERGENT THINKING

Make decisions
Clarify
Make sense
Decrease
Create hierarchies
Refine
Cluster
Connect
Test

ANALYTICAL THINKING
Left Brain
Traditional training of managers and engineers

Soiurce: Adapted from the center for Creati8ve Emergence

"

It's no longer good enough to be the best of the best, you need to be the only ones who do what you do.

JERRY GARCIA
Grateful Dead

DIVERGENT THINKING

Convergent thinking is a tool for problem solving in which the brain is applies a mechanized system or formula to some problem, where the solution is a number of steps from the problem. This kind of thinking is particularly appropriate in science6, engineering, maths and technology.

Convergent thinking is opposite from divergent thinking in which a person generates many unique, design solutions to a design problem. Divergent thinking is followed by convergent thinking, in which a designer assesses, judges, and strengthens those options. Divergent thinking is what we do when we do not know the answer, when we do not know

CONVERGENT THINKING

The design process is a series of divergent and convergent phases. During the divergent phase of design the designer creates a number of choices. The goal of this approach is to analyze alternative approaches to test for the most stable solution. Divergent thinking is what we do when we do not know the answer, when we do not know the next step. Divergent thinking is followed by convergent thinking, in which a designer assesses, judges, and strengthens those options.

"

Until Design
Thinking came to
the Mayo Clinic
we were better at
poking holes in new
concepts than filling
them.

ALAN DUNCAN
Mayo Clinic

"

Before you start
to research your
audience. Do a
diagnostic of your
organization to find
out how you can
remove obstacles
to innovation. Do
an exercise to help
get your team up
to speed working
together.

WARMING UP

INNOVATION DIAGNOSTIC

WHAT IS IT?

An innovation diagnostic is an evaluation of an organization's innovation capabilities. It reviews practices by stakeholders which may help or hinder innovation. An innovation diagnostic is the first step in preparing an implementing a strategy to create an organizational culture that supports innovation.

WHY USE THIS METHOD?

1. It helps organizations develop sustainable competitive advantage.
2. Helps identify innovation opportunities
3. Helps develop innovation strategy.

WHEN TO USE THIS METHOD

1. Know Context
2. Know User
3. Frame insights
4. Explore Concepts
5. Make Plans

HOW TO USE THIS METHOD

An innovation diagnostic reviews organizational and stakeholder practices using both qualitative and quantitative methods including

1. The design and development process
2. Strategic practices and planning.
3. The ability of an organization to monitor and respond to relevant trends.
4. Technologies
5. Organizational flexibility
6. Ability to innovate repeatedly and consistently

INNOVATION DIAGNOSTIC TEST

DOES MANAGEMENT COMMUNICATE THE NEED FOR INNOVATION?

1. There is no innovation in our organization
2. Innovation is not a high priority
3. Our managers sometimes talk about innovation
4. Our managers discuss innovation but not why it is needed
5. Managers regularly state the compelling need for innovation

WHAT IS YOUR ORGANIZATIONAL STRATEGY?

1. We make low cost goods or services
2. Efficient operations
3. We are a customer focused organization
4. Fast Follower
5. Market leaders

IS THE BUSINESS THAT YOU ARE IN UNDERSTOOD BY EMPLOYEES?

1. We are not sure
2. We may get different answers from different managers
3. The definition changes in
4. We have some clarity

5. We are very clear about what business we are in

IS YOUR ORGANIZATION INNOVATIVE?

1. No
2. Probably not
3. We would like to be
4. There is some innovation
5. We are clearly an innovative organization

HOW DOES YOUR COMPANY INNOVATE?

1. We react to market forces without innovation
2. There is little innovation
3. We do some incremental innovation
4. We do mainly incremental innovation but would like to do some breakthrough innovation
5. We manage a portfolio of incremental and more substantial innovation and manage risks

DOES YOUR MANAGEMENT SUPPORT INNOVATION?

1. No
2. No resources are allocated to innovation

3. Some resources are allocated
4. We have some resources and some involvement from managers in innovation
5. We have clearly defined resources allocated and senior management is actively involved in planning and managing innovation

DO YOU HAVE CROSS DISCIPLINARY DESIGN TEAMS?

1. Never
2. Rarely
3. Sometimes
4. Usually
5. Always

DO YOU USE OUTSIDE EXPERTS TO ASSIST IN YOUR INNOVATION PROCESS?

1. Never
2. Rarely
3. Sometimes
4. Usually
5. Always

HOW OFTEN DOES YOUR ORGANIZATION ENGAGE CUSTOMERS TO IDENTIFY THEIR UNMET NEEDS?

1. Never
2. Rarely
3. Sometimes
4. Usually
5. Always

HOW WOULD YOU DEFINE THE RISK TOLERANCE AT YOUR COMPANY?

1. We don't take any risks
2. We rarely take risks
3. Sometimes we take substantial risks
4. We manage our risk portfolio actively and take big risks when appropriate.

HOW ARE NEW IDEAS RECEIVED IN YOUR ORGANIZATION?

1. We fire people with new ideas
2. We rarely adopt new ideas
3. We sometimes adopt new ideas but they are mostly not considered
4. We regularly consider new ideas
5. We actively generate and adopt new ideas

Add up the numbers of each answer that you selected and calculate a total for all the questions

HOW WELL DID YOU SCORE?

SCORE 35 TO 45
HIGHLY INNOVATIVE ORGANIZATION

The highest level of innovation is where companies are able to create innovations that change how people live. The highest level of innovation also brings the highest level of risk, as many times this level of innovation involves products or services that no one has thought of and customers do not know they want. Revolutionary products and services, large investment, big risks high payoff

SCORE 25 TO 35
INNOVATIVE ORGANIZATION

The third level is the beginning of large financial and product risk, but it is also where the rewards are potentially larger. This level also requires that the business devote resources to monitoring progress and actively assessing risk throughout the development process. Evolutionary products, large investment, medium risk, some payoff

SCORE 15 TO 25
SOMEWHAT INNOVATIVE

The second level is a higher level of changes. Level Two changes include integrating new features into existing products on the market or creating differentiated versions of the same new product to sell to various demographic groups. These new features require what can be considered a medium level of investment and risk. Advancement of existing products medium investment and risk medium payoff

SCORE 0 TO 15
LOW INNOVATION

The first level emphasizes minimal changes to existing products, a low amount of new investment, and very low risk. Examples at this level would be changing the color of a product or putting a new logo design on a label. Essentially all companies are capable of achieving this level, as it does not require unique skills. Few new features on existing products, low investment and risk. Low payoff.

ACTIONPLAN

ACTION PLAN:						
OBJECTIVE:						
NO.	ITEM	PERSON	RESOURCE	DATE	ACTUAL	STATUS
1						
2						
3						
4						
5						
6						
7						
8						
9						
10						
11						
12						
13						

ACTIONPLAN

WHAT IS IT?

An action plan is a document that summarizes action items, due dates and other related information.

WHY USE THIS METHOD?

1. To focus team effort.
2. To monitor progress towards a goal.

CHALLENGES

1. Start with the final delivery date required and work backwards to assign delivery dates for individual actions.
2. The action plan should be displayed where it can be accessed by all team members.

HOW TO USE THIS METHOD

1. Team brainstorms actions needed to reach a goal and the times when each action should be completed.
2. The moderator draws the action plan on a white board.
3. Team members are assigned responsibility for individual actions.
4. The plan is reviewed by the team to ensure that there are no conflicts.
5. The plan is signed off on by the team.
6. The plan is posted in the project room for future reference.

WARMING UP EXERCISES INTRODUCTION

WHAT ARE WARMING UP EXERCISES?
A warming up exercise is a short exercise at the beginning of a design project that helps the design team work productively together as quickly as possible. The duration of an icebreaker is usually less than 30 minutes.

They are an important component of collaborative or team based design. The Design Thinking approach recognizes the value of designers working productively as members of a diverse cross-disciplinary teams with managers, engineers, marketers and other professionals.

RESOURCES
White board
Dry erase markers
Large table
Chairs
Post-it-notes
A comfortable space
Digital camera

WHY USE THIS METHOD?
When a designer works with others in a new team it is important that the group works as quickly as possible in a creative constructive dialogue. An icebreaker is a way for team members to quickly start working effectively;y together. It is a worthwhile investment of half an hour at the beginning of a project and can be fun. Ice breakers help start people thinking creatively, exchanging ideas and help make a team work effectively. For meetings in a business setting in which contribute.

WHEN USE THIS METHOD
1. When team members do not know each other
2. When team members come from different cultures
3. When team needs to bond quickly
4. When team needs to work to a common gaol quickly.
5. When the discussion is new or unfamiliar.
6. When the moderator needs to know the participants.

COMMON GROUND WARMING UP EXERCISE

WHAT IS IT?

A warming up exercise is an exercise that is used at the beginning of a design project or workshop to help to stimulate constructive interaction. It helps everyone to engage in the dialogue and contribute effectively.

WHY USE THIS METHOD?

1. Helps create a comfortable and productive environment.
2. Helps people get to know each other.
3. Helps participants engage the group and tasks.
4. Helps participants contribute effectively.
5. Creates a sense of community.

CHALLENGES

1. Be aware of time constraints.
2. Should limit the time to 15 to 30 minutes
3. Make it simple
4. It should be fun
5. You should be creative
6. Be enthusiastic
7. If something isn't working move on.
8. Consider your audience
9. Keep in mind technology requirements such as a microphone or projector.
10. Chairs can be arranged in a circle to help participants read body language.
11. Select exercises appropriate for your group.

HOW TO USE THIS METHOD

1. The moderator ask the group to divide into pairs of participants
2. Each participant should select a group member that they do not know if possible.
3. Each person should interview the other person that they are paired with and make a list of 5 to ten things that they have in common.
4. One person from each pair should then present the list to the larger group.

RESOURCES

White board
Dry erase markers
Large table
Chairs
Post-it-notes
A comfortable space
Digital camera

DESERT ISLAND WARMING UP EXERCISE

WHAT IS IT?

A warming up exercise is an exercise that is used at the beginning of a design project or workshop to help to stimulate constructive interaction. It helps everyone to engage in the dialogue and contribute effectively,

WHY USE THIS METHOD?

1. Helps create a comfortable and productive environment.
2. Helps people get to know each other.
3. Helps participants engage the group and tasks.
4. Helps participants contribute effectively.
5. Creates a sense of community.

CHALLENGES

1. Be aware of time constraints. Should limit the time to 15 to 30 minutes
2. Make it simple
3. It should be fun
4. You should be creative
5. Consider your audience
6. Keep in mind technology requirements such as a microphone or projector.
7. Chairs can be arranged in a circle to help participants read body language.

WHEN TO USE THIS METHOD

1. Define intent
2. Explore Concepts

HOW TO USE THIS METHOD

1. Moderator introduces the warming up exercise.
2. Each person has 30 second to list all of the things that they should take. Each person should list at least 3 things.
3. Each person should defend why their 3 items should be one of the chosen items selected by their team.
4. Each team can vote for three items preferred by their team.
5. Each of the teams presents the 3 items that they have agreed upon to the larger group.

RESOURCES

White board
Dry erase markers
Large table
Chairs
Post-it-notes
A comfortable space
Digital camera

DIVERSITY WARMING UP EXERCISE

WHAT IS IT?

A warming up exercise is an exercise that is used at the beginning of a design project or workshop to help to stimulate constructive interaction. It helps everyone to engage in the dialogue and contribute effectively,

WHY USE THIS METHOD?

1. Helps create a comfortable and productive environment.
2. Helps people get to know each other.
3. Helps participants engage the group and tasks.
4. Helps participants contribute effectively.
5. Creates a sense of community.

CHALLENGES

1. Be aware of time constraints.
2. Should limit the time to 15 to 30 minutes
3. Make it simple
4. It should be fun
5. You should be creative
6. Be enthusiastic
7. If something isn't working move on.
8. Consider your audience
9. Keep in mind technology requirements such as a microphone or projector.
10. Chairs can be arranged in a circle to help participants read body language.
11. Select exercises appropriate for your group.

HOW TO USE THIS METHOD

12. The moderator introduces the exercise.
13. Place a number of objects or cards on the floor that represent the relative positions of the continents on a map of the earth.
14. The moderator asks each person to move to the spot where they were born.
15. When the group is in position the moderator asks each person to tell the group one thing about the place they were born.
16. Allow one or two minutes per person.
17. When this is complete the moderator asks the group to move to the place where they have spent the most of their adult life and tell the group one thing about that place.

RESOURCES

White board
Dry erase markers
Large table
Chairs
Post-it-notes
A comfortable space

EXPECTATIONS WARMING UP EXERCISE

WHAT IS IT?

A warming up exercise is an exercise that is used at the beginning of a design project or workshop to help to stimulate constructive interaction. It helps everyone to engage in the dialogue and contribute effectively,

WHY USE THIS METHOD?

1. Helps create a comfortable and productive environment.
2. Helps people get to know each other.
3. Helps participants engage the group and tasks.
4. Helps participants contribute effectively.
5. Creates a sense of community.

CHALLENGES

1. Be aware of time constraints. Should limit the time to 15 to 30 minutes
2. Make it simple
3. It should be fun
4. You should be creative
5. Be enthusiastic
6. If something isn't working move on.
7. Consider your audience
8. Keep in mind technology requirements such as a microphone or projector.
9. Chairs can be arranged in a circle to help participants read body language.
10. Select exercises appropriate for your group.

WHEN TO USE THIS METHOD

1. Define intent

HOW TO USE THIS METHOD

1. Each team member introduces themselves
2. Each team member outlines what is their expectations of the project.
3. Each team member shares their vision of the best possible outcome for the project.
4. Allow about 2 minutes per person

RESOURCES

White board
Dry erase markers
Large table
Chairs
Post-it-notes
A comfortable space
Digital camera

HOPES AND HURDLES WARMING UP EXERCISE

WHAT IS IT?

Hopes and hurdles is a brainstorm that identifies factors that may help or hinder the success of success of a project:

1. Business drivers and hurdles
2. User and employee drivers and hurdles
3. Technology drivers and hurdles
4. Environmental drivers and hurdles.
5. Vendors
6. Competitive benchmarking.

WHY USE THIS METHOD?

1. This method helps identify where Resources should be focused for most return on investment.
2. Enables stakeholders to understand other stakeholders expectations.

CHALLENGES

1. It provides a tangible focus for discussion.
2. It draws out tacit knowledge from your team.
3. It helps build team consensus.
4. It drives insights
5. Do not get too detailed
6. Some information may be sensitive.

HOW TO USE THIS METHOD

1. Define the problem.
2. Find a moderator
3. Brainstorm hopes and hurdles
   - Which are our own advantages?
   - What are we able to do quite well?
   - What strategic Resources can we rely upon?
   - What could we enhance?
   - What should we avoid to do?
   - What are we doing poorly?
4. Collect the ideas on a white board or wall with post-it-notes.
5. Organize the contributions into two lists.
6. Prioritize each element
7. Use the lists to create strategic options.

RESOURCES

White board
Marker pens
Post-it notes
Flip chart
Video Camera
Camera

INTERVIEW WARMING UP EXERCISE

WHAT IS IT?

A warming up exercise is an exercise that is used at the beginning of a design project or workshop to help to stimulate constructive interaction. It helps everyone to engage in the dialogue and contribute effectively,

WHY USE THIS METHOD?

1. Helps create a comfortable and productive environment.
2. Helps people get to know each other.
3. Helps participants engage the group and tasks.
4. Helps participants contribute effectively.
5. Creates a sense of community.

CHALLENGES

1. Be aware of time constraints. Should limit the time to 15 to 30 minutes
2. Make it simple
3. It should be fun
4. You should be creative
5. Consider your audience
6. Keep in mind technology requirements such as a microphone or projector.
7. Chairs can be arranged in a circle to help participants read body language.

WHEN TO USE THIS METHOD

1. Define intent
2. Explore Concepts

HOW TO USE THIS METHOD

1. Moderator introduces the warming up exercise.
2. The group is paired into groups of two people who do not know each other.
3. The paired groups spend five minutes interviewing each other.
4. The interviewer introduces the interviewee to the group.
5. 3 minutes per person.

RESOURCES

White board
Dry erase markers
Large table
Chairs
Post-it-notes
A comfortable space
Digital camerar

JUMPSTART STORYTELLING

WHAT IS IT?
A warming up exercise is an exercise that is used at the beginning of a design project or workshop to help to stimulate constructive interaction. It helps everyone to engage in the dialogue and contribute effectively,

WHY USE THIS METHOD?
1. Stories reveal what is happening.
2. Stories inspire us to take action.
3. Stories are remembered.
4. Stories share and imbed values.
5. Stories connect people.

WHO INVENTED IT?
Seth Kahan

RESOURCES
Paper
Pens
White board
Dry-erase markers
Post-it-notes.

CHALLENGES
1. Be aware of time constraints. Should limit the time to 15 to 30 minutes
2. Make it simple
3. It should be fun
4. You should be creative
5. Consider your audience

6. Keep in mind technology requirements such as a microphone or projector.
Chairs can be arranged in a circle to help participants read body language.

HOW TO USE THIS METHOD
1. Divide the participants into groups of 5
2. Ask everyone to provide a story that is related to the objective of the workshop.
3. Each person gets 90 seconds.
4. Ask the participants to remember the story that resonated the most with them;
5. Reform the groups of 5 with different people.
6. Ask everyone to retell their story.
7. Note how the story improves with each retelling.
8. 90 seconds per story.
9. Ask each participant to reassess which story resonates with them the most.
10. Ask everyone to remember the person who told the most powerful, relevant, engaging story.
11. When clusters appear invite the people the group favored to retell their story to the whole group.

MILESTONES WARMING UP EXERCISE

WHAT IS IT?

A warming up exercise is an exercise that is used at the beginning of a design project or workshop to help to stimulate constructive interaction. It helps everyone to engage in the dialogue and contribute effectively,

WHO INVENTED IT?

Ava S, Butler 1996

WHY USE THIS METHOD?

1. Helps create a comfortable and productive environment.
2. Helps people get to know each other.
3. Helps participants engage the group and tasks.
4. Helps participants contribute effectively.
5. Creates a sense of community.

CHALLENGES

1. Be aware of time constraints.
2. Should limit the time to 15 to 30 minutes
3. Make it simple
4. It should be fun
5. You should be creative
6. Be enthusiastic
7. If something isn't working move on.
8. Consider your audience
9. Keep in mind technology requirements such as a microphone or projector.
10. Chairs can be arranged in a circle to help participants read body language.
11. Select exercises appropriate for your group.

HOW TO USE THIS METHOD

1. The moderator creates a milestone chart on a white board
2. The moderator estimates the age of the oldest members of the group and on a horizontal line write years from the approximate birth year of the older members to the present at 5 year intervals.
   1960 1965 1970 1975.
3. Using post-it notes each participant adds three personal milestones to the chart. One milestone per post-it-note under the year that the milestone occurred.
4. During the break participants read the milestones.

RESOURCES

White board
Dry erase markers
Large table
Chairs
Post-it-notes
A comfortable space
Digital camera

"

Frameworks help give structure to your research. If you are not sure where to start with research consider using a framework

DISCOVERY FRAMEWORKS

ETHNOGRAPHIC FRAMEWORKS
INTRODUCTION

If you are not sure where to start with research consider using a framework such as one of the following. This is a summary of some of the more common frameworks.

9 DIMENSIONS
Spradley, J. P. (1980) and Robson, C. (2002).

SPACE - layout of the physical setting; rooms, outdoor spaces, etc.
ACTORS - the names and relevant details of the people involved
ACTIVITIES - the various activities of the actors
OBJECTS - physical elements: furniture etc.
ACTS - specific individual actions
EVENTS - particular occasions, e.g. meetings
TIME - the sequence of events
GOALS - what actors are attempting to accomplish
FEELINGS - emotions in particular contexts

AEIOU
The Doblin Group/eLab
A - Activities are goal directed sets of actions-things which people want to accomplish
E - Environments include the entire arena where activities take place
I - Interactions are between a person and someone or something else, and are the building blocks of activities
O - Objects are building blocks of the environment, key elements sometimes put to complex or unintended uses, changing their function, meaning and context
U - Users are the consumers, the people providing the behaviors, preferences and needs (E-Lab 1997)
Descriptions from Christina Wasson's Ethnography in the field of design

A(X4)
Rothstein, P. (2001).
Atmosphere
Actors
Artifacts
Activities
4/ Bringing the Outside In
Sotirin, P. (1999).
Territory - including space and architecture
Stuff - furniture, possession, private/public, visual signs, technology
People - flows, dress, bodies, nonverbal behaviors, authority, affection
Talk - conversation, vocabularies

POSTA

Tracked as far as Pat Sachs
(Social Solutions) and Gitte Jordan
(Institute for Research on Learning)
P - Person
O - Objects
S - Situations
T - Time
A - Activity
6/ POEMS
Kumar and Whitney, 2003
P - People
O - Objects
E - Environments
M - Messages
S - Services

Source: Jono Hey

AEIOU

WHAT IS IT?

One of a number of ethnographic frameworks have been developed to give structure to observations and to ensure that the researcher doesn't miss important data.

Activities: Goal directed sets of actions which people want to accomplish.
Environments: where activities take place
Objects: located in an environment. Their use, function, meaning and context.
Users: The people and their behaviors, preferences and needs.

Source Recording ethnographic observations: palojono

WHO INVENTED IT?

The AEIOU framework was originated in 1991 at Doblin by Rick Robinson, Ilya Prokopoff, John Cain, and Julie Pokorny.

WHY USE THIS METHOD?

1. To give structure to research
2. In order to collect most important information.
3. To provide some certainty in the uncertain environment of fieldwork

CHALLENGES

"AEIOU framework suffers from a number of obvious limitations; it has no place to identify broad cultural patterns and ignores questions of change, history, and political economy. Such an overly exclusive focus on the microlevel was particularly characteristic of ELab's earliest days. By the time I worked there, researchers were developing various ways to incorporate macro level issues into their analyses. The AEIOU framework was still used for certain purposes, but its limitations were recognized."
Source: Christina Worsing"

HOW DO YOU USE IT?

1. Materials are gathered via ethnographic methods: notes, photos, videos, interviews, field observation, etc.
2. During field observation, use the AEIOU framework as a lens to observe the surrounding environment.
3. Record observations under the appropriate headings.
4. Supplement direct observations with photos or video tape when appropriate.
5. Review and cluster observations to disseminate higher-level themes and patterns.
Source: Ehnohub

LATCH

WHAT IS IT?

One of a number of ethnographic frameworks have been developed to give structure to observations and to ensure that the researcher doesn't miss important data.

1. **Location** Compare information sources.
2. **Alphabet** Used for very large volume of data.
3. **Time** Used for events that occur over a measurable duration of time.
4. **Category** Grouped by similarity of characteristics.
5. **Hierarchy** Information is organized on a scale

WHO INVENTED IT?

Richard Saul Wurman, 1996

WHY USE THIS METHOD?

1. To give structure to research
2. In order to collect most important information.
3. To provide some certainty in the uncertain environment of fieldwork

RESOURCES

Computer
Notebook
Pens
Video camera
Digital camera
Digital voice recorder
Release forms
Interview plan or structure
Questions, tasks and discussion items

SPOOL

GOALS

1. What is the user trying to accomplish?
2. How will the user know when they are done? What will be different?
3. How does the user describe their goals?
4. How do the user's actions fit into the objectives of the organization?
5. Who established the goals for the user? Were they self anointed or were they assigned by someone else?
6. Are the user's immediate goals part of a larger scope? (For example, the new point-of-sale application is one piece of delivering an entire new line of business.)

PROCESS

1. What are the steps the user will follow?
2. Who defined the steps?
3. How prepared is the user for each step? (Do they have it all laid out or
4. does it seem to be ad-hoc?)
5. How does information flow from one step to the next?
6. What are the various roles (such as creator, contributor, editor, or
7. approver) that are involved?
8. How long does the process take?
9. What artifacts (such as design documents, emails, or white board drawings)
10. are used?
11. How do the various team members communicate with each other?
12. What other tools are used during the process?

INPUTS & OUTPUTS

1. What materials and information will the user need to successfully use the interface?
2. Who will they get that information from?
3. What do they do when the information isn't complete?
4. What will they need from the interface to continue with their overarching goals?
5. Who do they give those results to?
6. What happens after they've turned them over? (Does the user move on to something else or do they have more interactions?)

EXPERIENCE

1. What similar things has the user done in their past?
2. Is this something that repeats itself or is the use a first-time occasion?
3. What journals or magazines do they read?
4. What kind of "organizational memory" helps the user avoid mistakes of the past?
5. How has the organization survived without this design in the past?
6. What competitors systems have users taken advantage of?
7. How will the user learn how to use the tool?
8. What training has the user received?
9. What conferences has the user attended?

CONSTRAINTS

1. What physical, temporal, or financial constraints are likely to impose themselves on the user's work?
2. What ideals are subverted by reality as the work progresses?
3. What constraints can the user predict in advance? What can't be predicted?

PHYSICAL ENVIRONMENT

1. How much room does the user have to work?
2. Do they have a place to store the documentation?
3. What materials on their desk?
4. What access do they have to necessary information (such as user manuals)?
5. What is taped to their monitor?

TOOLS IN USE

1. What hardware and software does the user currently use?
2. Do they participate in on-line forums?

RELATIONSHIPS

1. What are the interactions between the primary user and other people who are affected by the tool?
2. Does the user interact with other people who use the tool?

Source Jared M. Spool

NINE DIMENSIONS

WHAT IS IT?

One of a number of ethnographic frameworks have been developed to give structure to observations and to ensure that the researcher doesn't miss important data.

1. **Space:** Layout of the physical setting, rooms outdoor spaces etc.
2. **Actors:** The names and details of the people involved
3. **Activities:** the various activities of the actors
4. **Objects:** Physical elements: furniture etc
5. **Acts:** Specific Individual actions
6. **Events:** Particular occasions Eg meetings
7. **Time:** The sequence of events
8. **Goals:** What actors are attempting to accomplish
9. **Feelings:** Emotions in particular contexts

Source Recording ethnographic observations: palojono

WHO INVENTED IT?

Spradley, J. P. 1980

WHY USE THIS METHOD?

10. To give structure to research
11. In order to collect most important information.
12. To provide some certainty in the uncertain environment of fieldwork

RESOURCES

Computer
Notebook
Pens
Video camera
Digital camera
Digital voice recorder
Release forms
Interview plan or structure
Questions, tasks and discussion items

POSTA

WHAT IS IT?

One of a number of ethnographic frameworks have been developed to give structure to observations and to ensure that the researcher doesn't miss important data.

1. **People**
2. **Objects**
3. **Settings**
4. **Time**
5. **Activities**

WHO INVENTED IT?

May have been invented by Pat Sachs Social Solutions and Gitte Jordan Institute for Research on Learning

WHY USE THIS METHOD?

1. To give structure to research
2. In order to collect most important information
3. To provide some certainty in the uncertain environment of fieldwork

HOW TO USE THIS METHOD

Observe participant in the work setting around, observing what they do and how they interact with other people and tools in their environment. Or they may focus on key objects or artifacts in the environment, with special attention to the various roles that they play (functional, psychological and social). During another observation, the team may take notes and photo-graphs of the work setting and try to understand how the configuration of space mediates the work. Finally, they chart activities, including both formal work flow and informal work practices.

RESOURCES

Computer
Notebook
Pens
Video camera
Digital camera
Digital voice recorder
Release forms
Interview plan or structure
Questions, tasks and discussion items

"

Develop a deep understanding of your end-users through engaging them observing and listening to them explain their point of view, their problems and their needs.

This phase involves both creative and analytical thinking

RESEARCH
EMPATHIZE
DISCOVER

"

Innovation is all about people. Innovation thrives when the population is diverse, accepting and willing to cooperate.

VIVEK WADHWA
Entrepreneur Researcher and Writer.

ASSEMBLE YOUR TEAM

Select a diverse cross disciplinary group of people. Have different disciplines, different genders, ages, cultures, represented for the most successful results. Have some T shaped people. These are people who have more than one area of experience or training such as design and management. They will help your team collaborate productively.

DEFINE YOUR TARGET AUDIENCE

Creating a projected user models will keep the development team rooted to a realistic user requirements and minimizes user frustration with the real product. Having a deep understanding of users can help development team better understand the wants & needs of the targeted customers. This will help the development team relate better with the target user. Understanding user tasks helps in developing design solutions that will ensure that the user expectations are met & avoid design errors and customer frustration. Use research methods such as interviewing, observation, empathy maps and user experience maps to better understand your audience. Market segmentation is basically the division of market into smaller segments. It helps identify potential customers and target them.

Types of segmentation
1. Behavior segmentation
2. Benefit segmentation
3. Psychographic segmentation
4. Geographic segmentation
5. Demographic segmentation

1. What is your target group's goals emotions, experiences, needs and desires?
2. Information collected from just a few people is unlikely to be representative of the whole range of users.
3. What are the user tasks and activities?
4. How will the user use the product or service to perform a task?
5. What is the context of the user?
6. Where are they? What surrounds them physically and virtually or culturally?
7. How large is your user group?

When defining your target audience consider factors such as:
1. Age
2. Gender
3. Occupation
4. Industry
5. Travel
6. Citizenship status
7. Marital state
8. Income
9. Culture
10. Occupation
11. Language
12. Religion
13. Location
14. Education
15. Nationality
16. Mobility
17. Migration
18. Mental state
19. Abilities
20. Disabilities
21. Health

TEAM BUILDING EXERCISE

A team building exercise is a short exercise at the beginning of a Design Thinking project that helps the design team work productively together as quickly as possible. The duration of an exercise is usually less than 30 minutes. I describe some examples of exercises in the following chapter.

They are an important component of collaborative or team based design. The Design Thinking approach recognizes the value of designers working productively as members of a diverse cross-disciplinary teams with managers, engineers, marketers and other professionals.

SHARE WHAT YOU KNOW

1. In the project kick off meeting ask every team member to introduce themselves and to describe in 3 minutes what experience they have that may be relevant to the project.
2. The moderator can list areas of knowledge on a white board.

IDENTIFY WHAT YOU NEED TO KNOW

Arrange a project kick-off meeting. Invite your team and important stakeholders. On a white board or flip chart create two lists. Ask each person to introduce themselves and describe what they know or have experienced that may be useful for implementing the project. Brainstorm with your group the areas that are unknown

and how that information may be obtained. Formulate a research plan and assign responsibilities, tasks and deliverables with dates.

UNCOVER NEEDS

1. "What causes the problem?"
2. "What are the impacts of the problem?"
3. ""What are possible solutions?"
4. Probe about workarounds How do people adapt their environment to solve problems that they have?
5. Ask what their single biggest obstacle is to achieve what they are trying to achieve How can you help them?
6. Ask what's changing in their world What are the trends?
7. Observe people
8. Can you see problems they have that they perhaps do not even recognize are problems?
9. Ask other stakeholders

DEFINE THE GOALS

A goal is the intent or intents of the design process.

1. Write a detailed description of the design problem.
2. Define a list of needs that are connected to the design problem.
3. Make a list of obstacles that need to be overcome to solve the design problem.
4. Make a list of constraints that apply to the problem.
5. Rewrite the problem statement to articulate the above requirements.

UNCOVER PEOPLES STORIES

A powerful story can help ensure the success of a new product, service or experience. Storytelling can be an effective method of presenting a point of view. Research can uncover meaningful stories from end that illustrate needs or desires. These stories can become the basis of new designs or actions and be used to support decisions. Stories can be an effective way of communicating complex ideas and inspiring people to change.

1. The stories help to get buy-in from people throughout the design process and may be used to help sell a final design.
2. Real life stories are persuasive.
3. They are different to advertising because they are able to influence a design if uncovered from users during the early research phases and provide authenticity.

Challenges
1. A story with too much jargon will lose an audience.
2. Not everyone has the ability to tell vivid stories.
3. Stories are not always generalizable.

An effective story:
1. Meets information needs for your audience
2. Offer a new vantage point
3. Tell real world stories
4. Evoke the future
5. Share emotion
6. Communicate transformations
7. Communicate who you are.
8. Describe actions
9. Show cause and effect
10. Speak from your experience.
11. Describe how actions created change
12. Omit what is irrelevant.
13. Share your passion
14. Be honest and real
15. Build trust
16. Transmits values
17. Share a vision
18. Share knowledge
19. Your story should differentiate you.
20. Use humor
21. Engage the audience
22. Craft the story for your audience.
23. Pose a problem and offer a resolution
24. Use striking imagery
25. The audience must be able to act on your story.

AFFINITY DIAGRAMS

WHAT IS IT?

Affinity diagrams are a tool for analyzing large amounts of data and discovering relationships which allow a design direction to be established based on the affinities. This method may uncover important hidden relationships.

Affinity diagrams are created through consensus of the design team on how the information should be grouped in logical ways.

WHO INVENTED IT?

Jiro Kawaita, Japan, 1960

WHY USE THIS METHOD?

Traditional design methods are less useful when dealing with complex or chaotic problems with large amounts of data. This method helps to establish relationships of affinities between pieces of information. From these relationships insights can be determined which are the starting point of design solutions. It is possible using this method to reach consensus faster than many other methods.

HOW TO USE THIS METHOD

1. Select your team
2. Place individual opinions or answers to interview questions or design concepts on post-it-notes or cards.
3. Spread post-it-notes or cards on a wall or large table.
4. Group similar items.
5. This can be done silently by your design team moving them around as they each see affinities. Work until your team has consensus.
6. Name each group with a different colored card or Post-it-note above the group.
7. Repeat by grouping groups.
8. Rank the most important groups.
9. Photograph results
10. Analyze affinities and create insights.
11. 5 to 20 participants

RESOURCES

White board
Large wall spaces or tables
Dry-erase markers
Sharpies
Post-it notes

HOW TO CREATE AN AFFINITY DIAGRAM

1 Collect more than 150 pieces of research data through ethnographic techniques such as interviews or observation. Put each piece of data on one card or post it note.

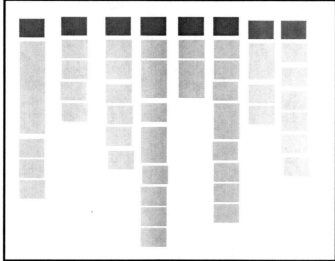

3 Ask your team without talking to arrange the post it notes into associated groups in vertical columns. Add a different colored header which describes what connects the data in each group.

2 When you return to your office spread the post it notes or cards randomly on a large wall or table

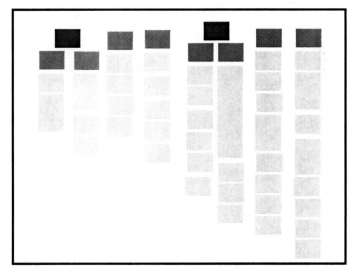

4 Crete super headers in a different color if groups can be combined. Organize groups into a hierarchy of importance of design issues to be addressed

ANTHROPUMP

WHAT IS IT?

This method involves the research videotaping one or more participant's activities. The videos are replayed to the participants and they are asked to explain their behavior.

WHO INVENTED IT?

Rick Robinson, John Cain, E- Lab Inc.,

WHY USE THIS METHOD?

Used for collecting data before concept and for evaluating prototypes after concept phases of projects,

CHALLENGES

Best conducted by someone who has practice observing human interactions in a space.

RESOURCES

Video camera
Video projector
Note pad
White board
Dry erase markers

HOW TO USE THIS METHOD

1. People are first captured on video while interacting with products.
2. The participants are then asked to watch the tapes while researchers question them about what they see, how they felt, etc. In effect, research subjects analyses their own actions and experiences.
3. The company invites people who have been captured on video to watch their tapes as researchers pose questions about what's happening.
4. E Lab videotapes and dissects these follow-up sessions, analyzing research subjects analyzing themselves.

"

For good ideas
and true innovation,
you need human
interaction, conflict,
argument, debate

MARGARET HEFFERNAN
CEO businessperson and writer

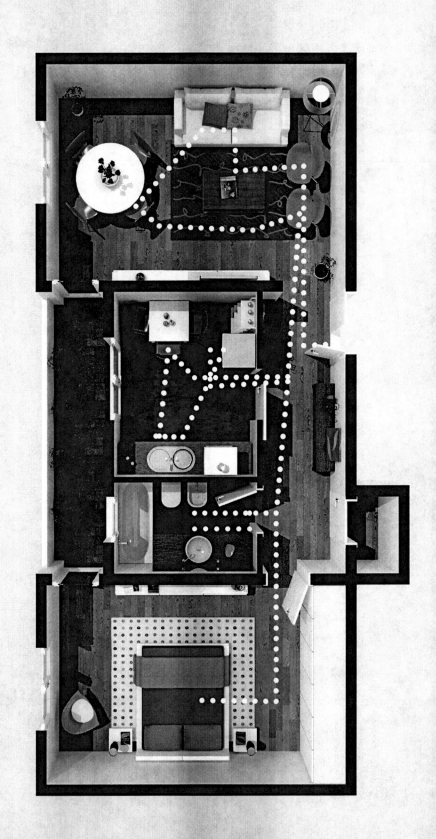

BEHAVIORAL MAP

WHAT IS IT?

Behavioral mapping is a method used to record and analyze human activities in a location. This method is used to document what participants are doing and time spent at locations and traveling. Behavioral maps can be created based on a person or a space

WHO INVENTED IT?

Ernest Becker 1962

WHY USE THIS METHOD?

1. This method helps develop an understanding of space layouts, interactions and experiences and behaviors.
2. Helps understand way finding.
3. Helps optimize use of space.
4. A limitation of this method is that motivations remain unknown.
5. Use when you want to develop more efficient or effective use of space in retail environments, exhibits, architecture and interior design.

HOW TO USE THIS METHOD

1. Decide who are the users.
2. Ask what is the purpose of the space?
3. Consider what behaviors are meaningful.
4. Consider different personas.
5. Participants can be asked to map their use of a space on a floor plan and can be asked to reveal their motivations.
6. Can use shadowing or video ethnographic techniques.
7. Create behavioral map.
8. Analyze behavioral map
9. Reorganize space based on insights.

RESOURCES

A map of the space.
Video camera
Digital still camera
Notebook
Pens

BENCHMARKING MATRIX FOR PRODUCT DESIGN

CRITERIA	A	B	C	D	E	F	G	H	I
USABILITY	1	2	3	1	4	1	1	2	3
SPEED TO MARKE	2	1	1	2	2	4	2	1	4
BRAND COMPATIBILITY	3	3	4	1	3	0	3	1	2
ROI	2	3	1	1	4	1	1	3	3
FITS STRATEGY	1	1	1	4	0	3	1	2	2
AESTHETIC APPEAL	2	4	0	2	2	4	0	4	4
DIFFERENTIATION	2	2	2	0	1	1	3	3	0
TOOLING COST	2	2	1	1	1	2	0	4	3
FITS DISTRIBUTION	2	2	3	1	2	1	4	0	3
USES OUR FACTORY	3	3	5	3	0	3	2	1	3
FITS TRENDS	1	3	2	2	1	3	4	3	2
TOTAL	21	26	23	18	20	23	21	24	29

BENCHMARKING

WHAT IS IT?
Benchmarking is a method for organizations to compare their products, services or customer experiences with other industry products, services and experiences in order to identify the best practices.

WHO INVENTED IT?
Robert Camp Xerox, 1989 Benchmarking: the search for industry best practices that lead to superior performance.

WHY USE THIS METHOD?
1. A tool to identify, establish, and achieve standards of excellence.
2. A structured process of continually searching for the best methods, practices, and processes and either adopting them
3. The practice of measuring your performance against world-class organizations.

WHEN TO USE THIS METHOD
1. Define intent
2. Know Context
3. Know User
4. Frame insights

CHALLENGES
1. Can be expensive
2. Organizations often think their companies were performining above the average for the industry when they are not.

HOW TO USE THIS METHOD
1. Identify what you would like to be bench marked,
2. Define the process,
3. Identify potential partners
4. Identify similar industries and organizations.
5. Identify organizations that are leaders.
6. Identify data sources
7. Identify the products or organizations to be bench marked
8. Select the benchmarking factors to measure.
9. Undertake benchmarking
10. Visit the "best practice" companies to identify leading edge practices
11. Analyze the outcomes
12. Target future performance
13. Adjust goal
14. Modify your own product or service to conform with best practices identified in benchmarking process.

RESOURCES
Post-it-notes
Pens
Dry-erase markers
White board
Paper

CULTURAL INVENTORY

WHAT IS IT?

It is a survey focused on the cultural assets of a location or organization.

WHO INVENTED IT?

Julian Haynes Steward may have been the first to use the term in 1947.

WHY USE THIS METHOD?

1. Can be used in strategic planning
2. Can be used to solve problems.

CHALLENGES

1. Requires time and resources

HOW TO USE THIS METHOD

1. Create your team
2. Collect existing research
3. Review existing research and identify gaps
4. Host a meeting of stakeholders
5. Promote the meeting
6. Ask open-ended questions about the culture and heritage
7. Set a time limit of 2 hours for the meeting.
8. Plan the collection phase
9. Compile inventory. This can be in the form of a web site
10. Distribute the inventory and obtain feedback.

RESOURCES

Diary
Notebooks
Pens
Post-it notes
Voice recorder
Post cards
Digital Camera

CULTURAL PROBES

WHAT IS IT?

A cultural probe is a method of collecting information about people, their context and their culture. The aim of this method is to record events, behaviors and interactions in their context. This method involves the participants to record and collect the data themselves.

WHO INVENTED IT?

Bill Gaver Royal College of Art London 1969

WHY USE THIS METHOD?

1. This is a useful method when the participants that are being studied are hard to reach for example if they are travelling.
2. It is a useful technique if the activities being studied take place over an extended period or at irregular intervals.
3. The information collected can be used to build personas.

CHALLENGES

It is important with this method to select the participants carefully and give them support during the study.

HOW TO USE THIS METHOD

1. Define the objective of your study.
2. Recruit your participants.
3. Brief the participants
4. Supply participants with kit. The items in the kit are selected to collect the type of information you want to gather and can include items such as notebooks, diary, camera, voice recorder or post cards.
5. You can use an affinity diagram to analyze the data collected

RESOURCES

Diary
Notebooks
Pens
Post-it notes
Voice recorder
Post cards
Digital Camera

CAMERA JOURNAL

WHAT IS IT?

The research subjects record their activities with a camera and notes. The researcher reviews the images and discusses them with the participants.

WHY USE THIS METHOD?

1. Helps develop empathy for the participants.
2. Participants are involved in the research process.
3. Helps establish rapport with participants.
4. May reveal aspects of life that are seldom seen by outsiders.

CHALLENGES

1. Should obtain informed consent.
2. May not be ideal for research among particularly vulnerable people.
3. May be a relatively expensive research method.
4. May be time consuming.
5. Best used with other methods.
6. Technology may be unreliable.
7. Method may be unpredictable'.
8. Has to be carefully analyzed

HOW TO USE THIS METHOD

1. Define subject of study
2. Define participants
3. Gather data images and insight statements.
4. Analyze data.
5. Identify insights
6. Rank insights
7. Produce criteria for concept generation from insights.
8. Generate concepts to meet needs of users.

RESOURCES

Cameras
Voice recorder
Video camera
Note pad
Pens

DAY IN THE LIFE

WHAT IS IT?
A study in which the designer observes the participant in the location and context of their usual activities, observing and recording events to understand the activities from the participant's point of view. This is sometimes repeated. Mapping a 'Day in the Life' as a storyboard can provide a focus for discussion.

WHO INVENTED IT?
ALex Bavelas 1944

WHY USE THIS METHOD?
1. This method informs the design process by observation of real activities and behaviors.
2. This method provides insights with relatively little cost and time.

CHALLENGES
1. Choose the participants carefully
2. Document everything. Something that seems insignificant may become significant later.

HOW TO USE THIS METHOD
1. Define activities to study
2. Recruit participants
3. Prepare
4. Observe subjects in context.
5. Capture data,
6. Create storyboard with text and timeline.
7. Analyze data
8. Create insights.
9. Identify issues
10. Identify needs
11. Add new/more requirements to concept development

RESOURCES
Camera
Notebook
Video camera
Voice recorder
Pens

DIARY STUDY

WHAT IS IT?

This method involves participants recording specific events, feelings or interactions, in a diary supplied by the researcher. User Diaries help provide insight into behavior. Participants record their behavior and thoughts. Diaries can uncover behavior that may not be articulated in an interview or easily visible to outsiders.

WHO INVENTED IT?

Gordon Allport, may have been the first to describe diary studies in 1942.

WHY USE THIS METHOD?

1. Can capture data that is difficult to capture using other methods.
2. Useful when you wish to gather information and minimize your influence on research subjects.
3. When the process or event you're exploring takes place intermittently or
4. When the process or event you're exploring takes place over a long period.

CHALLENGES

1. Process can be expensive and time consuming.
2. Needs participant monitoring.
3. It is difficult to get materials back.

WHEN TO USE THIS METHOD

1. Know Context
2. Know User
3. Frame insights

HOW TO USE THIS METHOD

1. A diary can be kept over a period of one week or longer.
2. Define focus for the study.
3. Recruit participants carefully.
4. Decide method: preprinted, diary notebook or on line.
5. Prepare diary packs. Can be preprinted sheets or blank 20 page notebooks with prepared questions or on line web based diary.
6. Brief participants.
7. Distribute diaries directly or by mail.
8. Conduct study. Keep in touch with participants.
9. Conduct debrief interview.
10. Look for insights.

RESOURCES

Diary
Preprinted diary sheets
Online diary
Pens
Disposable cameras
Digital camera
Self addressed envelopes

DESIGN WORKSHOP

WHAT IS IT?

A design workshop is a strategic design method that involves bringing the design team together with stakeholders to explore issue related to explore issues related to the people who are being designed for or to create design solutions.

WHY USE THIS METHOD?

1. Fast and inexpensive.
2. Increased probability of implementation.
3. Stakeholders can share information.
4. Promotes trust.

CHALLENGES

1. Managing work flow can be challenging.
2. Stakeholders may have conflicting visions.

WHEN TO USE THIS METHOD

1. Know Context
2. Know User
3. Frame insights
4. Explore Concepts

HOW TO USE THIS METHOD

1. See charrettes and creative toolkits.

RESOURCES

1. Paper flip chart
2. White board
3. Colored markers
4. Cards
5. Masking tape
6. Rolls of butcher paper
7. Post-it notes
8. Adhesive dots
9. Glue
10. Pins
11. Pens
12. Scissors
13. Spray adhesive
14. Screen
15. Laptop
16. Projector
17. Extension leads
18. Video Camera
19. Digital Camera
20. Chairs
21. Tables

CHARRETTE

WHAT IS IT?

A design charrette is a collaborative design workshop usually held over one day or several days. Charrettes are a fast way of generating ideas while involving diverse stakeholders in your decision process. Charrettes have many different structures and often involve multiple sessions. The group divides into smaller groups. The smaller groups present to the larger group.

WHO INVENTED IT?

The French word, "charrette" spelt with two r's means "cart" This use of the term is said to originate from the École des Beaux Arts in Paris during the 19th century, where a cart, collected final drawings while students finished their work.

WHY USE THIS METHOD?

1. Fast and inexpensive.
2. Increased probability of implementation.
3. Stakeholders can share information.
4. Promotes trust.

CHALLENGES

1. Managing work flow can be challenging.
2. Stakeholders may have conflicting visions.

WHEN TO USE THIS METHOD

1. Define intent
2. Know context and user
3. Frame insights
4. Explore concepts
5. Make Plans

RESOURCES

Large space
Tables
Chairs
White boards
Dry-erase markers
Camera
Post-it-notes

CREATIVE TOOLKITS

WHAT IS IT?

Collections of modular objects that can be used for participatory modeling and prototyping to inform and inspire design teams. Often used in creative codesign workshops. It is a generative design method which facilitates creative play. The elements can be reused in a number of research sessions in different geographic locations.

WHO INVENTED IT?

Pioneered by Liz Sanders and Lego Johan Roos and Bart Victor 1990s.

WHY USE THIS METHOD?

Helps develop:
1. Problem solving
2. Change management
3. Strategic thinking
4. Decision making
5. Services, product and experience redesign
6. Can be fun
7. Identify opportunities
8. Re frame challenges
9. Leverages creative thinking of the team

HOW TO USE THIS METHOD

1. Form cross-disciplinary team 5 to 20 members. It's best to have teams of not more than 8

2. Identify design problem. Create agenda.
3. Start with a warming up exercise.
4. Write design problem in visible location such as white board.
5. Workshop participants first build individual prototypes exploring the problem.
6. Divide larger group into smaller work groups of 3 to 5 participants.
7. Ask each participant to develop between 1 and design solutions. Can use post-it notes or cards.
8. Through internal discussion each group should select their preferred group design solution.
9. The group builds a collective model incorporating the individual contributions.
10. Each group build a physical model of preferred solution and presents it to larger group.
11. Larger group selects their preferred design solutions by discussion and voting.
12. Capture process and ideas with video or photographs.
13. Debriefing and harvest of ideas.

1. Copy paper
2. Magnets
3. Snaps
4. Masking tape
5. Duct tape (color would be ideal)
6. Tape
7. Post-it notes
8. Glue sticks
9. Paper clips, (asst colors ideal)
10. Decorative brads (square, crystal)
11. Hole punch
12. Scissors
13. Stapler (with staples)
14. Hot glue
15. Glue guns
16. Rulers
17. Pipe Cleaners
18. Colored card
19. Zip ties
20. Foam core sheets
21. Velcro
22. Rubber bands, multicolored
23. Assorted foam shapes
24. Markers
25. Scissors
26. Glue sticks
27. Tape
28. Glue guns
29. Straws
30. Paper Clips
31. Construction Paper
32. ABS sheets
33. Felt
34. Foam sheets
35. String
36. Foil
37. Butcher paper
38. Stickers
39. Pipe cleaners
40. Popsicle sticks
41. Multicolored card

EMPATHY PROBES

WHAT IS IT?

This method involves participants recording specific events, feelings or interactions, in a diary supplied by the researcher. User Diaries help provide insight into behavior. Participants record their behavior and thoughts. Diaries can uncover behavior that may not be articulated in an interview or easily visible to outsiders.

WHO INVENTED IT?

Gordon Allport, may have been the first to describe diary studies in 1942.

WHY USE THIS METHOD?

Can capture data that is difficult to capture using other methods.

1. Cultural probes are appropriate when you need to gather information from users with minimal influence on their actions,
2. When the process or event you're exploring takes place intermittently or
3. When the process or event you're exploring takes place over a long period.

CHALLENGES

1. Process can be expensive and time consuming.
2. Needs participant monitoring.
3. Diary can fit into users' pocket.
4. It is difficult to get materials back.

WHEN TO USE THIS METHOD

1. Know Context
2. Know User
3. Frame insights

HOW TO USE THIS METHOD

1. A diary can be kept over a period of one week or longer.
2. Define focus for the study.
3. Recruit participants carefully.
4. Decide method: preprinted, diary notebook or on-line.
5. Prepare diary packs. Can be preprinted sheets or blank 20 page notebooks with prepared questions or on-line web based diary.
6. Brief participants.
7. Distribute diaries directly or by mail.
8. Conduct study. Keep in touch with participants.
9. Conduct debrief interview.
10. Look for insights.

RESOURCES

Diary
Preprinted diary sheets
Online diary
Pens
Disposable cameras
Digital camera
Self addressed envelopes

EMPATHY TOOLS

WHAT IS IT?

Empathy tools are aids or tools that help designers empathize with the people they are designing for. They can be used to test a prototype design or in activities such as role playing or body storming.

WHO INVENTED IT?

Brandt, E. and Grunnet, C 2000

WHY USE THIS METHOD?

1. To help a designer understand the experiences of people that they are designing for.

CHALLENGES

1. Empathy tools are imperfect approximations of user experiences.

WHEN TO USE THIS METHOD

1. Know Context
2. Know User
3. Frame insights
4. Explore Concept

HOW TO USE THIS METHOD

1. Wear heavy gloves to experience less sensitivity in your hands
2. Wear fogged glasses to experience less acute vision
3. Wear black glasses to eat to experience issues locating food and utensils.
4. Spend a day in a wheelchair.
5. Wear earplugs to experience diminished hearing

RESOURCES

Wheelchair
Fogged glasses
Blackened glasses
Gloves
Earplugs
Crutches
Walking stick

EYETRACKING

WHAT IS IT?

Eye tracking is a group of methods of studying and recording a person's eye movements over time. The most widely used current designs are video-based eye trackers. One of the most prominent fields of commercial eye tracking research is web usability but this method is also used widely for evaluating retail interiors and products.

WHO INVENTED IT?

Louis Émile Javal 1879
Alfred L. Yarbus 1950s

WHY USE THIS METHOD?

1. Examine which details attract attention.
2. To record where a participant's attention is focused . For example on a supermarket shelf eyetracking can reveal which products colors and graphics attract the most attention from shoppers.

CHALLENGES

1. Each method of eye tracking has advantages and disadvantages, and the choice of an eye tracking system depends on considerations of cost and application.
2. A poorly adjusted system can produce unreliable information.

TYPES OF SYSTEMS

1. Measures eye movement with a device attached to the eye. For example a contact lens with a magnetic field sensor.
2. Non contact measurement of eye movement. For example infrared, is reflected from the eye and sensed by a video camera.
3. Measures eye movement with electrodes placed around the eyes.

TYPES OF OUTPUTS

1. Heat maps
2. Gaze plots
3. Gaze replays

RESOURCES

Eye tracking device
Software
Laptop computer

"

I keep six honest serving men. They taught me all I knew Their names are what and why and when and how and where and who

RUDYARD KIPLING
English short-story writer, poet, and novelist

FIVE WHYS

WHAT IS IT

Five Whys is an iterative question method used to discover the underlying cause of a problem. For every effect there is a root cause. The primary goal of the technique is to determine the underlying cause of a problem by repeating the question "Why?"

WHO INVENTED IT

The technique was originally developed by Sachichi Toyoda Sakichi Toyoda was a Japanese inventor and industrialist. He was born in Kosai, Shizuoka. The son of a poor carpenter, Toyoda is referred to as the "King of Japanese Inventors". He was the founder of the Toyota Motor company. The method is still an important part of Toyota training, culture and success.

WHY USE THIS METHOD

1. When we fix the root cause the problem does not reoccur

HOW TO USE THIS METHOD

1. Five whys could be taken further to a sixth, seventh, or higher level, but five is generally sufficient to get to a root cause.
2. Gather a team and develop the problem statement in agreement
3. Establish the time and place that the problem is occurring
4. Ask the first "why" of the team: why is this problem taking place?
5. Ask four more successive "whys," repeating the process
6. You will have identified the root cause when asking "why" yields no further useful information.
7. Discuss the last answers and settle on the most likely systemic cause.
8. Fix the root problem

FLY-ON-THE-WALL

WHAT IS IT?

Observation method where the observer remains as unobtrusive as possible and observes and collects data relevant to a research study in context with no interaction with the participants being observed. The name derived from the documentary film technique of the same name.

WHO INVENTED IT?

ALex Bavelas 1944
Lucy Vernile, Robert A. Monteiro 1991

WHY USE THIS METHOD?

1. Low cost
2. No setup necessary
3. Can observe a large number of participants.
4. Objective observations
5. Compared to other methods such as focus groups, setup, data collection, and processing are much faster.

CHALLENGES

1. No interaction by the observer.
2. Observer cannot delve deeper during a session.
3. No interruption allowed
4. Observer cannot obtain details on customer comments during a session

HOW TO USE THIS METHOD

1. Define activity to study
2. Select participants thoughtfully
3. Choose a context for the observation
4. Carefully observe the interaction or experience. This is best done by members of your design team.
5. It is important to influence the participants as little as possible by your presence.
6. Observe but do not interact with participants while observing them in context.
7. Capture Data
8. Identify issues
9. Identify needs
10. Create design solutions based on observed and experienced human needs.

RESOURCES

Digital camera
Video camera
Notebook
Pens
Voice recorder

FOCUS GROUPS

WHAT IS IT?

Focus groups are discussions usually with 6 to 12 participants led by a moderator. Focus groups are used during the the design of products, services and experiences to get feedback from people

They are often conducted in the evening and take on average two hous. 8 to 12 questions are commonly explored in discussion.

WHO INVENTED IT?

Robert K. Merton 1940 Bureau of Applied Social Research.

WHY USE THIS METHOD?

1. Low cost per participant compared to other research methods.
2. Easier than some other methods to manage

CHALLENGES

1. Removes participants from their context
2. Requires a skilled moderator
3. Focus group study results may not be not be generalizable.
4. Focus group participants can influence each other.

HOW TO USE THIS METHOD

1. Select a good moderator.
2. Prepare a screening questionnaire.
3. Decide incentives for participants.
4. Select facility.
5. Recruit participants. Invite participants to your session well in advance and get firm commitments to attend. Remind participants the date of the event.
6. Participants should sit around a large table. Follow discussion guide.
7. Describe rules. Provide refreshments.
8. First question should encourage talking and participation.
9. The moderator manages responses and asks important questions
10. Moderator collects forms and debriefs focus group.
11. Analyze results while still fresh.
12. Summarize key points.
13. Run additional focus groups to deepen analysis.

RESOURCES

Sound and video recording equipment
White board
Post-it-notes

INTERVIEWING

WHAT IS IT?

Interviewing is a method of ethnographic research that has been described as a conversation with a purpose.

WHY USE THIS METHOD?

1. Contextual interviews uncover tacit knowledge about people's context.
2. The information gathered can be detailed.
3. The information produced by contextual inquiry is relatively reliable

CHALLENGES

1. End users may not have the answers
2. Contextual inquiry may be difficult to challenge even if it is misleading.
3. Keep control
4. Be prepared
5. Be aware of bias
6. Be neutral
7. Select location carefully

WHEN TO USE THIS METHOD

1. Know Context
2. Know User
3. Frame insights

HOW TO USE THIS METHOD

1. Contextual inquiry may be structured as 2 hour one on one interviews.

2. The researcher does not usually impose tasks on the user.
3. Go to the user's context. Talk, watch listen and observe.
4. Understand likes and dislikes.
5. Collect stories and insights.
6. See the world from the user's point of view.
7. Take permission to conduct interviews.
8. Do one-on-one interviews.
9. The researcher listens to the user.
10. 2 to 3 researchers conduct an interview.
11. Understand relationship between people, product and context.
12. Document with video, audio and notes.

RESOURCES

Computer
Notebook
Pens
Video camera
Release forms
Interview plan or structure
Questions, tasks and discussion items
Confidentiality agreement

INTERVIEW GUIDE

HOW TO CREATE AN INTERVIEW GUIDE

1. Plan in advance what you want to achieve
2. Research the topic
3. Select a person to interview.
4. Meet them in their location if possible.
5. Set a place, date, and time.
6. Be sure he or she understands how long the interview should take and that you plan to record the session.
7. Start with an open-ended question. It is a good way to put the candidate at ease,
8. Tape record the interview if possible.
9. Decide what information you need
10. Write down the information you'd like to collect through the interview. Now frame your interview questions around this information.
11. Prepare follow-up questions to ask.
12. Research the person that you are interviewing
13. Check your equipment and run through your questions.
14.
15. Use neutral wording
16. Do not ask leading questions or questions that show bias.
17. Leave time for a General Question in the End
18. The last question should allow the interviewee to share any thoughts or opinions that they might want to share, such as "Thank you for all that valuable information, is there anything else you'd like to add before we end?"

1. Bring your questions to the interview
2. Explore the answers but return to your list of questions to follow your guide.
3. Record details such as the subjects name contact and details
4. Take detailed notes
5. Use empathy tools to encourage your participant to share information.
6. Final question: "Is there anything you think I should have asked that I didn't?"
7. Transcribe the interview
8. Write out both sides of the conversation, both question and answer.
9. Never change what the interviewee said or how they said it.
10. Outline the important points.
11. Edit the transcript for clarity, flow, and length.
12. Tell a story Now that you've gathered all of this great information and have accurately recorded it. It is important that you find a way to effectively document and share the story in a way that celebrates and accurately describes the story you were told.
13. Add details from your notes appearance and personality of your subject, ambient sounds, smells, visuals.
14. Check the facts.

Source: adapted from The Art of Interview" by Anne Williams

CONTEXTUAL INQUIRY

WHAT IS IT?

Contextual inquiry involves one-on-one observations and interviews of activities in the context. Contextual inquiry has four guiding principles:
1. Context
2. Partnership with users.
3. Interpretation
4. Focus on particular goals.

WHO INVENTED IT?

Whiteside, Bennet, and Holtzblatt 1988

WHY USE THIS METHOD

1. Contextual interviews uncover tacit knowledge about people's context.
2. The information gathered can be detailed.
3. The information produced by contextual inquiry is relatively reliable

CHALLENGES

1. End users may not have the answers
2. Contextual inquiry may be difficult to challenge even if it is misleading.

HOW TO USE THIS METHOD

1. Contextual inquiry may be structured as 2 hour one on one interviews.
2. The researcher does not usually impose tasks on the user.
3. Go to the user's context. Talk, watch listen and observe.
4. Understand likes and dislikes.
5. Collect stories and insights.
6. See the world from the user's point of view.
7. Take permission to conduct interviews.
8. Do one-on-one interviews.
9. The researcher listens to the user.
10. 2 to 3 researchers conduct an interview.
11. Understand relationship between people, product and context.
12. Document with video, audio and notes.

CONTEXTUAL LADDERING

WHAT IS IT?

Contextual laddering is a one-on-one interviewing technique done in context. Answers are further explored by the researcher to uncover root causes or core values.

WHO INVENTED IT?

Gutman 1982, Olsen and Reynolds 2001.

WHY USE THIS METHOD?

1. Laddering can uncover underlying reasons for particular behaviors.
2. Laddering may uncover information not revealed by other methods.
3. Complement other methods
4. Link features and product attributes with user/customer values

CHALLENGES

1. Analysis of data is sometimes difficult.
2. Requires a skilled interviewer who can keep the participants engaged.
3. Laddering may be repetitive
4. Sometimes information may not be represented hierarchically.

HOW TO USE THIS METHOD

1. Interviews typically take 60 to 90 minutes.
2. The introduction. The researcher gives information about the length of the interview, content, confidentiality and method of recording.
3. The body of the interview. The researcher investigates the user in context and documents the information gathered.
4. Ask participants to describe what kinds of features would be useful in or distinguish different products.
5. Ask why.
6. If this answer doesn't describe the root motivation ask why again.
7. Repeat step 3. until you have reached the root motivation.
8. Wrap up. Verification and clarification

RESOURCES

Note pad
Confidentiality agreement
Digital voice recorder
Video camera
Digital still camera
Interview plan or structure
Questions, tasks and discussion items

CONVERSATION CARDS

WHAT IS IT?
Cards used for initiating conversation in a contextual interview and to help subjects explore.

WHO INVENTED IT?
Originator unknown. Google Ngram indicates the term first appeared around 1801 in England for a collection of "Moral and Religious Anecdotes particularly adapted for the entertainment and instruction of young persons, and to support instead of destroying serious conversation"

WHY USE THIS METHOD?
1. Questions are the springboard for conversations.
2. Can be used to initiate sensitive conversations.

CHALLENGES
1. How will data from the cards be used?
2. How will cards be evaluated?
3. How many cards are necessary to be representative?
4. What are potential problems relating card engagement
5. Use one unit of information per question.

HOW TO USE THIS METHOD
1. Decide on goal for research.
2. Formulate about 10 questions related to topic
3. Create the cards.
4. Recruit the subjects.
5. Undertake pre interview with sample subject to test.
6. Use release form if required.
7. Carry light equipment.
8. Record answers verbatim.
9. Communicate the purpose and length of the interview.
10. Select location. It should not be too noisy or have other distracting influences
11. Work through the cards.
12. Video or record the sessions for later review.
13. Analyze
14. Create Insights

RESOURCES
Conversation Cards.
Notebook
Video Camera
Pens
Interview plan or structure
Questions, tasks and discussion items
Interview cards

EMOTIONCARDS

WHAT IS IT?

Emotion cards are a field method of analyzing and quantifying peoples emotional response to a design. The method classifies emotions into sets of emotions which each can be associated with a specific recognizable facial expression.

The emotion card tool consists of sixteen cartoon-like faces, half male and half female, each representing distinct emotions. Each face represents a combination of two emotion dimensions,Pleasure and Arousal. Based on these dimensions, the emotion cards can be divided into four quadrants: Calm-Pleasant, Calm-Unpleasant, Excited-Pleasant, and Excited-Unpleasant.

WHO INVENTED IT?

Bradley 1994

WHY USE THIS METHOD?

1. It is an inexpensive method.
2. The results are easy to analyze.
3. Emotional responses are subtle and difficult to measure.
4. Emotion cards is a cross-cultural tool.
5. Facial emotions are typically universally recognized

CHALLENGES

1. Emotions of male and female faces are interpreted differently.
2. Sometimes users want to mark more than one picture to express a more complex emotional response.

HOW TO USE THIS METHOD

1. Decide the goal of the study.
2. Recruit the participants.
3. Brief the participants.
4. When each interaction is complete the researcher asks the participant to select one of a number of cards that shows facial expressions that they associate with the interaction.

RESOURCES

Emotion cards
Notebook
Pens
Video camera
Release forms
Interview plan or structure
Questions, tasks and discussion items
Emotion cards

E-MAIL INTERVIEW

WHAT IS IT?

With this method an interview is conducted via an e-mail exchange.

WHY USE THIS METHOD?

1. Extended access to people.
2. Background noises are not recorded.
3. Interviewee can answer the questions at his or her own convenience
4. It is not necessary to take notes
5. It is possible to use on-line translators.
6. Interviewees do not have to identify a convenient time to talk.

CHALLENGES

1. Interviewer may have to wait for answers.
2. Interviewer is disconnected from context.
3. Lack of communication of body language.

HOW TO USE THIS METHOD

1. Choose a topic
2. Identify a subject.
3. Contact subject and obtain approval.
4. Prepare interview questions.
5. Conduct interview
6. Analyze data.

RESOURCES

Computer
Internet connection
Notebook
Pens
Interview plan or structure
Questions, tasks and discussion items
Confidentiality agreement

EXTREME USER INTERVIEW

WHAT IS IT?

Interview experienced or inexperienced users of a product or service. in order to discover useful insights that can be applied to the general users.

WHY USE THIS METHOD?

Extreme user's solutions to problems can inspire solutions for general users. Their behavior can be more exaggerated than general users so it is sometimes easier to develop useful insights from these groups.

CHALLENGES

1. Keep control
2. Be prepared
3. Be aware of bias
4. Be neutral
5. Select location carefully

HOW TO USE THIS METHOD

1. Do a time line of your activity and break it into main activities
2. Identify very experienced or very inexperienced users of a product or service in an activity area.
3. Explore their experiences through interview.
4. Discover insights that can inspire design.
5. Refine design based on insights.

RESOURCES

Computer
Notebook
Pens
Video camera
Release forms
Interview plan or structure
Questions, tasks and discussion items
Confidentiality agreement

GROUP INTERVIEW

WHAT IS IT?

This method involves interviewing a group of people.

WHY USE THIS METHOD?

People will often give different answers to questions if interviewed on=on=-one and in groups. If resources are available it is useful to interview people in both situations.

CHALLENGES

1. Group interview process is longer than an individual interview

RESOURCES

Computer
Notebook
Pens
Video camera
Release forms
Interview plan or structure
Questions, tasks and discussion items
Confidentiality agreement

HOW TO USE THIS METHOD

1. Welcome everyone and introduce yourself
2. Describe the process.
3. Ask everyone to introduce themselves.
4. Conduct a group activity or warming-up exercise.
5. Break the larger group into smaller groups of 4 or 5 people and give them a question to answer. Ask each participant to present their response to the larger group.
6. Allow about 25 minutes.
7. Ask each interviewee to write a summary
8. Collect the summaries.
9. Ask if have any further comments.
10. Thank everyone and explain the next steps.
11. Give them your contact details.

GUIDED STORYTELLING

WHAT IS IT?
Guided storytelling is interview technique, where the designer asks a participant to walk you through a scenario of use for a concept.

Directed story telling guides participants to describe their experiences and thoughts on a specific topic.

WHO INVENTED IT?
Whiteside, Bennet, and Holtzblatt 1988

WHY USE THIS METHOD?
1. Guided storytelling uncovers tacit knowledge.

CHALLENGES
1. Keep control
2. Be prepared
3. Be aware of bias
4. Be neutral
5. Select location carefully

HOW TO USE THIS METHOD
1. Contextual inquiry may be structured as 2 hour one on one interviews.
2. The researcher does not usually impose tasks on the user.
3. Go to the user's context. Talk, watch listen and observe.

4. Understand likes and dislikes.
5. Collect stories and insights.
6. See the world from the user's point of view.
7. Take permission to conduct interviews.
8. Do one-on-one interviews.
9. The researcher listens to the user.
10. 2 to 3 researchers conduct an interview.
11. Understand relationship between people, product and context.

RESOURCES
Computer
Notebook
Pens
Video camera
Release forms
Interview plan or structure
Questions, tasks and discussion items
Confidentiality agreement

MAN IN THE STREET INTERVIEW

WHAT IS IT?

Man in the street interviews are impromptu interviews usually recorded on video. They are usually conducted by two people, a researcher and a cameraman.

WHY USE THIS METHOD?

1. Contextual interviews uncover tacit knowledge.
2. The information gathered can be detailed.

CHALLENGES

1. Keep control
2. Be prepared
3. Be aware of bias
4. Be neutral
5. Ask appropriate questions
6. Select location carefully
7. Create a friendly atmosphere, interviewee to feel relaxed.
8. Clearly convey the purpose of the interview.
9. This method results in accidental sampling which may not be representative of larger groups.

HOW TO USE THIS METHOD

1. Decide on goal for research.
2. Formulate about 10 questions related to topic
3. Use release form if required.
4. Conduct a preliminary interview.
5. Select location. It should not be too noisy or have other distracting influences
6. Approach people, be polite. Say, "Excuse me, I work for [your organization] and I was wondering if you could share your opinion about [your topic]."
7. If someone does not wish to respond, select another subject to interview.
8. Limit your time. Each interview should be no be longer than about 10 minutes.
9. Conduct 6 to 10 interviews

RESOURCES

Notebook
Pens
Video camera
Digital voice recorder
Release forms
Interview plan
Questions, and tasks

NATURALISTIC GROUP INTERVIEW

WHAT IS IT?

Naturalistic group interview is an interview method where the participants know each other prior to the interview and so have conversations that are more natural than participants who do not know each other.

WHY USE THIS METHOD?

1. This method has been applied in research in Asia where beliefs are informed by group interaction.
2. Can help gain useful data in cultures where people are less willing to share their feelings.

CHALLENGES

1. Familiarity of participants can lead to Group-think.

HOW TO USE THIS METHOD

1. The interview context should support natural conversation.
2. Select participants who have existing social relationships.
3. Group the participants in natural ways so that the conversation   is as close as possible to the type of discussion they would have in their everyday life.
4. Groups should be no larger than four people for best results.

RESOURCES

Notebook
Pens
Video camera
Digital voice recorder
Release forms
Interview plan
Questions, and tasks
Use local moderator

OCTAGON

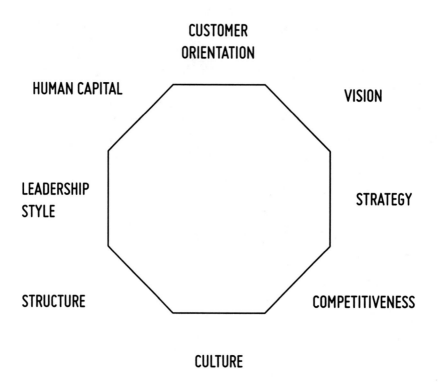

OCTAGON

WHAT IS IT?

The Octagon is a method that can be used in interviews with organizational stakeholders to help understand the intangible factors of an organization's culture and leadership style.

WHO INVENTED IT?

Bossard Consulting

WHY USE THIS METHOD?

1. To gain an understanding of stakeholders in an organization.

CHALLENGES

1. Obtain authorization to use statements.

HOW TO USE THIS METHOD

1. Select a group of managers or stakeholders in an organization.
2. Conduct interviews with each stakeholder and ask each to supply a short single sentence comment on each of the Octagon headings.
3. Analyze the statements.
4. Create a list of insights.

RESOURCES

Pen
Paper
Note pad
Prepared forms with questions.

ONE-ON-ONE INTERVIEW

WHAT IS IT?

The one-on-one interview is an interview that is between a researcher and one participant in a face-to-face situation.

WHY USE THIS METHOD?

1. The best method for personal information
2. Works well with other methods in obtaining information to inform design.
3. Can be used to exchange ideas or to gather information to inform design

CHALLENGES

1. Keep control
2. Be prepared
3. Be aware of bias
4. Be neutral
5. Select location carefully
6. Record everything
7. Combine one on one interviews with group interviews.

HOW TO USE THIS METHOD

1. May be structured as 2 hour one on one interviews.
2. Select the questions and the subjects carefully.
3. Create interview guide,
4. Conduct a preinterview to refine the guide.
5. The researcher does not usually impose tasks on the user.
6. Go to the user's context. Talk, watch listen and observe.
7. Understand likes and dislikes.
8. Collect stories and insights.
9. See the world from the user's point of view.
10. Take permission to conduct interviews.
11. Understand relationship between person, product and context.
12. Document with video, audio and notes.

RESOURCES

Notebook
Pens
Video camera
Digital voice recorder
Release forms
Interview plan
Questions, and tasks

PHOTO ELICITATION INTERVIEW

WHAT IS IT?

Photos are used by a researcher as a focus to discuss the experiences, thoughts and feelings of participants.

WHY USE THIS METHOD?

1. A method sometimes used to interview children.
2. Photos can make staring a conversation with a participant easier.
3. Photos can uncover meaning which is not uncovered in a face to face interview.

CHALLENGES

1. Photos can create ethical questions for the researcher.
2. A researcher may show bias in selecting subject of photos.

HOW TO USE THIS METHOD

1. Define the context.
2. Select the participants
3. Either researcher or participant may take the photos.
4. Researcher analyses photos and plans the interview process
5. Researcher shows the photos to the participant and discusses their thoughts in relation to the photographs.
6. The interview is analyzed by the researcher.
7. The researcher creates a list of insights.

RESOURCES

Notebook
Pens
Video camera
Release forms
Interview plan
Questions, and tasks
Digital voice recorder
Photographs

STRUCTURED INTERVIEW

WHAT IS IT?

In a structured interview the researcher prepares a list of questions, script or an interview guide that they follow during the interview. Most interviews use a structured method.

WHY USE THIS METHOD?

1. A structured interview is often used for phone interviews.
2. It is easy to analyze the results.
3. Structured interviews are often used by quantitative researchers.

CHALLENGES

1. Respondents may be less likely to discuss sensitive experiences.

WHEN TO USE THIS METHOD

1. Know Context
2. Know User
3. Frame insight

HOW TO USE THIS METHOD

1. The researcher should follow the script exactly.
2. The interviewer is required to show consistency in behavior across all interviews

RESOURCES

Computer
Notebook
Pens
Video camera
Release forms
Interview plan
Questions, and tasks
Confidentiality agreement

UNSTRUCTURED INTERVIEW

WHAT IS IT?

Unstructured interviews are interviews where questions can be modified as needed by the researcher during the interview.

WHY USE THIS METHOD?

1. A useful technique for understanding how a subject may perform under pressure.
2. Unstructured interviews are used in ethnographies and case studies
3. Respondents may be more likely to discuss sensitive experiences.

CHALLENGES

1. Interviewer bias is unavoidable

HOW TO USE THIS METHOD

1. Researchers need a list of topics to be covered during the interview

RESOURCES

Computer
Notebook
Pens
Video camera
Release forms
Interview plan
Questions, and tasks
Confidentiality agreement

TELEPHONE INTERVIEW

WHAT IS IT?
With this method an interview is conducted via telephone.

WHY USE THIS METHOD?
Wide geographical access
1. Allows researcher to reach hard to reach people.
2. Allows researcher to access closed locations.
3. Access to dangerous or politically sensitive sites

CHALLENGES
1. Lack of communication of body language.
2. Interviewer is disconnected from context.

WHEN TO USE THIS METHOD
Know Context
Know User
Frame insight

HOW TO USE THIS METHOD
1. Choose a topic
2. Identify a subject.
3. Contact subject and obtain approval.
4. Prepare interview questions.
5. Conduct interview
6. Analyze data.

RESOURCES
Computer
Notebook
Pens

MAGIC THING

WHAT IS IT?

A Magic Thing is a prop that is a focus for ideas in the context where an proposed design will be used. It can be a material such as wood or hard foam without surface detail. Participants carry a "magic thing" with them as they undertake their activities in context to imagine how a portable device could function.

WHO INVENTED IT?

Jeff Hawkins. Howard 2002. Jeff Hawkins, one of the inventors of the Palm Pilot PDA, carried a small block of wood to help him brainstorm interaction in various environments.

WHY USE THIS METHOD?

1. It is a form of physical prototype that simulates interaction when little information is available.

CHALLENGES

1. The researcher can put some imaginary constraints on the device so that it's technological capabilities are not too far from reality.

HOW TO USE THIS METHOD

1. The researcher briefs the participants on a design scenario.
2. The participants are given a prop, their magic thing.
3. The participants are briefed on the technological capabilities of the magic thing.
4. The participants and design team then act out scenarios in context.
5. The role playing is recorded by video or user diaries.
6. The material is analyzed and insights identified.

RESOURCES

A magic thing such as a block of wood about the size of a proposed device.
Video camera

METHOD BANK

WHAT IS IT?

A method bank is a central bank where design methods are documented by an organization's employees and can be accessed and applied by other employees.

WHO INVENTED IT?

1. Lego have compiled a Design Practice and emerging methods bank.
2. Microsoft have a methods bank in their Online User Experience best practice intra-net.
3. Starbucks have a methods bank in their on-line work flow management tool

WHY USE THIS METHOD?

1. This approaches helps document tacit knowledge within an organization.

HOW TO USE THIS METHOD

1. Methods are uploaded to the intra-net bank.
2. The bank may include descriptions, video, images charts or sketches.

RESOURCES

Intra-net
Camera
Video camera
Templates
Data base.
Computers

MOBILE DIARY STUDY

WHAT IS IT?

A mobile diary studies is a method that uses portable devices to capture a person's experiences in context when and where they happen such as their work place or home. Participants can create diary entries from their location on mobile phones or tablets.

WHY USE THIS METHOD?

1. Most people carry a mobile phone.
2. It is a convenient method of recording diary entries.
3. It is easier to collect the data than collecting written diaries.
4. Collection of data happens in real time.
5. Mobile devices have camera, voice and written capability.

CHALLENGES

1. Can miss non verbal feedback.
2. Technology may be unreliable

HOW TO USE THIS METHOD

1. Define intent
2. Define audience
3. Define context
4. Define technology
5. Automated text messages are sent to participants to prompt an entry.
6. Analyze data

RESOURCES

Smart phones,
Cameras,
Laptops and
Tablets

OBSERVATION

WHAT IS IT?

This method involves observing people in their natural activities and usual context such as work environment. With direct observation the researcher is present and indirect observation the activities may be recorded by means such as video or digital voice recording.

WHY USE THIS METHOD?

1. Allows the observer to view what users actually do in context.
2. Indirect observation uncovers activity that may have previously gone unnoticed

CHALLENGES

1. Observation does not explain the cause of behavior.
2. Obtrusive observation may cause participants to alter their behavior.
3. Analysis can be time consuming.
4. Observer bias can cause the researcher to look only where they think they will see useful information.

HOW TO USE THIS METHOD

1. Define objectives
2. Define participants and obtain their cooperation.
3. Define The context of the observation: time and place.
4. In some countries the law requires that you obtain written consent to video people.
5. Define the method of observation and the method of recording information. Common methods are taking written notes, video or audio recording.
6. Run a test session.
7. Hypothesize an explanation for the phenomenon
8. Predict a logical consequence of the hypothesis
9. Test your hypothesis by observation
10. Analyze the data gathered and create a list of insights derived from the observations.

RESOURCES

Note pad
Pens
Camera
Video camera
Digital voice recorder

COVERT OBSERVATION

WHAT IS IT?

Covert observation is to observe people without them knowing. The identity of the researcher and the purpose of the research are hidden from the people being observed.

WHY USE THIS METHOD?

1. This method may be used to reduce the effect of the observer's presence on the behavior of the subjects.
2. To capture behavior as it happens.
3. Researcher is more likely to observe natural behavior

CHALLENGES

1. The method raises serious ethical questions.
2. Observation does not explain the cause of behavior.
3. Can be difficult to gain access and maintain cover
4. Analysis can be time consuming.
5. Observer bias can cause the researcher to look only where they think they will see useful information.

HOW TO USE THIS METHOD

1. Define objectives.
2. Define participants and obtain their cooperation.
3. Define The context of the observation: time and place.
4. In some countries the law requires that you obtain written consent to video people.
5. Define the method of observation and the method of recording information. Common methods are taking written notes, video or audio recording.
6. Run a test session.
7. Hypothesize an explanation for the phenomenon.
8. Predict a logical consequence of the hypothesis.
9. Test your hypothesis by observation
10. Analyze the data gathered and create a list of insights derived from the observations.

RESOURCES

Camera
Video Camera
Digital voice recorder

DIRECT OBSERVATION

WHAT IS IT?

Direct Observation is a method in which a researcher observes and records behavior events, activities or tasks while something is happening recording observations as they are made.

WHO INVENTED IT?

Radcliff-Brown 1910
Bronislaw Malinowski 1922
Margaret Mead 1928

WHY USE THIS METHOD?

1. To capture behavior as it happens.

CHALLENGES

1. Observation does not explain the cause of behavior.
2. Analysis can be time consuming.
3. Observer bias can cause the researcher to look only where they think they will see useful information.
4. Obtain a proper sample for generalization.
5. Observe average workers during average conditions.
6. The participant may change their behavior because they are being watched.

HOW TO USE THIS METHOD

1. Define objectives.
2. Make direct observation plan
3. Define participants and obtain their cooperation.
4. Define The context of the observation: time and place.
5. In some countries the law requires that you obtain written consent to video people.
6. Define the method of observation and the method of recording information. Common methods are taking written notes, video or audio recording.
7. Run a test session.
8. Hypothesize an explanation for the phenomenon.
9. Predict a logical consequence of the hypothesis.
10. Test your hypothesis by observation
11. Analyze the data gathered and create a list of insights derived from the observations.

RESOURCES

Note pad
Pens
Camera
Video Camera
Digital voice recorder

INDIRECT OBSERVATION

WHAT IS IT?

Indirect Observation is an observational technique whereby some record of past behavior is used than observing behavior in real time. Humans cannot directly sense some things, we must rely on indirect observations with tools such as thermometers, microscopes, telescopes or X-rays

WHY USE THIS METHOD?

1. To capture behavior or an event as it happens in it's natural setting.
2. Indirect observation uncovers activity that may have previously gone unnoticed
3. May be inexpensive
4. Can collect a wide range of data

CHALLENGES

1. Observation does not explain the cause of behavior.
2. Analysis can be time consuming.
3. Observer bias can cause the researcher to look only where they think they will see useful information.
4. Obtain a proper sample for generalization.
5. Observe average workers during average conditions.
6. The participant may change their behavior because they are being watched.

HOW TO USE THIS METHOD

1. Define objectives.
2. Make direct observation plan
3. Define participants and obtain their cooperation.
4. Define The context of the observation: time and place.
5. In some countries the law requires that you obtain written consent to video people.
6. Define the method of observation and the method of recording information.
7. Run a test session.
8. Hypothesize an explanation for the phenomenon.
9. Predict a logical consequence of the hypothesis.
10. Test your hypothesis by observation
11. Analyze the data gathered and create a list of insights derived from the observations.

RESOURCES

Note pad
Pens
Camera
Video Camera
Digital voice recorder

NONPARTICIPANT OBSERVATION

WHAT IS IT?

The observer does not become part of the situation being observed or intervene in the behavior of the subjects. Used when a researcher wants the participants to behave normally. Usually this type of observation occurs in places where people normally work or live

WHY USE THIS METHOD?

1. To capture behavior as it happens.

CHALLENGES

1. Observation does not explain the cause of behavior.
2. Analysis can be time consuming.
3. Observer bias can cause the researcher to look only where they think they will see useful information.
4. Obtain a proper sample for generalization.
5. Observe average workers during average conditions.
6. The participant may change their behavior because they are being watched.

HOW TO USE THIS METHOD

1. Determine research goals.
2. Select a research context
3. The site should allow clear observation and be accessible.
4. Select participants
5. Seek permission.
6. Gain access
7. Gather research data.
8. Analyze data
9. Find common themes
10. Create insights

RESOURCES

Note pad
Pens
Camera
Video Camera
Digital voice recorder

PARTICIPANT OBSERVATION

WHAT IS IT?
Participant observation is an observation method where the researcher participates. The researcher becomes part of the situation being studied. The researcher may live or work in the context of the participant and may become an accepted member of the participant's community. This method was used extensively by the pioneers of field research.

WHO INVENTED IT?
Radcliff-Brown 1910
Bronislaw Malinowski 1922
Margaret Mead 1928

WHY USE THIS METHOD?
1. The goal of this method is to become close and familiar with the behavior of the participants.
2. To capture behavior as it happens.

CHALLENGES?
1. My be time consuming
2. May be costly
3. The researcher may influence the behavior of the participants.
4. The participants may not show the same behavior if the observer was not present.
5. May be language barriers
6. May be cultural barriers
7. May be risks for the researcher.
8. Be sensitive to privacy, and confidentiality.

HOW TO USE THIS METHOD
1. Determine research goals.
2. Select a research context
3. The site should allow clear observation and be accessible.
4. Select participants
5. Seek permission.
6. Gain access
7. Gather research data.
8. Analyze data
9. Find common themes
10. Create insights

RESOURCES
Note pad
Pens
Camera
Video Camera
Digital voice recorder

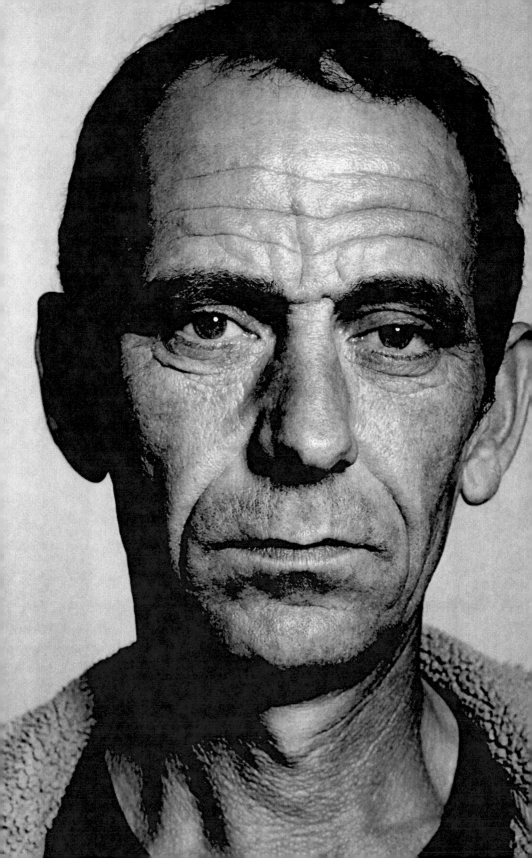

OVERT OBSERVATION

WHAT IS IT?
A method of observation where the subjects are aware that they are being observed

WHO INVENTED IT?
Radcliff-Brown 1910
Bronisław Malinowski 1922
Margaret Mead 1928

WHY USE THIS METHOD?
1. To capture behavior as it happens.

CHALLENGES
1. Observation does not explain the cause of behavior.
2. Analysis can be time consuming.
3. Observer bias can cause the researcher to look only where they think they will see useful information.

HOW TO USE THIS METHOD
1. Define objectives.
2. Define participants and obtain their cooperation.
3. Define The context of the observation: time and place.
4. In some countries the law requires that you obtain written consent to video people.
5. Define the method of observation and the method of recording information. Common methods are taking written notes, video or audio recording.
6. Run a test session.
7. Hypothesize an explanation for the phenomenon.
8. Predict a logical consequence of the hypothesis.
9. Test your hypothesis by observation
10. Analyze the data gathered and create a list of insights derived from the observations.

RESOURCES
Note pad
Pens
Camera
Video Camera
Digital voice recorder

STRUCTURED OBSERVATION

WHAT IS IT?

Particular types of behavior are observed and counted like a survey. The observer may create an event so that the behavior can be more easily studied. This approach is systematically planned and executed.

WHY USE THIS METHOD?

1. Allows stronger generalizations than unstructured observation.
2. May allow an observer to study behavior that may be difficult to study in unstructured observation.
3. To capture behavior as it happens.
4. A procedure is used which can be replicated.

CHALLENGES

1. Observation does not explain the cause of behavior.
2. Analysis can be time consuming.
3. Observer bias can cause the researcher to look only where they think they will see useful information.

HOW TO USE THIS METHOD

1. Define objectives.
2. Define participants and obtain their cooperation.
3. Define The context of the observation: time and place.
4. In some countries the law requires that you obtain written consent to video people.
5. Define the method of observation and the method of recording information. Common methods are taking written notes, video or audio recording.
6. Run a test session.
7. Hypothesize an explanation for the phenomenon.
8. Predict a logical consequence of the hypothesis.
9. Test your hypothesis by observation
10. Analyze the data gathered and create a list of insights derived from the observations.

RESOURCES

Note pad
Pens
Camera
Video Camera
Digital voice recorder

UNSTRUCTURED OBSERVATION

WHAT IS IT?

This method is used when a researcher wants to see what is naturally occurring without predetermined ideas. We use have an open-ended approach to observation and record all that we observe

WHY USE THIS METHOD?

1. To capture behavior as it happens.
2. Observation is the most direct measure of behavior

CHALLENGES

1. Replication may be difficult.
2. Observation does not explain the cause of behavior.
3. Analysis can be time consuming.
4. Observer bias can cause the researcher to look only where they think they will see useful information.
5. Data cannot be quantified
6. In this form of observation there is a higher probability of observer's bias.

HOW TO USE THIS METHOD

1. Select a context to explore
2. Take a camera, note pad and pen
3. Record things and questions that you find interesting
4. Record ideas as you form them
5. Do not reach conclusions.
6. Ask people questions and try to understand the meaning in their replies.

RESOURCES

Note pad
Pens
Camera
Video Camera
Digital voice recorder

PERSONA TEMPLATE

PERSONA NAME

DEMOGRAPHICS

Age   Income
Occupation   Gender
Location   Education

CHARACTERISTIC S

GOALS

What does this person want to achieve in life?

MOTIVATIONS

Incentives   Achievement
Fear   Power
Growth   Social

FRUSTRATIONS

What experiences does this person
wish to avoid?

QUOTE

Characteristic quote

BRANDS

What brands does this persona purchase or wish to purchase?

CHARACTERISTICS

EXTROVERT   INTROVERT FREE TIME

TRAVEL   LUXURY GOODS

TECHNICAL SAVVY   SPORTS

SOCIAL NETWORKING   MOBILE APPS

PERSONAS

WHAT IS IT?

"A persona is a archetypal character that is meant to represent a group of users in a role who share common goals, attitudes and behaviors when interacting with a particular product or service Personas are user models that are presented as specific individual humans. They are not actual people, but are synthesized directly from observations of real people."(Cooper)

WHO INVENTED IT?

Alan Cooper 1998

WHY USE THIS METHOD?

1. Helps create empathy for users and reduces self reference.
2. Use as tool to analyze and gain insight into users.
3. Help in gaining buy-in from stakeholders.

WHEN TO USE THIS METHOD

1. Know Context
2. Know User
3. Frame insights
4. Explore Concept

HOW TO USE THIS METHOD

1. Inaccurate personas can lead to a false understandings of the end users. Personas need to be created using data from real users.
2. Collect data through observation, interviews, ethnography.
3. Segment the users or customers
4. Create the Personas
5. Avoid Stereotypes
6. Each persona should be different. Avoid fringe characteristics. Personas should each have three to four life goals which are personal aspirations,
7. Personas are given a name, and photograph.
8. Design personas can be followed by building customer journeys

RESOURCES

Raw data on users from interviews or other research Images of people similar to segmented customers.
Computer
Graphics software

PERSONAL INVENTORY

WHAT IS IT?
This method involves studying the contents of a research subject's purse, or wallet. Study the things that they carry everyday.

WHO INVENTED IT?
Rachel Strickland and Doreen Nelson 1998

WHY USE THIS METHOD?
1. To provide insights into the user's lifestyle, activities, perceptions, and values.
2. to understand the needs priorities and interests

HOW TO USE THIS METHOD
1. Formulate aims of research
2. Recruit participants carefully.
3. "the participant is asked to bring their 'most often carried bag' and lay the objects they carry on a flat surface, talking through the purpose and last-use of each item. Things to look out for where the bag is kept in the home and what is clustered around it, what is packed/repacked on arrival/departure, and the use of different bags for different activities." *Jan Chipchase*
4. Document the contents with photographs and notes
5. ask your research subject to talk about the objects and their meaning.
6. Analyze the data.

RESOURCES
Camera
Note pad

SHADOWING

WHAT IS IT?

Shadowing is observing people in context.

The researcher accompanies the user and observes user experiences and activities.

It allows the researcher and designer to develop design insights through observation and shared experiences with users.

WHO INVENTED IT?

Alex Bavelas 1944

Lucy Vernile, Robert A. Monteiro 1991

WHY USE THIS METHOD?

1. This method can help determine the difference between what subjects say they do and what they really do.
2. It helps in understanding the point of view of people. Successful design results from knowing the users.
3. Define intent
4. Can be used to evaluate concepts.

CHALLENGES

1. Selecting the wrong people to shadow.
2. Hawthorne Effect, The observer can influence the daily activities under being studied.

HOW TO USE THIS METHOD

1. Prepare
2. Select carefully who to shadow.
3. Observe people in context by members of your design team.
4. Capture behaviors that relate to product function.
5. Identify issues and user needs.
6. Create design solutions based on observed and experienced user needs.
7. Typical periods can be one day to one week.

RESOURCES

Video camera
Digital still camera
Note pad
Laptop Computer

PATIENT STAKEHOLDER MAP

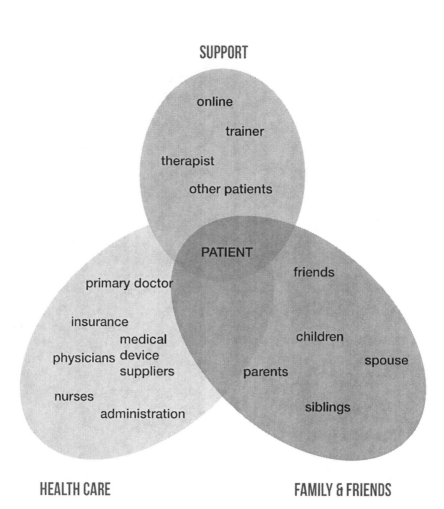

SUPPORT

online

trainer

therapist

other patients

PATIENT

friends

primary doctor

insurance

medical

children

physicians device

spouse

suppliers

parents

nurses

siblings

administration

HEALTH CARE

FAMILY & FRIENDS

STAKEHOLDER MAPS

WHAT IS IT
Stakeholders maps are used to document the key stakeholders and their relationship.

At the beginning of a design project it is important to identify the key stakeholders and their relationships. The map serves as a reference for the design team.

WHO INVENTED IT
Mitchell 1997

WHY USE THIS METHOD
1. Stakeholder mapping helps discover ways to influence other stakeholders.
2. Stakeholder mapping helps discover risks.
3. Stakeholder mapping helps discover positive stakeholders to involve in the design process.

CHALLENGES?
Stakeholder mapping helps discover negative stakeholders and their associated risks.

HOW TO USE THIS METHOD
1. Invite six known stakeholders to a meeting.
2. Give each stakeholder a block of post it notes.
3. Brainstorm with the group additional stakeholders
4. Cluster stockholders into relevant groups
5. Assign priorities for individual stakeholders based on the value of their potential feedback during the design process,
6. Map the stakeholders.
7. Can initially be documented on a white board, cards, post-it-notes and consolidated as a diagram through several iterations showing hierarchy and relationships.

THROUGHOTHEREYES

WHAT IS IT?

At several times during a design project it is useful to invite an outside group to review the state of the design and to tell your design team if they think that your design direction is real and good.

WHY USE THIS METHOD?

A design team can follow design directions that seem unworkable or unrealistic to end users because they may be remote from the end users of a product or service.

RESOURCES

Pen
Paper
White board
Dry erase markers

HOW TO USE THIS METHOD

1. Define your design problem clearly
2. Select a group of outside people who are representative of the end users of a product or service.
3. Prepare a presentation that may include prototypes or images and statements that clearly communicate the favored concept direction.
4. Prepare a question guide to help your design team obtain useful feedback
5. Review your design with the outside group.
6. Refine your design based on the feedback
7. Provide feedback to the outside reviewers to let them know how their input has been useful.
8. It may be necessary to ask the external participants to sign a non disclosure agreement before to the design review.

WWWWWH

WHAT IS IT?

'Who, What, Where, When, Why, and How'?
is a method for getting a thorough understanding of the problem, It is used to obtain basic information in police investigations. A well known golden rule of journalism is that if you want to know the full story about something you have to answer all the five W's. Journalists argue your story isn't complete until you answer all six questions.

1. Who is involved?
2. What occurred?
3. When did it happen?
4. Where did it happen?
5. Why did it occur?

WHO INVENTED IT?

Hermagoras of Temnos, Greece 1st century BC.

WHY USE THIS METHOD?

This method helps create a story that communicates clearly the nature of an activity or event to stakeholders.

HOW TO USE THIS METHOD

1. Ask the questions starting with the 5 w's and 1 h question words.
2. Identify the people involved
3. Identify the activities and make a list of them.
4. Identify all the places and make a list of them.
5. Identify all the time factors and make a list of them.
6. Identify causes for events of actions and make a list of them.
7. Identify the way events took place and make a list of them.
8. Study the relationships between the information.

RESOURCES

Computer
Notebook
Pens
Video camera
Digital camera
Digital voice recorder
Release forms
Interview plan or structure
Questions, tasks and discussion items

SOME W W W W W H QUESTIONS

WHO
1. Is affected?
2. Who believes that the problem affects them?
3. Needs the problem solved?
4. Does not want the problem to be solved?
5. Could stand in the way of a solution?

WHEN
1. Does it happen
2. Doesn't it happen?
3. Did it start?
4. Will it end?
5. Is the solution needed?
6. Might it happen in the future?
7. Will it be a bigger problem?
8. Will it improve?

WHERE
1. Does it happen?
2. Doesn't it happen
3. Else does it happen?
4. Is the best place to solve the problem

WHY
1. Is this situation a problem?
2. Do you want to solve it?
3. Do you not want to solve it?
4. Does it not go away?
5. Would someone else want to solve it?
6. Can it be solved?
7. Is it difficult to solve?

WHAT
1. May be different in the future
2. Are its weaknesses?
3. Do you like?
4. Makes you unhappy about it?
5. Is flexible?
6. Is not flexible?
7. Do you know?
8. Do you not understand?
9. How have you solved similar problems?
10. Are the underlying ideas?
11. Are the values involved?
12. Are the elements of the problem and how are they related?
13. What can you assume to be correct
14. Is most important
15. Is least important
16. Are your goals?
17. Do you need to discover?

"

Design thinking is an
approach to problem
finding that assumes
people often work on
the wrong problems and
can leverage and improve
outcomes by reframing
them.

BILL BURNETT
Director Stanford Design Program

"

We are visual animals.
Over 80% of the
information processed
by our brains from our
senses comes through
our eyes. The design
thinking process involves
communicating visually
where possible. Her are
some tools that you can
uses to communicate the
meaning of complex data.

VISUALIZATION TOOLS

BARCHART

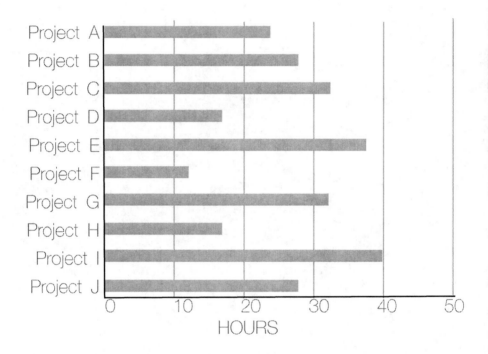

BARCHART

WHAT IS IT?

A simple bar chart is useful to present information for a quick problem or opportunity analysis. It provides a comparison of quantities of items or frequencies of events within a particular time period.

WHO INVENTED IT?

The first bar graph appeared in the 1786 book The Commercial and Political Atlas, by William Playfair (1759-1823)

WHY USE THIS METHOD?

1. To display a "snapshot" comparison of categories.
2. To depict the relationship between variations over time.
3. To illustrate process variability or trends.
4. To indicate a potential problem area (high or low frequencies).

CHALLENGES

1. Care should be taken not to insert more than five bars or cover more than five time periods. This would make the Bar Chart cluttered and difficult to interpret.

WHEN TO USE THIS METHOD

1. Frame insights

HOW TO USE THIS METHOD

1. Collect data from sources
2. Draw the vertical and horizontal axes.
3. Decide on the scale
4. Draw a bar for each item.
5. Label the axes

RESOURCES

Pen
Paper
Graph paper
Computer
Graphics software

LINKINGDIAGRAM

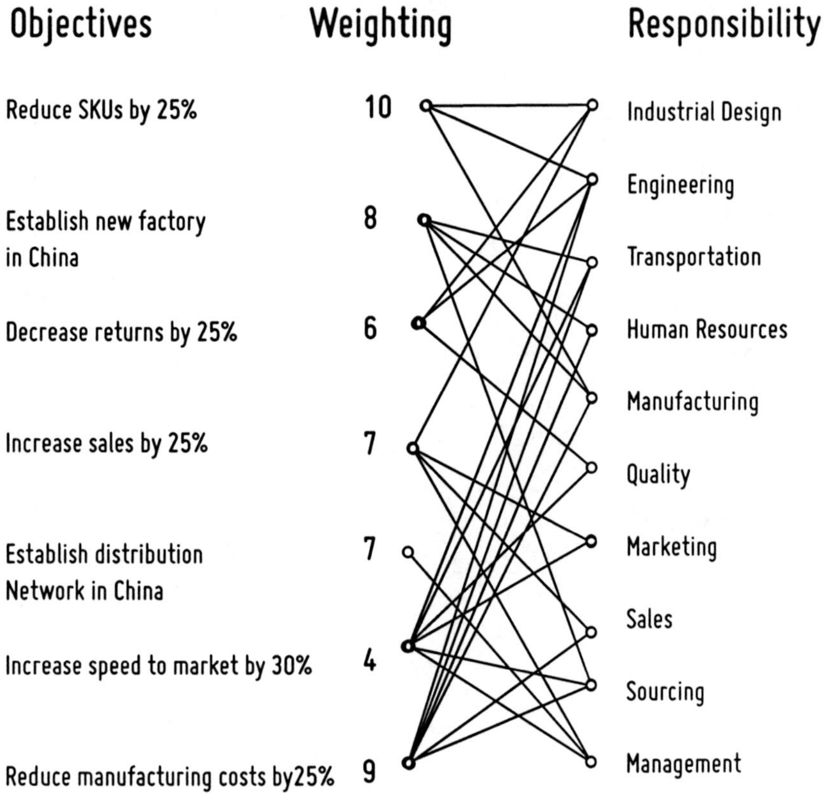

Objectives	Weighting	Responsibility

Objectives (column):
- Reduce SKUs by 25%
- Establish new factory in China
- Decrease returns by 25%
- Increase sales by 25%
- Establish distribution Network in China
- Increase speed to market by 30%
- Reduce manufacturing costs by25%

Weighting (column):
10
8
6
7
7
4
9

Responsibility (column):
- Industrial Design
- Engineering
- Transportation
- Human Resources
- Manufacturing
- Quality
- Marketing
- Sales
- Sourcing
- Management

LINKING DIAGRAM

WHAT IS IT?

A linking diagram is a graphical method of displaying relationships between factors in data sets.

WHY USE THIS METHOD?

1. To analyze relationships of complex data

RESOURCES

Pen
Paper
White board
Dry erase markers

HOW TO USE THIS METHOD

1. Select a problem to analyze.
2. Team brainstorms two lists of factors that relate to the problem such as outcomes and actions.
3. Team rates the items by importance. 1-10, 10 being most important.
4. Draw lines between related items in each list.
5. Review and refine
6. List insights
7. Take actions based on the insights.

ONION MAP

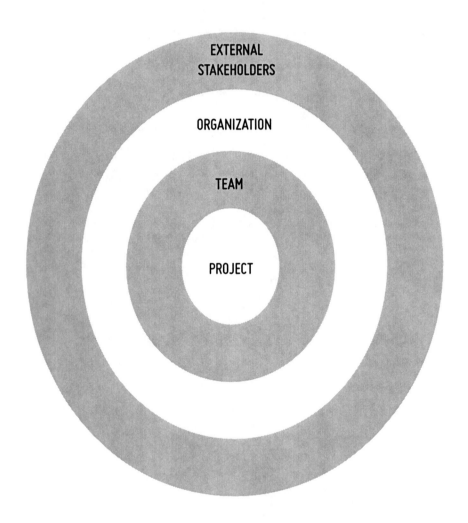

ONION MAP

WHAT IS IT?

An onion map is a chart that shows dependencies of a system. The items in each circle depend on the items in the smaller circle.

WHO INVENTED IT?

Onion models have been used for centuries to indicate hierarchical levels of dependency. Peter Apian's 1539 Cosmographia used an onion model to illustrate the pre-Copernican model of the universe.

WHY USE THIS METHOD?

1. It is an effective way of describing complex relationships
2. It provides a focus for team discussion and alignment
3. It is fast
4. It is inexpensive.

HOW TO USE THIS METHOD

1. Define the system to be represented by the onion diagram.
2. Create a circle to define the innermost level of dependency
3. Create concentric circles around the inner circle to represent progressively higher levels of dependency
4. Name the levels.

RESOURCES

Pen
Paper
Software
Computer
White board
Dry-erase markers

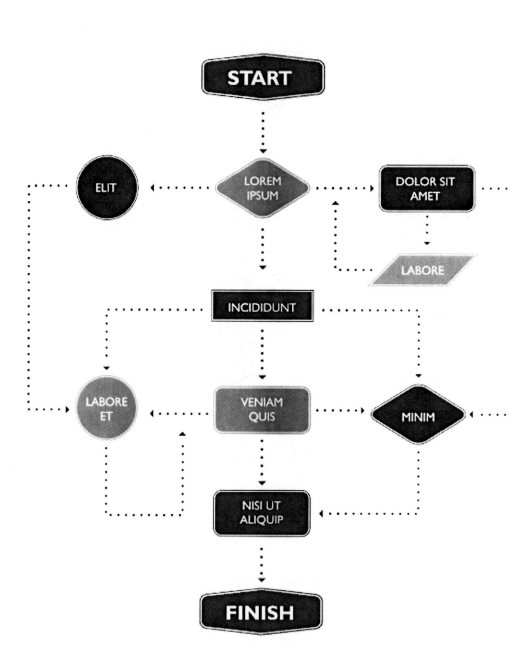

PROCESS FLOW DIAGRAM

WHAT IS IT?

A process flowchart is a type of diagram that represents a process, showing the steps as boxes

WHO INVENTED IT?

Frank Gilbreth, American Society of Mechanical Engineers. 1921

WHY USE THIS METHOD?

1. To represent a flow of process or decisions or both.

CHALLENGES

1. Use standard symbols.
2. Arrows should show the direction of flow.
3. A junction is indicated by two incoming and one outgoing line.
4. The two most common types of boxes are for a process step and for a decisions.

RESOURCES

Pen
Paper
White board
Dry erase markers.

HOW TO USE THIS METHOD

1. Define the process boundaries
2. Complete the big picture first.
3. Draw a start box.
4. Draw the first box below the start box. Ask, 'What happens first?'.
5. Add further boxes below the previous box, Ask 'What happens next?'.
6. Connect the boxes with arrows
7. Describe the process to be charted
8. Review.

RADAR CHART

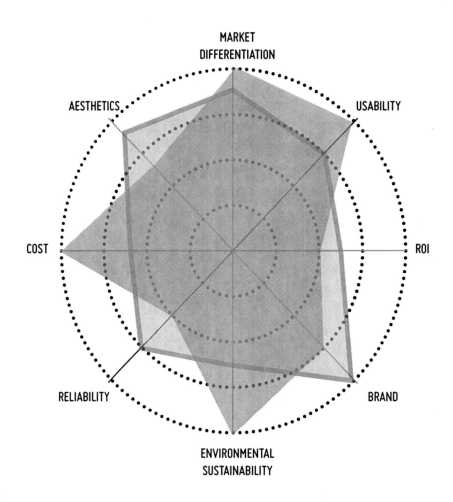

RADAR CHART

WHAT IS IT?

The radar chart is a star shape chart that allows information to be logged radially for a number of variables. The radar chart is also known as a web chart, spider chart, star chart, star plot, cobweb chart, irregular polygon, polar chart, or kiviat diagram.

WHO INVENTED IT?

Georg von Mayr 1877

CHALLENGES

1. Radar charts may not provide information for trade off decisions.

WHY USE THIS METHOD?

1. A spider diagram is a way of displaying a great deal of information in a condensed form,

HOW TO USE THIS METHOD

1. Draw a circle on paper
2. For each item to evaluate draw a line from the center to the circle.
3. Write the item on the intersection between the line and the circle.
4. Draw spider lines from the inside to the outside of the circle (see photo).
5. Gather the participants around the chart
6. Ask them to put one dot for each item: If highly ranked the dot should be close top the center; if poorly ranked the dot should be close to the circle.
7. Present and discuss the result with the group.

RESOURCES

Paper
Pens
Computer
Graphic software

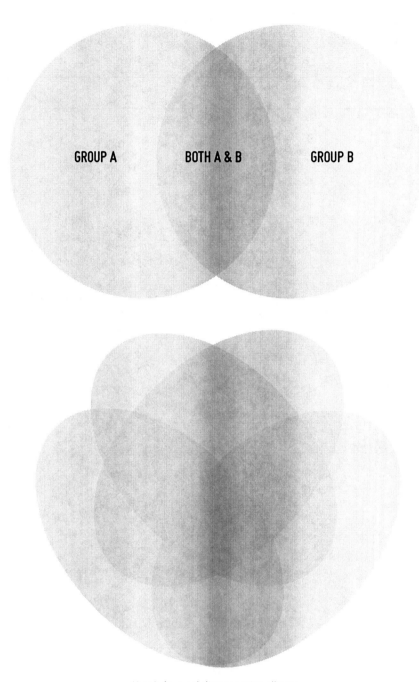

Venn's four-set diagram using ellipses

VENN DIAGRAM

WHAT IS IT?
Venn diagrams normally are constructed from overlapping circles. Circles represent groups of things with a shared attribute. The interior of the circle and the areas of overlap symbolically represents the elements of discreet sets.

WHO INVENTED IT?
John Venn 1880

WHY USE THIS METHOD?
1. A useful tool for simplifying and communicating data related to user populations and design features
2. Explaining systems of taxonomy
3. Displaying organizational systems
4. Exploring different classes of items

RESOURCES
Paper
Pens
Software

"

Make sense from your research. What are the insights? What is connected? What are the unmet needs and desires of your audience? How can your design be unique, and better than what is already out there?

SYNTHESIS

"

One of the symptoms
of an absence of
innovation is the fact
that you lose your
jobs

STEVE JOBS
Apple

SYNTHESIS

Synthesis is the convergent part of the design process.
In this stage we review the research, make connections, uncover insights, distill the data. We make sense of the information

ACTIONABLE INSIGHTS

Design Thinking provides insights that are based on unrecognized or unmet needs. An insight is a fresh point of view based on a deep understanding of the way of thinking and behavior. An insight occurs by mentally connecting two or more things that have not been connected before. These things may be things that many people have seen or experienced but not connected before. A goal of Design Thinking is to build actionable insights

USER NEED STATEMENT

The user need statement or question is the desires or needs of end users expressed in their own words.

User Need Statement
I am a doctor who has a hard time keeping babies warm.

POINT OF VIEW STATEMENT

A point-of-view (POV) is reframing of a design challenge into an actionable problem statement.
The POV is used as the basis for design ideation. The POV defines the design intent.

The POV helps reframe the design problem into an actionable focus for the generation of ideas.

tool: a device used to carry out a particular function

technique: a way to carry out a particular task

method: a particular procedure for accomplishing something in a systematic way

methodology: a system of methods used in a particular area of activity

mindset: an established set of attitudes, or frame of reference

culture: the customs, designs, social institutions of a particular nation, people or group. A set of learned beliefs values and behaviors shared by a group of people.

Source: adapted from Liz Sanders

ASSUMPTION SURFACING

WHAT IS IT?
This is a method of analyzing your assumptions, considering alternative assumptions and prioritizing solutions.

WHO INVENTED IT?
Richard O. Mason, Ian Mitroff 1981

WHY USE THIS METHOD?
1. The purpose of this method is to analyze assumptions to understand which are most plausible and may have the highest impact.
2. A method for approaching ill-structured or "wicked" problems
3. To compare and to evaluate systematically the assumptions of different people.
4. To examine the relationship between underlying assumption

RESOURCES
Pen
Paper
White board
Dry Erase markers

WHEN TO USE THIS METHOD
1. Define intent

HOW TO USE THIS METHOD
1. List the decisions that you have made.
2. For each decision list the assumptions that you made
3. Under each assumption list an alternative counter assumption.
4. Delete from your list choices where it makes little difference whether the original assumption or the counter assumption are correct.
5. Analyze the remaining assumptions on a 2x2 matrix high low impact on one axis and high low plausibility on the other axis.
6. High impact and plausibility assumptions should be given high priority.

The brain processes visual information faster than written language. Visual tools improve memory, organization, critical thinking and planning. Visual communication invites collaboration.

BACKCASTING

WHAT IS IT?

Backcasting is a method for planning the actions necessary to reach desired future goals. This method is often applied in a workshop format with stakeholders participating. The future scenarios are developed for periods of between 1 and 20 years in the future. The participants first identify their goals and then work backwards to identify the necessary actions to reach those goals.

WHO INVENTED IT?

AT&T 1950s, Shell 1970s

WHY USE THIS METHOD?

1. It is inexpensive and fast
2. Backcasting is a tool for identifying, planning and reaching future goals.
3. Backcasting provides a strategy to reach future goals.

CHALLENGES

1. Need a good moderator
2. Needs good preparation

HOW TO USE THIS METHOD

A typical backcasting question is"How would you define success for yourself in 2015?

1. Define a framework
2. Analyze the present situation in relation to the framework
3. Prepare a vision and a number of desirable future scenarios.
4. Back-casting: Identify the steps to achieve this goal.
5. Further elaboration, detailing
6. Step by step strategies towards achieving the outcomes desired.
7. Ask do the strategies move us in the right direction? Are they flexible strategies?. Do the strategies represent a good return on investment?
8. Implementation, policy, organization embedding, follow-up

RESOURCES

Post-it-notes
White board
Pens
Dry-erase markers
Cameras

BENEFITS MAP

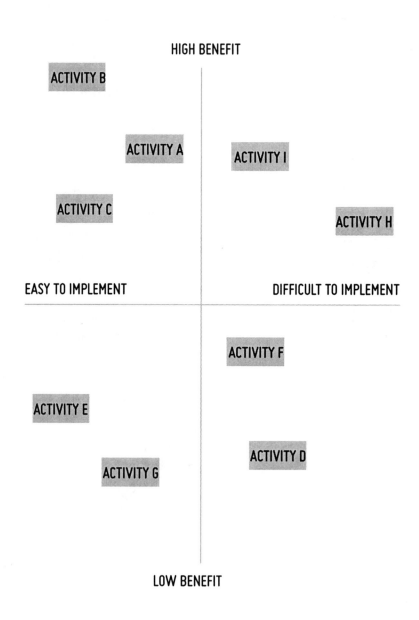

HIGH BENEFIT

ACTIVITY B

ACTIVITY A

ACTIVITY I

ACTIVITY C

ACTIVITY H

EASY TO IMPLEMENT

DIFFICULT TO IMPLEMENT

ACTIVITY F

ACTIVITY E

ACTIVITY D

ACTIVITY G

LOW BENEFIT

BENEFITS MAP

WHAT IS IT?

The benefits map is a simple tool that helps your team decide what will give you the best return on investment for time invested

WHY USE THIS METHOD?

1. Aids communication and discussion within the organization.
2. It is human nature to do tasks which are not most urgent first.
3. To gain competitive advantage,
4. Helps build competitive strategy
5. Helps build communication strategy
6. Helps manage time effectively

CHALLENGES

1. Can be subjective

HOW TO USE THIS METHOD

1. Moderator draws axes on white board or flip chart.
2. Worthwhile activity at the start of a project.
3. Map individual tasks.
4. Interpret the map.
5. Create strategy.
6. Tasks which have high benefit with low investment may be given priority.

RESOURCES

Pen
Paper
White board
Dry erase markers

"

[end-users] are the precedent for every action you take. You will measure your success based on the value you bring to them. Actively involve them in your work to help you understand the problem and get feedback on ideas along the way.

IBM
Design Tinking

BLUE OCEAN STRATEGY

WHAT IS IT?

Blue Ocean Strategy is a business strategy proposed by W. Chan Kim and Renée Mauborgne. The authors propose that companies can experience high growth and profits by exploiting "blue ocean" or uncontested, differentiated market spaces.

Blue Ocean strategy:
1. Create uncontested market space
2. Make competition irrelevant.
3. Create and capture new demand.
4. Break the value-cost trade off.
5. Align the whole system of a company's activities in pursuit of differentiation and low cost.

Red Ocean Strategy
6. Compete in existing market place.
7. Beat the competition.
8. Exploit existing demand.
9. Make the value-cost trade off.
10. Align the whole system of a company's activities with it's strategic choice of differentiation or low cost.

WHO INVENTED IT?

W. Chan Kim and Renée Mauborgne 2004

WHY USE THIS METHOD?

1. BOS contains a road map for assessing a company and its business and strategy.
2. Useful for mature companies that need new strategy.
3. A number of methods that help an an organization understand what value they are delivering.

CHALLENGES

1. Blue Ocean Strategy does not define where or how to find Blue Oceans.
2. Some critics of the Blue Ocean approach suggest that the strategy is a new way of packaging old ideas.

C-BOX

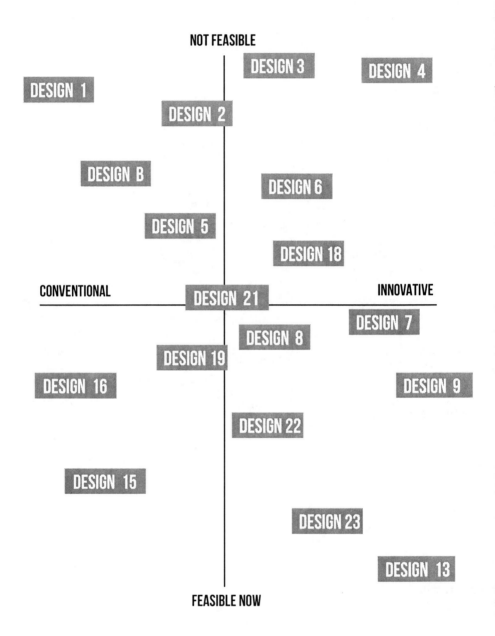

C-BOX

WHAT IS IT?

A C-box is a type of perceptual map that allows comparison and evaluation of a large number of ideas generated in a brainstorming session by a design team. The method allows everyone to contribute in a democratic way. It can be used to identify the most feasible and innovative ideas. It is up to your team to decide the level of innovation that they would like to carry forward from the idea generation or divergent phase of the project to the convergent or refinement and implementation phases.

WHO INVENTED IT?

Marc Tassoul, Delft 2009

WHY USE THIS METHOD?

1. It is democratic
2. It is quick and productive
3. It is inexpensive

.

HOW TO USE THIS METHOD

1. The moderator defines the design problem
2. You group can be optimally from 4 to 20 people.
3. On a white board or large sheet of paper create two axes. You can also use tape on a large wall.
4. Innovation on the horizontal and feasibility on the vertical axes creating 4 quadrants
5. The scale on the innovation ranges from not innovative at the left hand to highly innovative on the right hand end.
6. Alternative axes are attractiveness and functionality.
7. Brainstorm concepts. Each team member to generate 5 to 10 concepts over 30 minutes. One idea per post-it note. Hand out more post-it notes if required.
8. Each team member then presents each idea taking one to three minutes per idea depending on time available.
9. With the group's input discuss the ideas and precise position on the map.
10. Position each post-it-note according to the group consensus.

CONTEXTMAP

TRENDS | POLITICAL | ECONOMIC | USER NEEDS | TECHNOLOGY | UNCERTAINTIES | TRENDS

CONTEXT MAP

WHAT IS IT?

A context map is a tool for representing complex factors affecting an organization or design visually. Context maps are sometimes used by directors or organizations as a tool to enable discussion of the effects of change and related interacting business, cultural and environmental factors in order to create a strategic vision for an organization. A context map can be used to analyze trends

WHO INVENTED IT?

Joseph D. Novak Cornell University 1970s.

WHY USE THIS METHOD?

Uses include:
1. New knowledge creation
2. Documenting the knowledge existing informally within an organization.
3. Creating a shared strategic vision

RESOURCES

Template
White board
Paper flip chart
Pens
Dry-erase markers
Post-it-notes

HOW TO USE THIS METHOD

1. Put together a team of between 4 and 20 participants with diverse backgrounds and outlooks.
2. Appoint a good moderator
3. Prepare a space. Use a private room with a white board or large wall.
4. Distribute post-it notes to each participant.
5. Brainstorm the list of factors one at a time.
6. These can include Trends, technology, trends, political factors, economic climate customer needs, uncertainties.
7. Each participant can contribute.
8. All contributions are recorded on the white board or on the wall with the post-it-notes.
9. When all factors have been discussed prioritize each group of contributions to identify the most critical.
10. This can be done by rearranging the post-it-notes or white board notes.
11. Video the session and photograph the notes after the session.
12. Analyze the map and create strategy.

DECISIONRINGS

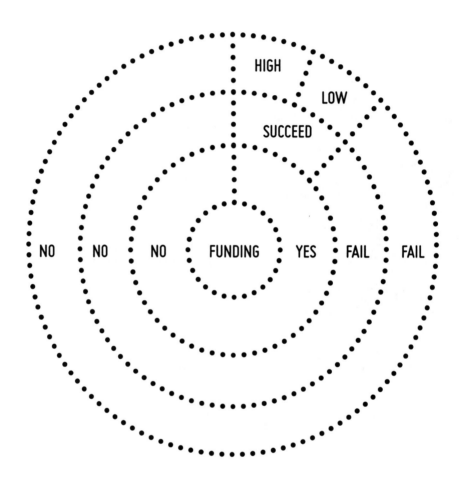

DECISION RINGS

WHAT IS IT?
Decision rings are a graphical way of visualizing the likelihood or benefit of the outcome of decisions.

WHY USE THIS METHOD?
A visual way of representing a problem.

RESOURCES
Pen
Paper
Computer
Software

HOW TO USE THIS METHOD
1. Draw a number of concentric circles.
2. If your problem decision involves n stages, draw n+1 concentric circles.
3. Split the first ring into segments equal to the number of choices for the first decision.
4. Divide the next stage into segments based on the segments of the previous stage
5. Divide each subsequent segment into the number of boxes equal to the alternative solutions.
6. Divide each subsequent box into boxes proportional to the probability of the associated outcome
7. Repeat for each decision stage.

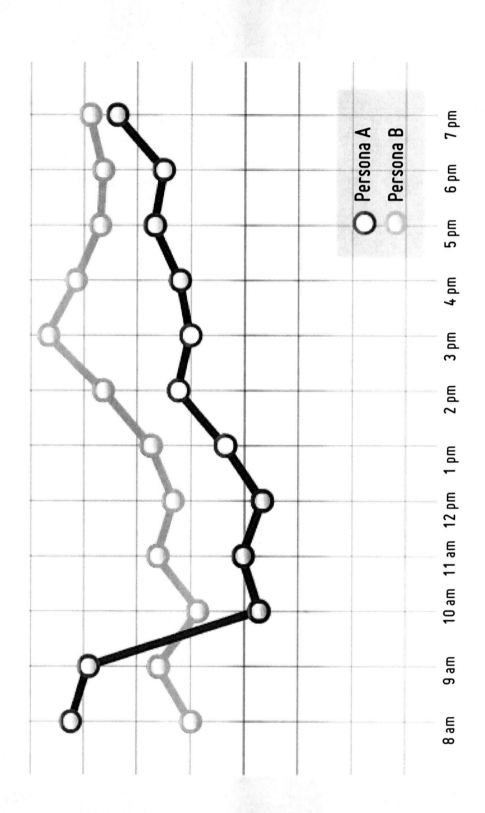

EMOTIONAL JOURNEY MAP

WHAT IS IT?

An emotional journey map is a map that visually illustrates people's emotional experience throughout an interaction with an organization or brand.

WHY USE THIS METHOD?

1. It provides a focus for discussion
2. It focuses on what may make your customers unhappy
3. Provides a visually compelling story of customer experience.
4. Customer experience is more than interaction with a product.
5. By understanding the journey that your customers are making, you will be in a position to make informed improvements.

CHALLENGES

1. Customers often do not take the route in an interaction that the designer expects.
2. Failure to manage experiences can lead to lost customers.

HOW TO USE THIS METHOD

1. Define the activity of your map. For example it could be a ride on the underground train.
2. Collect internal insights
3. Research customer perceptions
4. Analyze research
5. Map journey.
6. Across the top of the page do a time line Break the journey into stages using your customer's point of view
7. Capture each persona's unique experience
8. Use a scale from 0 to 10. The higher the number, the better the experience.
9. Plot the emotional journey.
10. Analyze the lease pleasant emotional periods and create ideas for improving the experience during those periods.
11. Create a map for each persona.

RESOURCES

Paper
Pens
White board
Post-it-notes

EMPATHY MAPS

WHAT IS IT?

A mapping method that analyses each part of a user experience.. An Empathy Map gives a high level view of where an experience is good or bad. Used to improve a user experience.

The biggest single cause of failure of new products and services in the marketplace is that the organization creating the product or service did not understand completely the customer's perspective. This method helps draw out the main components of the customer experience so that problems can be identified and fixed.

Empathy Map is a tool that helps the design team empathize with people they are designing for. You can create an empathy map for a group of customers or a persona.

WHO INVENTED IT?

Scott Matthews and Dave Gray at PLANE now Dachis Group.

HOW LONG DOES IT TAKE?

One to three hours per persona.

WHY USE THIS METHOD?

This tool helps a design team understand the customers and their context. It is an outside in technique.

CHALLENGES

1. Emotions must be inferred by observing clues.
2. This method does not provide the same level of rigor as traditional personas but requires less investment.

WHEN TO USE THIS METHOD

1. Know Context
2. Know User
3. Frame insights

RESOURCES

1. Empathy map template
2. White board
3. or blackboard
4. or video projector
5. or Large sheet of paper
6. Dry-erase markers
7. Post-it-notes
8. Pens
9. Video Camera

HOW TO USE THIS METHOD

1. A team of 4 to 12 people is a good number for this method.
2. The best people to involve are people who have direct interaction with customers.
3. The team should represent various functions in your organization such as management, design, marketing, sales, and engineering. It is helpful to also include some stakeholders such as customers and others affected by the end design. The process will help draw out useful information from them.
4. This method can be used with personas.
5. The map should be based on real information from customers. This can be gathered from sources such as interviews, observation, web analytics, customer service departments and focus groups.
6. Segment your market then create a persona representing an average customer in each segment. Four to six personas are a good number.
7. Draw a circle to represent your target persona.
8. Divide the circle into sections that represent aspects of that persona's sensory experience. It is common to have boxes for seeing and hearing. Some experiences such as drinking coffee could include boxes for other senses such as taste and smell.
9. Place two boxes at the bottom of the map and label them "Pain" and "Gain".
10. Ask your team to describe from the persona's point of view their experience.
11. Populate the map by taking note of the following traits of your user as you review your notes, audio, and video from your fieldwork: What are they thinking, feeling, saying, doing, hearing, seeing?
12. Fill in the diagram with real, tangible, sensory experiences.
13. Once you have filled all of the top boxes move the post it notes for negative components of the experience into the lower pain box and positive into the gain box.
14. The pain box can serve as a start for identifying the problems to fix in the ideation phase.

HOW TO CREATE AN EMPATHY MAP

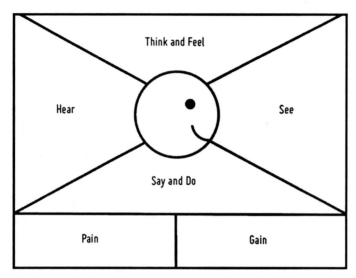

1 Create the Empathy Map template on a white board, on a large sheet of paper or project it on a wall.

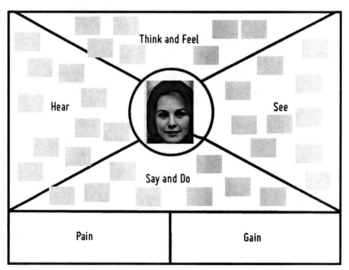

3 Populate top four boxes one at a time. You can have more than four boxes in the top section if for example smell and touch are important for your persona's experience.

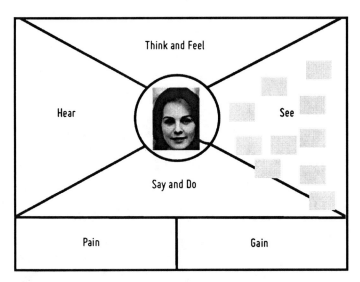

2 Populate one box with post it notes based on your research on the particular persona

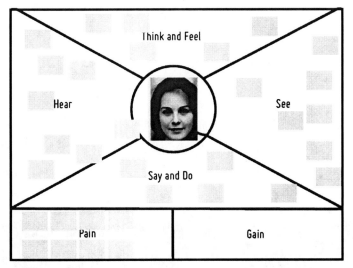

4 Move the negative experiences into the pain box. Move the positive experiences into the gain box. The pain box can be the basis for experiential problems to fix in the ideation phase.

EXPERIENCE MAP TEMPLATE

	ANTICIPATE	ENTER	ENGAGE	EXIT	REVIEW
CUSTOMER ACTIVITIES					
DOING					
THINKING					
FEELING					
EMOTIONAL EXPERIENCE					
OPPORTUNITIES					

EXPERIENCE MAPS

WHAT IS IT?

It is a diagram that allows a designer to describe the elements of a customer experience in clear concise terms.

WHY USE THIS METHOD?

1. Helps develop a consistent, predictable customer experience.
2. Identifies problems in a customer experience and how to fix them.
3. Presents an overview of your customer's experience from their point of view.
4. Helps reduce the number of dissatisfied customers
5. A tool for developing more loyal customers
6. Can be used with different personas.
7. A focus for discussion between departments of an organization that helps develop a consistent and superior customer experience.
8. Can be used to understand where to place resources most efficiently

WHEN TO USE THIS METHOD

1. Discovery or research phase
2. Synthesis phase

HOW TO USE THIS METHOD

1. Identify your team. Use a cross disciplinary team of 4 to 12 people with stakeholders.
2. Collect research data related to customer experience using ethnographic techniques such as interviews.
3. Identify the customer experience to be analyzed. Identify the context. Identify personas.
4. Break the customer experience down into sub activities and place each activity in a horizontal time-line
5. Below each activity describe what the customer is doing
6. Do one line of comments for what they are doing, one line for what they are thinking, and feeling.
7. Use post-it-notes to add positive and negative experiences to the relevant parts of the time line.
8. Brainstorm opportunities where customer experiences are negative.
9. When you are complete photograph the map and document it using a program such as Adobe Illustrator.
10. Circulate the map to stakeholders for feedback and refine.

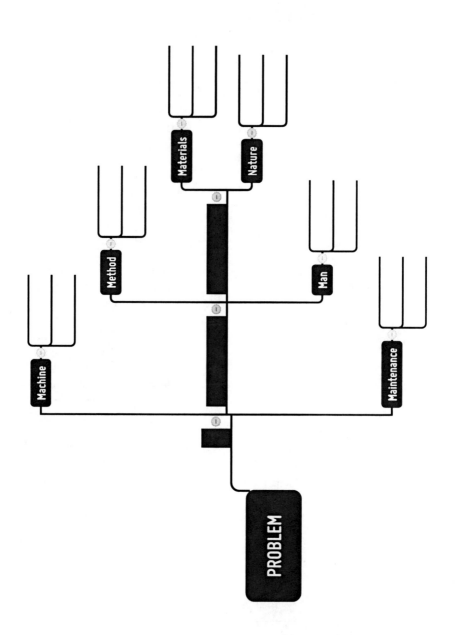

FISHBONE DIAGRAMS

WHAT IS IT?

Fishbone diagrams also called Ishikawa diagrams, are diagrams that show the causes of a specific event. Mazda Motors used an Ishikawa diagram to design the Miata sports car, The goal was was "Jinba Ittai" Horse and Rider as One. Every factor identified in the diagram was included in the final design. Ishikawa described the process as fishboning your problem and letting it cook overnight.

WHO INVENTED IT?

Kaoru Ishikawa University of Tokyo 1968

WHY USE THIS METHOD?

1. People tend to fix a problem by responding to an immediately visible cause while ignoring the deeper issues. This approach may lead to a problem reoccurring.
2. Use in the predesign phase to understand the root causes of a problem to serve as the basis for design.
3. Identifies the relationship between cause and effect.

HOW TO USE THIS METHOD

1. Prepare the six arms of the Ishikawa Diagram on a white board.
2. Define the problem clearly as a short statement in the head of the diagram.
3. Describe the causes of each bone and write them at the end of each branch. Use the 4 M's as categories; Machine, Man Methods, Materials.
4. Conduct the brainstorming session using brainstorming guidelines Ask each team member to define the cause of the problem. You may list as many causes as necessary. Typically 3 to 6 are listed.
5. Minor causes are then listed around the major causes.
6. Interpret the Ishikawa Diagram once it's finished.

RESOURCES

White board
Dry-erase markers
Room with privacy
Paper
Pens

FORCE FIELD DIAGRAM

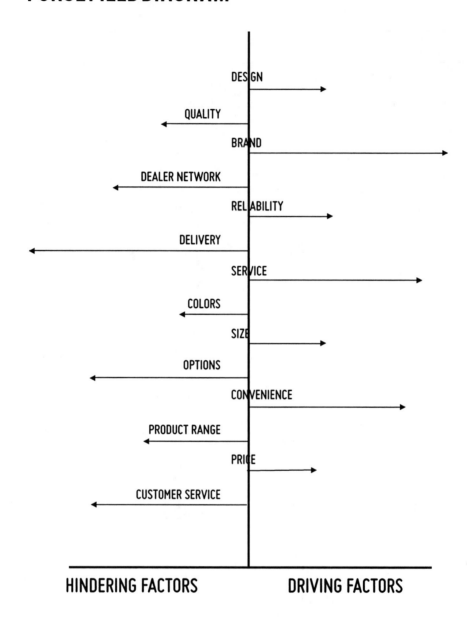

HINDERING FACTORS   DRIVING FACTORS

FORCE FIELD ANALYSIS

WHAT IS IT?
Force field analysis is a method of mapping and analyzing factors which assist or work against desired goals.

WHO INVENTED IT?
Kurt Lewin 1940s
John R. P. French 1947

WHY USE THIS METHOD?
1. Allows visual comparison of factors affecting the success of a project for discussion of solutions.

CHALLENGES
1. It is best to focus on barriers.
2. Assign a strategy to each barrier

HOW TO USE THIS METHOD
1. Select a moderator and a team of stakeholders.
2. The moderator describes the problem being focused on to the team
3. The moderator draws the letter T on a white board
4. The moderator writes the problem above the cross stroke on the T
5. The team brainstorms a list of forces working against the goal and the moderator lists them on the right hand of the upstroke on the letter T.
6. The team brainstorms a list or forces working towards the goal and the moderator writes them on the right hand of the upstroke on the letter T.
7. Forces listed can be internal and external.
8. They can be associated with the environment, the organization, people strategy, culture, values, competitors, conflicts or other factors.
9. Prioritize and quantify both lists of forces
10. The moderator draws a horizontal letter T and above the horizontal line draws arrows for each factor indicating their relative significance in the opinion of the team.
11. The moderator draws arrows for each negative factor below the line showing their relative significance.

RESOURCES
Pen
Paper
White board
Dry erase markers
Post-it notes.

FUTURE WHEEL

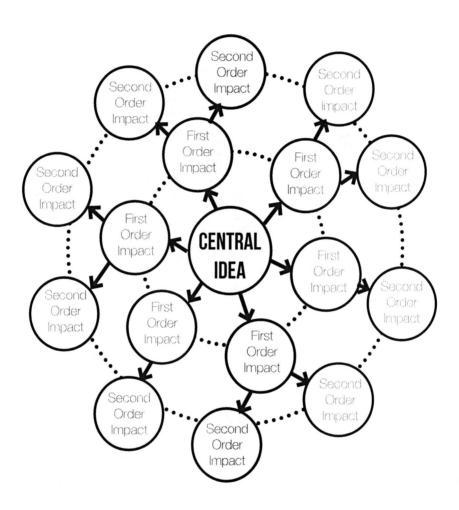

FUTURE WHEEL

WHAT IS IT?
The future wheel is a method to graphically represent and analyze the direct and indirect outcomes of a proposed change.

WHO INVENTED IT?
Jerome Glenn 1972

WHY USE THIS METHOD?
1. A method of envisioning outcomes of decisions.
2. Can be used to study possible outcomes of trends.
3. Helps create a consciousness of the future.

CHALLENGES
1. Can be subjective

WHEN TO USE THIS METHOD
1. Define intent

HOW TO USE THIS METHOD
1. Define the proposed change
2. Identify and graph the first level of outcomes
3. Identify and graph the subsequent level of outcomes
4. Link the dependencies
5. Identify insights
6. Identify the actions
7. Implement the actions

RESOURCES
Pen
Paper
White board
  Dry erase markers

MASLOWS HIERARCHY OF NEEDS

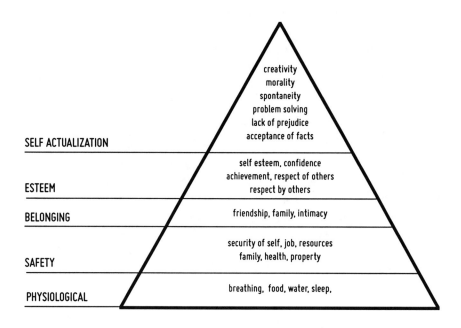

SELF ACTUALIZATION — creativity, morality, spontaneity, problem solving, lack of prejudice, acceptance of facts

ESTEEM — self esteem, confidence, achievement, respect of others, respect by others

BELONGING — friendship, family, intimacy

SAFETY — security of self, job, resources, family, health, property

PHYSIOLOGICAL — breathing, food, water, sleep,

MASLOWS HIERARCHY OF NEEDS

WHAT IS IT?
This is a psychological theory proposed by Abraham. The theory has been influential in design and marketing for half a century.

WHO INVENTED IT?
Abraham Maslow 1943

WHY USE THIS METHOD?
1. Maslow believed that these needs play a role in motivating behavior
2. Maslow believed that once these lower-level needs have been met, people move up to the next level of need

CHALLENGES
1. The hierarchy proposed by Maslow is not today universally accepted.
2. Today it is believed that needs are not a linear hierarchy as proposed by Maslow but are more complex, systematic and interconnected.

HOW TO USE THIS METHOD
The hierarchy as proposed by Maslow is:
1. Self actualization, The highest level,. personal growth and fulfilment
2. Esteem needs. Achievement, status, responsibility, reputation
   .
3. Social needs, friendships, romantic attachments, and families, social, community, or religious relationships.
4. Security needs. Protection, security, order, law, limits, stability
5. Physiological needs. Air, food, drink, shelter, warmth, sleep.

DESIGN THINKING MIND MAP

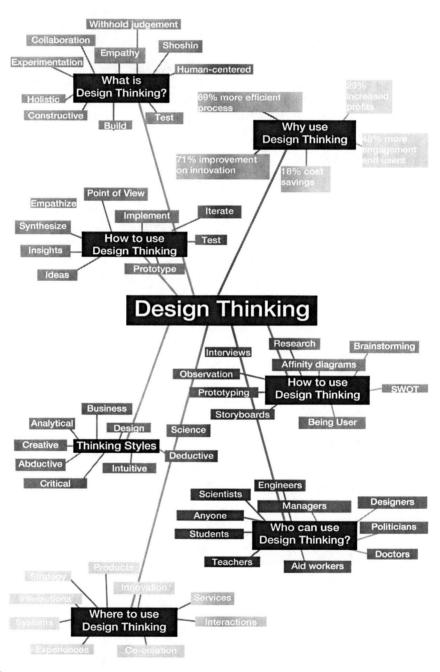

MIND MAPS

WHAT IS IT?
A mind map is a diagram used to represent the affinities or connections between a number of ideas or things. Understanding connections is the starting point for design. Mind maps are a method of analyzing information and relationships.

WHO INVENTED IT?
Porphry of Tyros 3rd century BC. Allan Collins, Northwestern University 1960, USA

WHY USE THIS METHOD?
1. The method helps identify relationships.
2. There is no right or wrong with mind maps. They help with they help with memory and organization.
3. Problem solving and brainstorming
4. Relationship discovery
5. Summarizing information
6. Memorizing information

CHALLENGES
Print words clearly, use color and images for visual impact.

HOW TO USE THIS METHOD
1. Start in the center with a key word or idea. Put box around this node.
2. Use images, symbols, or words for nodes.
3. Select key words.
4. Keep the key word names of nodes s simple and short as possible.
5. Associated nodes should be connected with lines to show affinities.
6. Make the lines the same length as the word/image they support.
7. Use emphasis such as thicker lines to show the strength of associations in your mind map.
8. Use radial arrangement of nodes.

RESOURCES
Paper
Pens
White board
Dry-erase markers

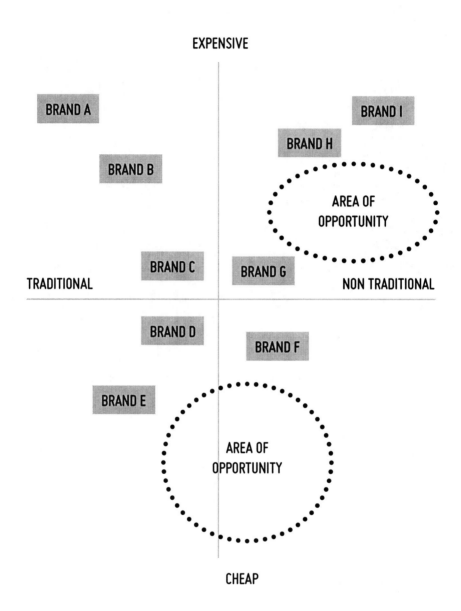

EXPENSIVE

BRAND A

BRAND I

BRAND H

AREA OF OPPORTUNITY

BRAND B

TRADITIONAL

BRAND C

BRAND G

NON TRADITIONAL

BRAND D

BRAND F

BRAND E

AREA OF OPPORTUNITY

CHEAP

PERCEPTUAL MAPS

WHAT IS IT?

Perceptual mapping is a method that creates a map of the perceptions of people of competing alternatives to be compared.

WHO INVENTED IT?

Unknown

WHY USE THIS METHOD?

1. Aids communication and discussion within the organization
2. To gain competitive advantage,
3. Helps build competitive strategy
4. Helps build communication strategy
5. Helps identify potential new products
6. Helps build brand strategy

CHALLENGES

1. Because the position of a product or service on the map is subjective, you can ask several people to locate the position through group discussion.
2. Works well for clearly defined functional attributes such as price, product features

HOW TO USE THIS METHOD

1. Define characteristics of product or service to map.
2. Identify competing brands, services or products to map.
3. Map individual items.
4. Interpret the map.
5. Create strategy.

RESOURCES

Pen
Paper
White board
Dry erase markers

SERVICE BLUEPRINT TEMPLATE

	ACTIVITY PHASE	ACTIVITY PHASE	ACTIVITY PHASE	ACTIVITY PHASE	ACTIVITY PHASE
CUSTOMER ACTIONS	What does user do?				
TOUCHPOINTS	objects and places of customer contact				
	what the customer finds unpleasant				
FRONT STAGE	What your Staff do				
BACK STAGE	What your Staff do				
OPPORTUNITIES	What your Staff do				

LINE OF INTERACTION

LINE OF VISIBILITY

SERVICE BLUEPRINTS

WHAT IS IT?

A blueprint is a process map often used to describe the delivery of services information is presented as a number of parallel rows of activities. These are sometimes called swim lanes. They may document activities over time such as:

1. Customer Actions
2. Touch points
3. Direct contact visible to customers
4. Invisible back office actions
5. Support Processes
6. Physical Evidence
7. Emotional Experience for customer.

WHO INVENTED IT?

Lynn Shostack 1983

WHEN TO USE THIS METHOD

1. Know Context
2. Know User
3. Frame insights

WHY TO USE THIS METHOD

1. Can be used for design or improvement of existing services or experiences.
2. Is more tangible than intuition.
3. Makes the process of service development more efficient.
4. A common point of reference for stakeholders for planning and discussion.
5. Tool to assess the impact of change.

HOW TO USE THIS METHOD

1. Define the service or experience to focus on.
2. A blueprint can be created in a brainstorming session with stakeholders.
3. Define the customer demographic.
4. See though the customer's eyes.
5. Define the activities and phases of activity under each heading.
6. Link the contact or customer touchpoints to the needed support functions
7. Use post-it-notes on a white board for initial descriptions and rearrange as necessary drawing lines to show the links.
8. Create the blueprint then refine iteratively.

RESOURCES

Paper
Pens
White board
Dry-erase markers
Camera
Blueprint templates
Post-it-notes

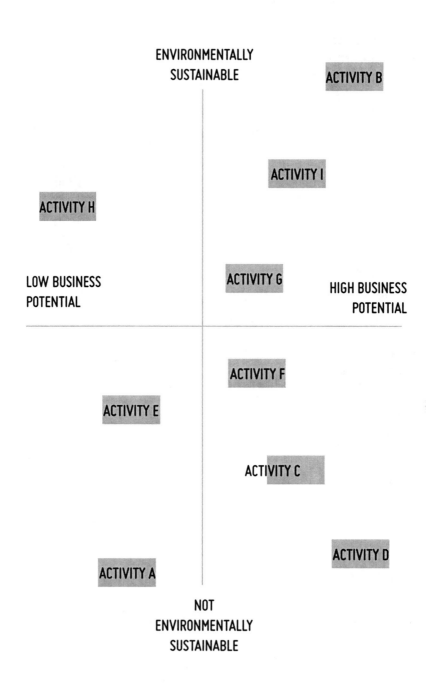

ENVIRONMENTALLY
SUSTAINABLE

ACTIVITY B

ACTIVITY I

ACTIVITY H

LOW BUSINESS
POTENTIAL

ACTIVITY G

HIGH BUSINESS
POTENTIAL

ACTIVITY F

ACTIVITY E

ACTIVITY C

ACTIVITY D

ACTIVITY A

NOT
ENVIRONMENTALLY
SUSTAINABLE

SUSTAINABILITY MAP

WHAT IS IT?

This method allows the team to assess the relative business potential and environmental impact of products and services.

WHY USE THIS METHOD?

1. Aids communication and discussion within the organization.
2. To gain competitive advantage with environmental sustainability,
3. Helps build competitive strategy
4. Helps build team alignment

CHALLENGES

1. Can be subjective

HOW TO USE THIS METHOD

1. Moderator draws grid on whiteboard or flip chart.
2. Team brainstorms
3. Interpret the map.
4. Create strategy.
5. Products and services which have both high environmental sustainability and good business proposition are given priority.

RESOURCES

1. Pen
2. Paper
3. White board
4. Dry erase markers

Define your audience

Define the problem
that you will solve and
the need that you will
address

Define your unique
point of view to guide
your ideation

DESIGN BRIEF &
POINT OF VIEW

BHAG

WHAT IS IT?

BHAG stands for Big Hairy Audacious Goal. It is a type of goal that is bigger than a usual mission statement.

Some examples of BHAGs are:

1. Google bhag is to make all digital information in the world accessible to people everywhere
2. Nokia bhag is to connect one billion people to the internet. For the first time.

WHO INVENTED IT?

J Collins and J Porras, 1996

WHY USE THIS METHOD?

1. Bold visions stimulate bold steps
2. BHAGs encourage you to set your sights high and long term.

WHEN TO USE THIS METHOD

Define intent

HOW TO USE THIS METHOD

1. It needs to motivate people and get them excited.
2. It shouldn't be in your comfort zone
3. It should take a herculean effort to achieve.
4. It should not be possible to achieve with incremental change.
5. BHAGs have time frames of 10-30 years.
6. The BHAG should be aligned to the organization's core values.

RESOURCES

Pen
Paper
White board
Dry erase markers

BOUNDARY EXAMINATION

WHAT IS IT?

Boundary examination is a way of refining the definition of a problem.

WHO INVENTED IT?

Edward De bono 1982

WHY USE THIS METHOD?

1. The boundary setting may be part of the problem.
2. The boundary may reflect biases.

RESOURCES

Pen
Paper
White board
Dry erase markers

HOW TO USE THIS METHOD

1. Define the problem with a written statement.
1. Underline the key words
1. Analyze each key word for underlying assumptions.
2. Consider how the meaning of the problem statement changes as the keywords are replaced by synonyms.
1. Redefine the problem boundary by substituting new keywords.

CHECKLIST: ENVIRONMENTALLY RESPONSIBLE DESIGN

Some of the ways in which we can work to improve the environmental performance of the products that we design:

1. Use environmentally responsible strategies appropriate to the product;
2. Reduce overall material content and increase the percentage of recycled material in products;
3. Reduce energy consumption of products that use energy;
4. Specify sustainability grown materials when using wood or agricultural materials;
5. Design disposable products or products that wear out to be more durable and precious;
6. Eliminate unused or unnecessary product features;
7. Design continuously transported products for minimal weight;
8. Design for fast, economical disassembly of major components prior to recycling;
9. Design products so that toxic components are easily removed prior to recycling;
10. Perform comprehensive environmental assessment;
11. Consider all of the ecological impacts from all of the components in the products over its entire life cycle, including extraction of materials from nature, conversion of materials into products, product use, disposal or recycling and transport between these phases;
12. Consider all ecological impacts including global warming, acid rain, smog, habitat damage, human toxicity, water pollution, cancer causing potential, ozone layer depletion and resource depletion;
13. Strive to reduce the largest ecological impacts,
14. Conduct life cycle impact assessment to comprehensively identify opportunities for improving ecological performance
15. Encourage new business models and effective communication
16. Support product 'take back' systems that enable product up-grading and material recycling;
17. Lease the product or sell the service of the product to improve long-term performance and end-of-life product collection;
18. Communicate the sound business value of being ecologically responsible to clients and commissioners
19. Discuss market opportunities for meeting basic needs and reducing consumption,

Source: adapted from design-sustainability.com

GOAL GRID

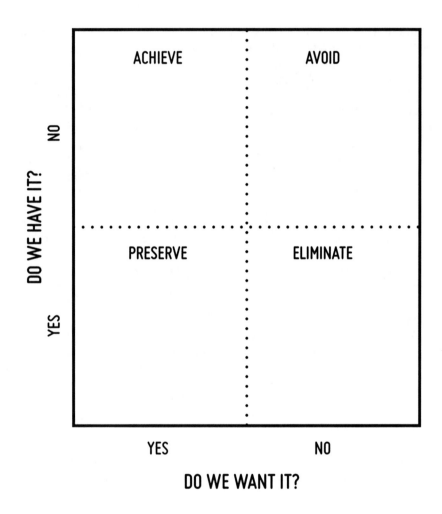

GOAL GRID

WHAT IS IT?

A goal grid is a method for clarifying goals.

"The Goals Grid also provides a structure for analyzing patterns in goals and objectives and for detecting potential conflict with the goals and objectives of others."
Fred Nickols

WHO INVENTED IT?

Ray Forbes, John Arnold and Fred Nickols 1992

WHY USE THIS METHOD?

A goal grid is a method for clarifying goals.

HOW TO USE THIS METHOD

1. The team brainstorms a list of goals.
2. The moderator asks the team these questions:
   - "Do we have it?"
   - "Do we want it?"
   - "What are we trying to achieve?"
   - "What are we trying to preserve?"
   - "What are we trying to avoid?"
   - "What are we trying to eliminate?"

RESOURCES

Pen
Paper
White board
Dry erase markers
Post-it notes.

REFRAMING THE PROBLEM

WHAT IS IT?
This method helps develop innovative solutions with a number of questions.

WHO INVENTED IT?
Tudor Rickards 1974 Manchester Business School

WHY USE THIS METHOD?
1. To create different perspectives and new ideas.

RESOURCES
1. Pen
2. Paper
3. White board
4. Dry Erase markers

REFERENCES
1. Rickards, Tudor (1974). Problem Solving Through Creativity. Wiley. pp. 198. ISBN 0-470-72045-X.
2. Rickards, Tudor; Runco, Mark A., Moger, Susan (2008). 978-0-415-77317-1 The Routledge Companion To Creativity. Routledge. pp. 400. ISBN 978-0-415-77317-1.

WHEN TO USE THIS METHOD
1. Define intent

HOW TO USE THIS METHOD
1. Define the problem that you would like to address.

Complete these sentences while considering your problem.
1. There is more than one way of looking at a problem. You could also define this problem in another way as."
2. "The underlying reason for the problem is."
3. "I think that the best solution is."
4. "If I could break all laws of reality I would try to solve it by."
5. "You could compare this problem to the problem of."
6. "Another, different way of thinking about it is"

REFRAMING MATRIX

PRODUCT PERSPECTIVE

1. Is there something wrong with the product or service?
2. Is it priced correctly?
3. How well does it serve the market?
4. Is it reliable?

PLANNING PERSPECTIVE

1. Are our business plans, marketing plans, or strategy at fault?
2. Could we improve these?

POTENTIAL PERSPECTIVE

1. How would we increase sales?
2. If we were to seriously increase our targets or our production volumes, what would happen with this problem?

PEOPLE PERSPECTIVE

1. What are the people impacts and people implications of the problem?
2. What do people involved with the problem think?
3. Why are customers not buying the product?

DESIGN PROBLEM

REFRAMING MATRIX

WHAT IS IT?

The reframing matrix is a method of approaching a problem by imagining the perspectives of a number of different people and exploring the possible solutions that they might suggest.

WHO INVENTED IT?

Michael Morgan 1993

WHY USE THIS METHOD?

1. This is a method for assisting in empathy which is an important factor in gaining acceptance and creating successful design.

CHALLENGES

The reframing is not done with stakeholders present or in context so may be subjective

RESOURCES

Pens
Paper
Post it notes
White board
Dry erase markers

HOW TO USE THIS METHOD

1. Define a problem.
2. On a white board or paper draw a large square and divide it into four quadrants.
3. Select 4 different perspectives to approach the problem. They could be four professions or four people or four other perspectives that are important for your problem.
4. With your team brainstorm a number of questions that you believe are important from the perspectives that you have selected.
5. The moderator writes the questions in the relevant quadrants of the matrix.
6. The group discusses each of these questions.
7. The answers are recorded and the perspectives are incorporated into the considerations for design solutions.

PREMORTEM

WHAT IS IT?
The premortem is a risk-mitigation planning tool that attempts to identify project threats at the outset.

WHO INVENTED IT?
Gary Klein, 1998

WHY USE THIS METHOD?
The premortem technique is low cost and high value

RESOURCES
Evaluation forms can be printed or online.

HOW TO USE THIS METHOD
1. Determine a period after completion of the project when it should be known whether the project was successful. It could be one or five years.
2. Imagine the project was a complete failure.
3. What could have been the cause?
4. Ask each team member to suggest ten reasons for the failure.
5. Think about the internal and external context and the stakeholders relationships.
6. Ask each team member to select one of the reasons for failure they have listed and describe it to the group.
7. Each person should present one reason.
8. Collect and review the full list of reasons from each participant.
9. Review the session and strengthen the strategy based on the premortem.

SWOT ANALYSIS

WHAT IS IT?

SWOT Analysis is a useful technique for understanding your strengths and weaknesses, and for identifying both the opportunities open to you and the threats you face.

WHO INVENTED IT?

Albert Humphrey 1965 Stanford University

WHY USE THIS METHOD?

1. SWOT analysis can help you uncover opportunities that you can exploit.
2. You can analysis both your own organization, product or service as well as those of competitors.
3. Helps develop a strategy of differentiation.
4. It is inexpensive

CHALLENGES

1. Use only verifiable information.
2. Have system for implementation.

HOW TO USE THIS METHOD

1. Explain basic rules of brainstorming.
2. Ask questions related to the SWOT categories.
3. Record answers on a white board or video
4. Categorize ideas into groups
5. Consider when evaluating "What will the institution gain or lose?"

RESOURCES

Post-it-notes
SWOT template
Pens
White board
Video camera
Dry-erase markers

SWOT TEMPLATE

Strengths

Weaknesses

Opportunities

Threats

SAMPLE SWOT QUESTIONS

STRENGTHS

1. Advantages of proposition
2. Capabilities
3. Competitive advantages
4. Marketing - reach, distribution
5. Innovative aspects
6. Location and geographical
7. Price, value, quality?
8. Accreditation, certifications
9. Unique selling proposition
10. Human resources
11. Experience,
12. Assets
13. Return on investment
14. Processes, IT, communications
15. Cultural, attitudinal, behavioral
16. Management cover, succession

WEAKNESSES

1. Value of proposition
2. Things we cannot do.
3. Things we are not good at
4. Perceptions of brand
5. Financial
6. Own known vulnerabilities
7. Time scales, deadlines and pressures
8. Reliability of data, plan predictability
9. Morale, commitment, leadership
10. Accreditation,
11. Cash flow, start-up cash-drain
12. Continuity, supply chain robustness

OPPORTUNITIES

1. Market developments
2. Competitors' vulnerabilities
3. New USP's
4. Tactics - surprise, major contracts
5. Business and product development
6. Information and research
7. Partnerships, agencies, distribution
8. Industrial trends
9. Technologies
10. Innovations
11. Global changes
12. Market opportunities
13. Specialized market niches
14. New exports or imports
15. Volumes, production, economies
16. Seasonal, weather, fashion influences

THREATS

1. Political effects
2. Legislative effects
3. Obstacles faced
4. Insurmountable weaknesses
5. Environmental effects
6. IT developments
7. Competitor intentions
8. Loss of key staff
9. Sustainable financial backing
10. Market demand
11. New technologies, services, ideas

"

Use the diverse perspectives of the team members to create 75 to 120 good design solutions. that effectively balance the needs of people, appropriate use of technology and business goals. Keep an open mind until the ideas have been tested and compared

IDEATION

USER STORIES SCENARIOS AND CASES

USER STORIES

A user story is a brief statement that identifies the user and her need. It makes an incisive abstract that can be associated with your personas. Because personas tend to be pretty general, you might have several user stories associated with one persona group. Here's an example user story for a hypothetical industrial parts database:

Here's another example of a user story that might apply to the same website designed to meet our first user's need:

"Jack owns a small landscaping business. He needs to be able to order replacement parts and have access to resources that will help him safely and properly service his equipment on his own."

USER SCENARIOS

A user scenario expands upon your user stories by including details about how a system might be interpreted, experienced, and used. Like user stories, you might imagine several scenarios for each persona group that you anticipate will make up your audience. Your scenarios should anticipate the user's goal, specify any assumed knowledge, and speculate on the details of the user's interaction experience.

Here's an example of a user scenario, again from our hypothetical industrial parts website: "Jerry has been helping his father manage an all-purpose machine shop in Western Massachusetts since he graduated from high school a decade ago. In the last year, Jerry's father has retired, leaving Jerry in charge. Their only commercial wood chipper, which Jerry's father purchased before Jerry began working with him, has broken down. He suspects that the hydraulic pump lever is broken. Jerry manages to locate the operator's manual for the chipper, and searches the web for the manufacturer's name and the model number. He finds several listings for his chipper online, and chooses the first one to view. On the chipper's listing page, he finds a link to a PDF of the owner's manual. He reads through it and finds a diagram showing the hydraulic pump and the part number for the lever. But there is nowhere on the page he is viewing that indicates he can order this part. He clicks a link to contact the manufacturer, who he hopes can point him in the right direction. One of Jerry's long-time clients, the local country club, is expecting to pick up the chipper in two weeks."

USE CASES

A use case is really just a long list of steps a user might take in trying to get something done. It starts with whatever event serves as a catalyst for their interaction with your system — so, how the user got there — and recounts each and every step they take until they've either successfully done what they need to do, or failed to do so.

Here's an example based upon Jerry's scenario from earlier: Jerry's commercial chipper breaks down. He: locates user manual and identifies name and model number enters name and model number in search field at Google. com hits "Enter" search results appear; scans page for name and model number finds no results that look correct enters chipper name in search field hits "Enter" search results appear; scans page finds listing for chipper clicks link detail page for chipper loads from manufacturer website scans page for model number identifies link for owner's manual clicks to download PDF opens PDF and scans for model number; finds his among three

models covered by manual scans PDF for part he suspects needs maintenance finds part number listed in hydraulic pump schematic tries to copy and paste part number; cannot, text is part of image writes part number on a sheet of paper returns to manufacturer website searches for part number in manufacturer website's search field clicks "Go" button search results page loads with no results scans navigation for a contact link clicks "Contact Us" contact page loads; scans and fills out form clicks "Submit."
This detailed case highlights several points at which Jerry's experience could be improved. With this case as a guide, improvements to the chipper's detail page can be made, such as prominently displaying model numbers, expanding the resources associated with specific models, including an on-page parts search, and adding a contact form. Cases like these can also be informed and/or verified by actual usability test sessions.

Source: Christopher Butler

DRAW 10 ROWS OF TEN FAST SMALL SKETCHES

10 X 10 SKETCH METHOD

WHAT IS IT?

This method is an approach to making early concept generation sketching more efficient in use of time than the method that stresses finished sketches early in the design process. It allows more time to explore ideas and so stresses the quality of thinking and the final solution. The 10 x 10 method involves creating ten rows with ten thumbnail sketches per row on each page.

WHY USE THIS METHOD?

1. It allows more exploration of alternative ideas in a shorter time
2. May lead to a final concept which is a better design than traditional approaches.
3. Prevents sketches from becoming jewelry in the mind of the designer and more important than the quality of the final design solution.

CHALLENGES

1. This method takes discipline

HOW TO USE THIS METHOD

1. Traditional design concept exploration involves a designer producing six to 12 alternative design concepts presented as attractive renderings
2. This method involves a designer making ten rows of ten simple fast cartoon like sketches per page.
3. Each sketch should be no larger than one inch by one inch.
4. The designer produces 5 to 20 pages of very fast sketches during first phase of concept exploration
5. Designs are reviewed and ranked by the design team following a discussion and presentation by the designer and a relatively small number are selected for iteration, recombination and further development.
6. At the next stage more finished and larger concept sketches are produced

RESOURCES

Paper
Fine line pens
Sharpie markers

SCENARIOS

WHAT IS IT?

A scenario is a narrative or story about how people may experience a design in a particular future context of use. They can be used to predict or explore future interactions with concept products or services. Scenarios can be presented by media such as storyboards or video or be written. They can feature single or multiple actors participating in product or service interactions.

WHO INVENTED IT?

Herman Kahn, Rand Corporation 1950, USA

WHY USE THIS METHOD?

1. Scenarios become a focus for discussion which helps evaluate and refine concepts.
2. Usability issues can be explored at a very early stage in the design process.
3. The are useful tool to align a team vision.
4. Scenarios help us create an end to end experience.
5. Interactive experiences involve the dimension of time.
6. Personas give us a framework to evaluate possible solutions.

CHALLENGES

1. Generate scenarios for a range of situations.
2. Include problem situations
3. Hard to envision misuse scenarios.

HOW TO USE THIS METHOD

1. Identify the question to investigate.
2. Decide time and scope for the scenario process.
3. Identify stakeholders and uncertainties.
4. Define the scenarios.
5. Create storyboards of users goals, activities, motivations and tasks.
6. Act out the scenarios.
7. The session can be videotaped.
8. Analyze the scenarios through discussion.
9. Summarize insights

RESOURCES

Storyboard templates
Pens
Video cameras
Props
White board
Dry-erase markers

"

I have not failed. I've just found 10,000 ways that will not work

Just because something doesn't do what you planned it to do doesn't mean it's useless

To have a great idea have a lot of them

THOMAS EDISON
Design Thinker

BRAINSTORMING

PREPARING FOR BRAINSTORMING

Come to the brainstorm session prepared.

1. Bring a lot of paper and markers.
2. Pens
3. Post-it-notes
4. Index cards
5. A flip chart
6. White board or wall
7. Video camera
8. Camera
9. One clear goal per brainstorming session.
10. Determine who will write things down and document the proceedings?
11. Allow one to two hours for a brainstorming session.
12. Recruit good people.
13. 8 to 12 people is a good number
14. Prepare brainstorm questions that you think will help guide the group.

CREATE A STRATEGY

1. What do you want to achieve?
2. What problem do you want solved?
3. Define the goal
4. How will you define the problem to the participants?
5. How long will the session be?
6. How many people will be involved?
7. What will be the mix of people?
8. Will there be a follow up session?
9. Will you send out information before the session?
10. Do the participants have the information that they need?
11. Who should you invite?
12. Assemble a diverse team.
13. Do the participants have the right skills and knowledge for the task?
14. Where will the brainstorm be held?
15. Who owns the intellectual property?
16. Will the session be free of interruptions?
17. How will you record the ideas?
18. What will you do with the information?
19. What brainstorming technique will be used and is it best for your purpose?
20. Be mindful of the scope brainstorm questions. Neither too broad nor too narrow.
21. 45-60 minutes for brainstorm time. Warm up 15-30 minutes.
22. Wrap up 15-30 minutes.

CHOOSING A TECHNIQUE

1. There are many different brainstorming methods.
2. Choose a method that suites your task and participants
3. Try different methods over time to find which ones work best for you.

REFRESHMENTS

1. An army marches on it's stomach
2. Offer tea, coffee water, soda.

FACILITATING

1. Encourage everyone to contribute.
2. Review the rules and ask group to enforce them.
3. Encourage an attitude of shoshin.
4. Ask participants to turn phones off or onto vibrate mode.
5. A facilitator isn't a leader.
6. Do not steer the discussion
7. Do not let particular people dominate the conversation.
8. Keep the conversations on topic.
9. Set realistic time limits for each stage and be sure that you keep on time.
10. 5. Have a brainstorm plan and stick to it.
11. The facilitator should create an environment where it is safe to suggest wild ideas.
12. Provide clear directions at the beginning of the meeting.
13. Clearly define the problem to be discussed.
14. Write the problem on the white board where everyone can see it.
15. Provide next steps at the end of the meeting.
16. Select final ideas by voting.
17. Use your camera or phone to take digital pictures of the idea output at the end of your meeting.
18. Good facilitation requires good listening skills
19. The facilitator should run the white board, writing down ideas as people come up with them,
20. Prevent people from interrupting others
21. Invite quieter people to contribute.
22. Hire a facilitator if necessary.
23. Start on time.
24. End on time.
25. Keep things moving
26. You can filter the best ideas after the session or get the team to vote on their preferred ideas during the session.
27. Listen
28. Write fast & be visual
29. Use humour and be playful
30. Thank the group after the session.
31. Provide next steps to the group after the meeting.
32. Keep participants engaged
33. Encourage inter activity
34. 100 ideas per hour.
35. Avoid social hierarchy
36. Organize small break-out sessions that cut across traditional office boundaries to establish teams.
37. Encourage passion.

Source Hasso Plattner Institute of

Design Standford University

RULES FOR BRAINSTORMING

38. "Defer judgment Separating idea generation from idea selection strengthens both activities. For now, suspend critique. Know that you'll have plenty of time to evaluate the ideas after the brainstorm.
39. Encourage wild ideas
40. One conversation at a time Maintain momentum as a group. Save the side conversations for later.
41. Headline Capture the essence quickly "
42. Focus on quantity not on quality."

POST-IT VOTING

1. Give every participant 4 stickers and have everyone put stickers next to their favorite ideas.
2. Each person tags 3 favorite ideas
3. Cluster favorite ideas
4. Clustering of stickers indicate possible strong design directions.

GROUP REVIEW

Ask everyone to review the boards of ideas, and discuss the specific ideas or directions they like and why.

Source adapted from Hasso Plattner Institute of Design

THE ENVIRONMENT

1. Select a space not usually used by your team.
2. Refreshments
3. Find a comfortable quiet room
4. Comfortable chairs
5. No interruptions
6. Turn phones off
7. Go off-site. A new environment might spur creativity and innovation by providing new stimuli. Helps participants mentally distance themselves from ordinary perceptions and ways of thinking.
8. Location matters:
9. Use big visible materials for writing on
10. Keep the temperature comfortable Adequate lighting
11. Suitable external noise levels
12. A circular arrangement of seats allows participants to read body language and with no "head of the table."
13. Seats should be not too far apart
14. Have a space with a lot of vertical writing space.

METHODS OF ARRANGING IDEAS

1. 2X2 matrix
2. Clustering
3. Continuum
4. Concentric circles
5. Time-line
6. Pyramid
7. Prioritization
8. Adoption curve

101METHOD

WHAT IS IT?

This is a brainstorming method focuses on creating volumes of ideas

WHY USE THIS METHOD?

1. Leverages the diverse experiences of a team.
2. A large volume of ideas helps overcome people's inhibitions to innovating.
3. Makes group problem solving fun.
4. Helps build team cohesion.
5. Everyone can participate.

CHALLENGES

1. Because the focus is on volume some ideas will not be useful.
2. Best used with other creativity methods

HOW TO USE THIS METHOD

1. Define a problem
2. Select a moderator
3. Select a diverse design team of 4 to 12 people and a moderator.
4. The moderator asks the team to each generate 101 solutions to the design problem in a defined time. Allow 30 to 60 minutes.
5. Analyze results and prioritize.
6. Develop actionable ideas.

RESOURCES

Pens
Post-it-notes
A flip chart
White board or wall
Refreshments

635 BRAINSTORMING PROCESS

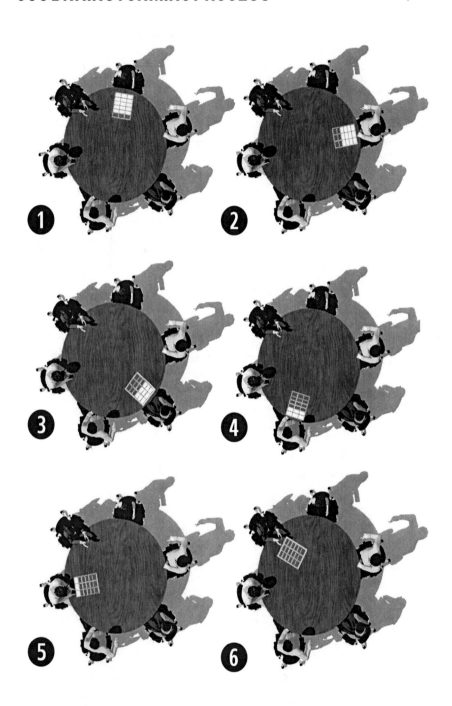

635 BRAINSTORMING

WHAT IS IT?
Method 635 is a structured form of brainstorming.

The outcome of each session is 108 ideas in 18 minutes.

WHO INVENTED IT?
Professor Bernd Rohrbach 1968

WHY USE THIS METHOD?
1. Can generate a lot of ideas quickly
2. Participants can build on each others ideas
3. Ideas are recorded by the participants
4. Democratic method.
5. Ideas are contributed privately.
6. Ideas are iteratively refined five times.
7. Does not need a moderator

WHEN TO USE THIS METHOD
1. Frame insights
2. Explore Concepts

HOW TO USE THIS METHOD
1. Your team should sit around a table.
2. Each team member is given a sheet of paper with the design objective written at the top.
3. The sheet can be divided into six rows of three boxes.
4. Each team member is given three minutes to generate three ideas.
5. Your participants then pass the sheet of paper to the person sitting on their left.
6. Each participant must come up with three new ideas.
7. The process can stop when sheets come around the table.
8. Repeat until ideas are exhausted. No discussion during the idea generating period.
9. Ideas can be sketches or written or a combination.
10. You can use an egg timer
11. You can also use post-it notes. One per box. This makes it easier to process the ideas after the session.
12. Analyze ideas as a group,
13. Put the ideas on a white board or wall cluster and vote for the preferred ideas.

RESOURCES
Large room
Large table
Paper
Pens
Post-it notes.

AOKI METHOD

WHAT IS IT?

The Aoki or MBS method is a structured brainstorming method that stresses input by all team members.

WHO INVENTED IT?

Sadami Aoki. Used by Mitsubishi

WHY USE THIS METHOD?

1. There is a hierarchy of ideas
2. This method requires that a quantity of ideas is generated.
3. Shifts you from reacting to a static snapshot of the problem and broadens your perspective toward the problem and the relationships and connections between its components

CHALLENGES

1. Group-think
2. Not enough good ideas
3. Taking turns
4. Freeloading
5. Inhibition
6. Lack of critical thinking
7. A group that is too large competes for attention.

HOW TO USE THIS METHOD

1. Warm Up: Participants generate ideas for 15 minutes.
2. Participants present their ideas verbally to the larger group.
3. The larger group continues to generate ideas during the individual presentations.
4. For one hour the individual team members further explain their ideas to the group
5. Idea maps are created by the moderator.

RESOURCES

Paper
Pens
White board
Dry-erase markers
Post-it-notes.

BODYSTORMING

WHAT IS IT?

Bodystorming is method of prototyping experiences. It requires setting up an experience - complete with necessary artifacts and people - and physically "testing" it. A design team play out scenarios based on design concepts that they are developing. The method provides clues about the impact of the context on the user experience.

WHO INVENTED IT?

Buchenau, Fulton 2000

WHY USE THIS METHOD?

1. You are likely to find new possibilities and problems.
2. Generates empathy for users.
3. This method is an experiential design tool. Bodystorming helps design ideation by exploring context.
4. It is fast and inexpensive.
5. It is a form of physical prototyping
6. It is difficult to imagine misuse scenarios

CHALLENGES

1. Some team members may find acting a difficult task.

HOW TO USE THIS METHOD

1. Select team.
2. Define the locations where a design will be used.
3. Go to those locations and observe how people interact. the artifacts in their environment.
4. Develop the prototypes and props that you need to explore an idea. Identify the people, personas and scenarios that may help you with insight into the design directions.,
5. Bodystorm the scenarios.
6. Record the scenarios with video and analyze them for insights.

RESOURCES

Empathy tools
A large room
White board
Video camera

BOUNDARY SHIFTING

WHAT IS IT?

Boundary shifting involves identifying features or ideas outside the boundary of the system related to the defined problem and applying to them to the problem being addressed.

WHY USE THIS METHOD?

1. It is fast and inexpensive.
2. Helps find innovative solutions

HOW TO USE THIS METHOD

1. Define the problem.
2. Research outside systems that may have related ideas or problems to the defined problem.
3. Identify ideas or solutions outside the problem system.
4. Apply the outside idea or solution to the problem being addressed.

RESOURCES

Pen
Paper
White board
Dry-erase markers

BRAINWRITING

WHAT IS IT?

Brainwriting is a similar method to the 635 method. Both terms are commonly used. Brainwriting generates written ideas.

WHO INVENTED IT?

Brahm & Kleiner, 1996

WHY USE THIS METHOD?

1. Moderation of Brainwriting is easier than brainstorming.
2. Brainwriting tends to produce more ideas than brainstorming
3. Can be conducted in 15 to 30 minutes
4. Brainwriting is better if participants are shy or from cultures where group interaction is more guarded.
5. Brainwriting reduces the problems of group-think.

CHALLENGES

1. Not enough good ideas
2. Freeloading
3. Inhibition
4. Lack of critical thinking

WHEN TO USE THIS METHOD

1. Explore Concepts

HOW TO USE THIS METHOD

1. Define the problem
2. Each participant should brainstorm three solutions in two minutes in written form.
3. Then have them pass the sheet of paper to their left.
4. Have the participants add to or build upon the existing suggestions by writing their own ideas underneath the original solutions. Allow 3 minutes.
5. The process should be repeated as many times as there are people around the table allowing an additional minute each time.
6. When you've finished post the ideas on a wall.
7. Get the group to vote on the most promising ideas.

RESOURCES

Pens
Post-it-notes
A flip chart
White board or wall
Refreshments.

DISNEY METHOD

WHAT IS IT?

The Disney Method is a parallel thinking technique. It was invented before Design Thinking evolved to it's current state but has many of the elements of the Design Thinking approach. It allows a team to discuss an issue from four perspectives. It involves parallel thinking to analyze a problem, generate ideas, evaluate ideas, and to create a strategy. It is a method used in workshops. The four thinking perspectives are Spectators, Dreamers, Realists and Critics.

WHO INVENTED IT?

Dilts, 1991

WHY USE THIS METHOD?

1. Allows the group to discuss a problem from four different perspectives

CHALLENGES

1. An alternative to De Bono Six Hat Method.
2. Can deliver a workable solution quickly.

HOW TO USE THIS METHOD

1. Have Four different brainstorming sessions in four different rooms.
2. At the end of each of the four sessions the participants leave the room and then at a later time reenter the next room then assuming the personas and perspectives of the next group. Time taken is often 60 to 90 minutes per session. The sessions adopt the following themes.
3. The spectator's view. Puts the problem in an external context. How would a consultant, a customer or an outside observer view the problem?
4. The Dreamers view. Looking for an ideal solution. What would our dream solution for this be? What if? Unconstrained brainstorm.
5. Realists view. The realists are convergent thinkers. How can we turn the dreamer's views into reality? Looking for ideas that are feasible, profitable, customer focused and can be implemented within 18 months.
6. The Critics view. What are the risks and obstacles? Who would oppose this plan? What could go wrong? Refine, improve or reject. Be constructive.

DOT VOTING

CONCEPT 1

● ● ● ● ● ●

CONCEPT 2

● ●

CONCEPT 3

● ● ● ●

CONCEPT 4

● ● ●

CONCEPT 5

●

CONCEPT 6

● ● ● ● ●

DOT VOTING

WHAT IS IT?

This is a way of efficiently selecting from a large number of ideas the preferred ideas to carry forward in the design process.

WHY USE THIS METHOD?

It is a method of selecting a favored idea by collective rather than individual judgment. It is a fast method that allows a design to progress. It leverages the strengths of diverse team member viewpoints and experiences.

CHALLENGES

1. The assessment is subjective.
2. Group-think
3. Not enough good ideas
4. Inhibition
5. Lack of critical thinking

RESOURCES

Large wall
Adhesive dots

HOW TO USE THIS METHOD

1. Gather your team of 4 to 12 participants.
2. Brainstorm ideas for example ask each team member to generate ten ideas as sketches.
3. Each idea should be presented on one post-it-note or page.
4. Each designer should quickly explain each idea to the group before the group votes.
5. Spread the ideas over a wall or table.
6. Ask the team to vote on their two or three favorite ideas and total the votes. You can use sticky dots or colored pins to indicate a vote or a moderator can tally the scores.
7. Rearrange the ideas so that the ideas with the dots are ranked from most dots to least.
8. Refine the preferred ideas.

"

Design thinking is a framework for "radical collaboration" intended to create a culture of creativity and innovation among diverse groups of people. It seeks to reawaken the "creative confidence" of individuals through visual thinking and intuition, skills often dormant since childhood.

KAREN COLLIAS
Design without borders

HEURISTIC IDEATION

WHAT IS IT?

Heuristic ideation method is used to create new concepts, ideas, products or solutions.

WHY USE THIS METHOD?

1. To create new connections and insights for products, services and experiences

WHO INVENTED IT?

Couger 1995, McFadzean 1998, McFadzean, Somersall, and Coker 1998, VanGundy 1988

RESOURCES

Pens
Markers
White board or flip chart
Dry erase markers

HOW TO USE THIS METHOD

1. The group will first make two lists of words
2. Each team member selects three words from the first list and connects each word to a different word in the second list.
3. Each team members develops these ideas into concepts and illustrates or describes each concept on an index card.
4. The index cards are places on a pin board and each concept is briefly described by the team member who generated the idea.
5. The team votes to prioritize the ideas

IDEA ADVOCATE

WHAT IS IT?
This method involves appointing advocates for ideas that were previously created during a brainstorming session.

WHO INVENTED IT?
Battelle Institute in Frankfurt, Germany

WHY USE THIS METHOD?
1. Idea advocate is a simplified form of the dialectical approach
2. To ensure fair examination of all ideas.
3. To give every presented idea equal chance of being selected.
4. To uncover the positive aspects of ideas

CHALLENGES
1. Consideration should be given to also assigning a devil 's advocate for a more balanced assessment of certain proposed ideas.
2. There should be little difference in status amongst the idea advocates.

HOW TO USE THIS METHOD
1. The team reviews a list of previously generated ideas.
2. Assign idea advocate roles to:
3. A team member who proposed an idea, will implement an idea, or argues for the selection of a design direction.
4. The idea advocates present arguments to the design team on why the idea is the best direction.
5. After the advocates have presented the team votes on their preferred idea.

RESOURCES
Pens
Markers
White board or flip chart
Dry erase markers

KJ METHOD

WHAT IS IT?

The KJ method is a form of brainstorming. The KJ method places emphasis on the most important ideas. It is one of the seven tools of Japanese quality management and incorporates the Buddhist value of structured meditation.

WHO INVENTED IT?

Kawakita Jiro

WHY USE THIS METHOD?

1. There is a hierarchy of ideas
2. This method generates many ideas.
3. This method highlights the connections between ideas which is the starting point for a design solution.

CHALLENGES

1. Group-think
2. Not enough good ideas
3. Taking turns
4. Freeloading
5. Inhibition
6. Lack of critical thinking
7. A group that is too large competes for attention.

RESOURCES

Paper
Pens
White board
Dry-erase markers
Post-it-notes.

HOW TO USE THIS METHOD

1. The moderator frames the design challenge.
2. Team members generate ideas in up to 25 words on post-it notes.
3. Cards are shuffled and then handed out again to the participants.
4. Each participant should not get any of their own cards back.
5. Each post-it note is read out by the participants, and all participants review the post-it notes that they hold to find any that seem to go with the one read out, so building a 'group'.
6. Organize post-it notes into groups.
7. Group the groups until you have no more than ten groups.
8. Sort categories into subcategories of 20-30 cards.
9. Refine groups into 10 post-it notes or less.
10. Use a white board or smooth wall.
11. Write the individual post-it notes arranged in groups on the white board or arrange the post-it notes on a wall.
12. The moderator will read out the groups and record the participant's ideas about the relationships and meaning of the information gathered.

LOTUS TEMPLATE

A1	A2	A3	B1	B2	B3	C1	C2	C3
A4	**A**	A5	B4	**B**	B5	C4	**C**	C5
A6	A7	A8	B6	B7	B8	C6	C7	C8
D1	D2	D3	**A**	**B**	**C**	E1	E2	E3
D4	**D**	D5	**D**		**E**	E4	**E**	E5
D6	D7	D8	**F**	**G**	**H**	E6	E7	E8
F1	F2	F3	G1	G2	G3	H1	H2	H3
F4	**F**	F5	G4	**G**	G5	H4	**H**	H5
F6	F7	F8	G6	G7	G8	H6	H7	H8

LOTUS METHOD

WHAT IS IT?

The lotus blossom is a creativity technique that consists a framework for idea generation that starts by generating eight concept themes based on a central theme. Each concept then serves as the basis for eight further theme explorations or variations.

WHO INVENTED IT?

Yasuo Matsumura, Director of the Clover Management Research

WHY USE THIS METHOD?

1. This method requires that a quantity of 81 ideas is generated. To generate one good idea it is necessary to generate many ideas.
2. You can explore a spectrum of ideas from low risk to high risk or other spectrum.
3. Each idea can be developed in the outer boxes.

CHALLENGES

1. It is a somewhat rigid model. Not every problem will require the same number of concepts to be developed.

WHEN TO USE THIS METHOD

To generate concepts

HOW TO USE THIS METHOD

1. Draw up a lotus blossom template of 9 x 9 empty boxes.
2. Write the design problem in the center box of the diagram.
3. Write eight related ideas around the center.
4. Each idea then becomes the central idea of a new theme or blossom.
5. Follow step 3 with all central ideas.

RESOURCES

Paper
Pens
White board
or large sheet of paper
Dry-erase markers
Post-it-notes.

OUT OF THE BOX

WHAT IS IT?

This is a method to perform out-of-the box brainstorming to generate outrageous and wild ideas.

WHY USE THIS METHOD?

1. To generate wild ideas
2. To promote creative thinking among participants.

RESOURCES

1. Pen
2. Paper
3. White board
4. Dry erase markers
5. Post-it-notes

CHALLENGES

1. Avoid persona representations that may be harmful.
2. Group-think
3. Not enough good ideas
4. Taking turns
5. Freeloading
6. Inhibition
7. Lack of critical thinking
8. A group that is too large competes for attention.

WHEN TO USE THIS METHOD

1. Explore Concepts

HOW TO USE THIS METHOD

1. The moderator introduces this method.
2. The moderator shows the team several wild or out of the box ideas.
3. Participants generate concepts stressing that they must be wild and out of the box.
4. The moderator records the ideas on a white board.
5. The team reviews the ideas and selects some for further development and bringing back to reality.

RESOURCES

Pen
Paper
White board
Dry erase markers
Post-it-notes

NHK METHOD

WHAT IS IT?

The NHK method is a rigorous iterative process of brainstorming of ideas following a predetermined structure.

WHO INVENTED IT?

Hiroshi Takahashi

WHY USE THIS METHOD?

1. This method requires that a quantity of ideas is generated.

CHALLENGES

1. Group-think
2. Not enough good ideas
3. Taking turns
4. Freeloading
5. Inhibition
6. Lack of critical thinking
7. A group that is too large competes
         for attention.

RESOURCES

Paper
Pens
White board
Dry-erase markers
Post-it-notes.

HOW TO USE THIS METHOD

1. Define problem statement.
1. Each participant writes down five ideas on five separate cards.
2. Create groups of five participants
3. While each person explains their ideas, the others continue to record new ideas.
4. Collect, and create groups of related concepts.
5. Form new groups of two or three people Brainstorm for half an hour.
6. Groups organize ideas and present them to the larger group.
7. Record all ideas on the white board.
8. Form larger groups of ten people and work further brainstorm each of the ideas on the white board.

NOMINAL GROUP METHOD

WHAT IS IT?

The nominal group method is a brainstorming method that is designed to encourage participation of all members of the team and minimizes the possibility of more vocal members from dominating the discussion.

WHO INVENTED IT?

William Fox

WHY USE THIS METHOD?

1. To define and prioritize problems or opportunities
2. To understand the best solution to a problem
3. To create a plan to implement an opportunity

RESOURCES

White board
Dry erase markers
Blank postcards

WHEN TO USE THIS METHOD

1. Frame insights
2. Explore Concepts

HOW TO USE THIS METHOD

1. Distribute information about the process to participants before the meeting.
2. Participants drop anonymous suggestions into an unmonitored suggestion box written on blank postcards.
3. The suggestions are distributed to participants before the meeting so that they can think about them.
4. In the meeting the moderator writes the suggestions on to a white board
5. Each participant has the opportunity to speak in support or against any of the suggestions.
6. The moderator leads the team in to clarify each idea,
7. The moderator instructs each person to work silently and independently for five minutes, recording as many ideas, thoughts, or answers as possible on paper.
8. The moderator asks the group to list 5 to 10 ideas that the like the most, in order of importance, and to pass them to the moderator.
9. The moderator counts up the number of votes for each idea.
10. Each participant is given a number of votes that they record on blank postcards which are collected face down and tallied.

NYAKA

WHAT IS IT?

The Nyaka method is a form of brainstorming. The Nyaka method places emphasis on exploring problems and solutions to problems.

WHY USE THIS METHOD?

1. There is a hierarchy of ideas
2. This method generates many ideas.

CHALLENGES

1. Group-think
2. Not enough good ideas
3. Taking turns
4. Freeloading
5. Inhibition
6. Lack of critical thinking
7. A group that is too large competes for attention.

RESOURCES

Paper
Pens
White board
Dry-erase markers
Post-it-notes.

HOW TO USE THIS METHOD

1. Define a moderator
2. The moderator draws a vertical line on a white board.
3. Time limit of 30 minutes
4. The moderator asks the team to define as many things that are wrong with a design or service or experience as possible.
5. The moderator asks the team to define solutions for as many of the problems defined as possible.
6. Create a hierarchy of problems and a hierarchy of solutions for each problem.
7. A group size of 4 to 20 people is optimum.
8. For larger groups the moderator can break the group into groups of 4 or 5 people.

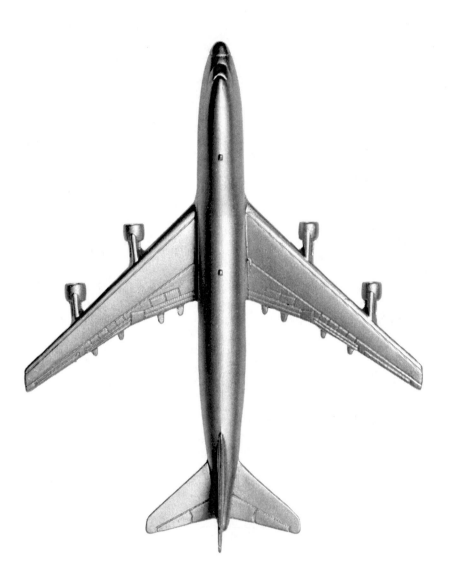

OBJECTSTORMING

WHAT IS IT?
A brainstorming technique that uses found objects for inspiration.

WHO INVENTED IT?
Alex Faickney Osborn 1953 is often credited with inventing brainstorming.

WHY USE THIS METHOD?
1. Leverages the diverse experiences of a team.
2. Makes group problem solving fun.
3. Helps build team cohesion.
4. Everyone can participate.

CHALLENGES
1. Group-think
2. Not enough good ideas
3. Taking turns
4. Freeloading
5. Inhibition
6. Lack of critical thinking
7. A group that is too large competes for attention.

HOW TO USE THIS METHOD
1. The moderator introduces the method to the group.
2. The problem is defined by the moderator.
3. The larger group is broken down into groups of 4 or 5 participants. The moderator collects a diverse collection of objects before the brainstorming session.
4. Each participant is given two objects and asked to use them as inspiration to generate 10 ideas
5. Allow 20 minutes
6. The participants are asked to vote for their three preferred solutions.
7. Select the top ideas for further development.

RESOURCES
Pens
Post-it-notes
A flip chart
White board or wall
Refreshments

PERSONAL

WHAT IS IT?

Recent research has suggested that some individuals are more creative working alone for brainstorming sessions rather than in groups. In this case the divergent idea generation is done by an individual and the convergent phase is done by the team.

WHO INVENTED IT?

Alex Faickney Osborn 1953 is often credited with inventing brainstorming.

WHY USE THIS METHOD?

1. Leverages the diverse experiences of a team.
2. Uses the creativity of the individual free from distractions.
3. Helps build empathy.

CHALLENGES

1. Some ideas that you generate using the tool may be impractical.
2. Best used with other creativity methods

HOW TO USE THIS METHOD

1. Define a problem
2. Find a quiet place
3. Generate as many ideas as possible in 30 minutes.
4. Get the team together and present the ideas to them.
5. Get the team to vote on which ideas they like the most. Two votes per person.
6. Analyze results and prioritize.
7. Develop actionable ideas.

RESOURCES

Pens
Post-it-notes
A flip chart
White board or wall
Refreshments

PERSONA BRAINSTORMING

WHAT IS IT?

This is a brainstorming method that uses the imagined perspectives of an identified persona or group identified as one of your client's customer groups such as students look at a design problem.

WHO INVENTED IT?

Alex Faickney Osborn 1953 is often credited with inventing brainstorming.

WHY USE THIS METHOD?

1. Leverages the diverse experiences of a team.
2. Helps build empathy.
3. Makes group problem solving fun.
4. Helps build team cohesion.
5. Everyone can participate.

CHALLENGES

1. Some ideas that you generate using the tool may be impractical.
2. Best used with other creativity methods

HOW TO USE THIS METHOD

1. Define a problem
2. Select a diverse design team of 4 to 12 people and a moderator.
3. Identify a persona to focus on. See personas.
4. Ask the team how they would deal with the problem if they were the persona
5. Analyze results and prioritize.
6. Develop actionable ideas.

RESOURCES

Pens
Post-it-notes
A flip chart
White board or wall
Refreshments

PINCARDS

WHAT IS IT?

The pin cards technique is a brainwriting process to generate ideas on colored cards that are sorted into groups and discussed. This method allows participants to think of more ideas during the writing process. This method can generate more ideas than some other brainstorming methods.

WHO INVENTED IT?

Wolfgang Schnelle

WHY USE THIS METHOD?

1. To generate ideas to solve a problem
2. To produce many ideas quickly and without filtering from other participants.

CHALLENGES

1. Cards need to be passed on quickly
2. Participants may feel time stressed.
3. Some participants may want to make their ideas confidential.

RESOURCES

Colored blank index cards
Pins
Pin Board
Pens
Markers

HOW TO USE THIS METHOD

1. The moderator writes the problem statement on a white board.
2. The participants should be seated around a large table.
3. The moderator distributes 10 cards of the same color to each participant.
4. Each participant receives different-colored cards.
5. Participants record one idea per card.
6. Ideas can be a cartoon sketch or a sentence
7. Completed cards are passed to the person on the participant's right hand side.
8. Participants can review cards from a person on their left hand side.
9. After 30 to 45 minutes all the participants pin the cards that they have to a wall.
10. Each participant should aim to produce at least 40 ideas.
11. The team sorts the cards into a number of groups by association. The type of association are determined by the group.
12. The participants prioritize the groups and combine the ideas in the favored group for further development.

RELATED CONTEXT

WHAT IS IT?

A method that involves discovering and projecting the thinking of another sector, brand, organization or context onto a design problem.

WHY USE THIS METHOD?

A method of discovering affinities that can facilitate innovative thinking and solutions.

1. Scenarios become a focus for discussion which helps evaluate and refine concepts.
2. Usability issues can be explored.
3. Scenarios help us create an end to end experience.
4. Personas give us a framework to evaluate possible solutions.

CHALLENGES

1. Strong personalities can influence the group in negative ways.
2. Include problem situations
3. Hard to envision misuse scenarios.

WHEN TO USE THIS METHOD

1. Know Context
2. Know User
3. Frame insights
4. Generate Concepts

HOW TO USE THIS METHOD

1. Identify a design problem
2. Put together a design team of 4 to 12 members with a moderator.
3. Brainstorm a list of sectors, organizations, or contexts that may imply a different approach or thinking to your design problem.
4. Imagine your design problem with the associated list.
5. Generate concepts for each relationship
6. Vote for favored directions using dot voting method.
7. Analyze and summarize insights.

RESOURCES

Post-it notes
White board
 Paper
Pens
Dry-erase markers

RESOURCES

WHAT IS IT?

This is a brainstorming method that uses the availability of resources to look at a design problem.

WHO INVENTED IT?

Alex Faickney Osborn 1953 is credited with inventing brainstorming.

WHY USE THIS METHOD?

1. Leverages the diverse experiences of a team.
2. Helps build empathy.
3. Makes group problem solving fun.
4. Helps build team cohesion.
5. Everyone can participate.

CHALLENGES

1. Some ideas that you generate using the tool may be impractical.
2. Best used with other creativity methods

HOW TO USE THIS METHOD

1. Define a problem
2. Select a diverse design team of 4 to 12 people and a moderator.
3. Identify a resource to limit or make more available such as finance, time, people, materials or process.
4. Ask the team how they would deal with the problem if the resource was changed as proposed
5. Analyze results and prioritize.
6. Develop actionable ideas.

RESOURCES

Pens
Post-it-notes
A flip chart
White board or wall
Refreshments

ROLESTORMING

WHAT IS IT?

Rolestorming is a brainstorming method where participants adopt other people's identity while brainstorming.

WHO INVENTED IT?

Rick Griggs 1980s

WHY USE THIS METHOD?

1. Helps reduce inhibitions which some team members may have in suggesting innovative solutions.

CHALLENGES

1. Avoid persona representations that may be harmful.
2. Group-think
3. Not enough good ideas
4. Taking turns
5. Freeloading
6. Inhibition
7. Lack of critical thinking
8. A group that is too large competes for attention.

HOW TO USE THIS METHOD

1. Select moderator
2. Conduct a traditional brainstorming session
3. At the conclusion of the first brainstorming session the moderator identifies a number of identities to be used for the second session
4. The identities can be any person not in the brainstorming group such as a competitor, a famous person, a boss. They should be known to the team members.
5. The Moderator asks some questions

How would this identity solve the problem?
What would this persona see as the problem?
Where would this persona see the problem?
Why would the persona see a problem?

6. Brainstorm in character.
7. Use words such as "My persona"
8. Share ideas.

SCAMPER

WHAT IS IT?

SCAMPER is a brainstorming technique and creativity method that uses seven words as prompts.

1. Substitute.
2. Combine.
3. Adapt.
4. Modify.
5. Put to another use.
6. Eliminate.
7. Reverse.

WHO INVENTED IT?

Alex Osborne

WHY USE THIS METHOD?

1. Scamper is a method that can help generate innovative solutions to a problem.
2. Leverages the diverse experiences of a team.
3. Makes group problem solving fun.
4. Helps get buy in from all team members for solution chosen.
5. Helps build team cohesion.
6. Everyone can participate.

CHALLENGES

1. Some ideas that you generate using the tool may be impractical.
2. Best used with other creativity methods

HOW TO USE THIS METHOD

1. Select a product or service to apply the method.
2. Select a diverse design team of 4 to 12 people and a moderator.
3. Ask questions about the product you identified, using the SCAMPER mnemonic to guide you.
4. Create as many ideas as you can.
5. Analyze
6. Prioritize.
7. Select the best single or several ideas to further brainstorm.

RESOURCES

Pens
Post-it-notes
A flip chart
White board or wall
Refreshments

SCAMPER QUESTIONS

SUBSTITUTE

1. What materials or resources can you substitute or swap to improve the product?
2. What other product or process could you substitute?
3. What rules could you use?
4. Can you use this product in another situation?

COMBINE

1. Could you combine this product with another product?
2. Could you combine several goals?
3. Could you combine the use of the product with another use?
4. Could you join resources with someone else?

ADAPT

1. How could you adapt or readjust this product to serve another purpose or use?
2. What else is the product like?
3. What could you imitate to adapt this product?
4. What exists that is like the product?
5. Could the product adapt to another context?

MODIFY

1. How could you change the appearance of the product?
2. What could you change ?
3. What could you focus on to create more return on investment?
4. Could you change part of the product?

PUT TO ANOTHER USE

1. Can you use this product in another situation?
2. Who would find this product useful?
3. How would this product function in a new context?
4. Could you recycle parts of this product to create a new product?

ELIMINATE

1. How could you make the product simpler?
2. What features, parts, could you eliminate?
3. What could you understate or tone down?
4. Could you make the product smaller or more efficient?
5. What components could you substitute to change the order of this product?

SCENARIOS

WHAT IS IT?

A scenario is a narrative or story about how people may experience a design in a particular future context of use. They can be used to predict or explore future interactions with concept products or services. Scenarios can be presented by media such as storyboards or video or be written. They can feature single or multiple actors participating in product or service interactions.

WHO INVENTED IT?

Herman Kahn, Rand Corporation 1950, USA

WHY USE THIS METHOD?

1. Scenarios become a focus for discussion which helps evaluate and refine concepts.
2. Usability issues can be explored at a very early stage in the design process.
3. The are useful tool to align a team vision.
4. Scenarios help us create an end to end experience.
5. Interactive experiences involve the dimension of time.
6. Personas give us a framework to evaluate possible solutions.

CHALLENGES

1. Generate scenarios for a range of situations.

2. Include problem situations
3. Hard to envision misuse scenarios.

WHEN TO USE THIS METHOD

1. Frame insights
2. Generate Concepts
3. Create Solutions

HOW TO USE THIS METHOD

1. Identify the question to investigate.
2. Decide time and scope for the scenario process.
3. Identify stake holders and uncertainties.
4. Define the scenarios.
5. Create storyboards of users goals, activities, motivations and tasks.
6. Act out the scenarios.
7. The session can be videotaped.
8. Analyze the scenarios through discussion.
9. Summarize insights

RESOURCES

Storyboard templates
Pens
Video cameras
Props
White board
Dry-erase markers

SENSORIAL METHOD

WHAT IS IT?

Design in northern Europe and the United States focuses on the visual sense which is only a component of the design experience. A design such as an Italian sports car gives greater consideration to other senses such as hearing, smell touch to give a consistent experience of through all senses to a product user.

WHO INVENTED IT?

Rob Curedale 1995

WHY USE THIS METHOD?

1. It gives a design a greater experience of quality than a design that focuses on the visual sense.
2. It gives a consistent experience.
3. It provides a more stimulating experience than a design that focuses on the visual experience.

CHALLENGES

1. Group-think
2. Not enough good ideas
3. Taking turns
4. Freeloading
5. Inhibition
6. Lack of critical thinking
7. A group that is too large competes
         for attention.

HOW TO USE THIS METHOD

1. The moderator frames the design challenge.
2. Team members generate ideas on post-it notes.
3. The team works through 20 minute brainstorming sessions in each sense, Vision, smell, touch hearing, taste.
4. Ask team members to generate 6 to 10 ideas each under each category.
5. Use up to 25 words for non visual senses and simple sketches for the visual ideas.
6. Organize post-it notes into groups through discussion with five concepts in each group, one idea from each sense group or five different senses in each group.
7. Ask team to vote on which groups have the most potential for further development.

RESOURCES

Paper
Pens
White board
Dry-erase markers
Post-it-notes.

"

Design thinking is
an approach to new
perspectives on value
creation through a
human-centered
co-creation process
focused on real
end-user needs
that yields the
highest value to all
stakeholders

BILL BURNETT
Director Stanford Design Program

WORDLISTS

VERB LIST	ADJECTIVE LIST	ADVERB LIST	PRODUCT LIST
walk	adaptable	accidentally	GPS
stand	adventurous	anxiously	marine
reach	affable	beautifully	printer
sit	affectionate	blindly	copy
jump	agreeable	boldly	chair
fly	ambitious	bravely	sofa
accept	amiable	brightly	video
allow	amicable	calmly	game
advise	amusing	carefully	camera
answer	brave	carelessly	desk
arrive	bright	cautiously	tv
ask	broad-minded	clearly	music
avoid	calm	correctly	floor
stop	careful	courageously	bookcase
agree	charming	cruelly	tools
deliver	communicative	daringly	fence
depend	compassionate	deliberately	cart
describe	conscientious	doubtfully	car
deserve	considerate	eagerly	house
destroy	convivial	easily	bean bag
disappear	courageous	elegantly	audio

329

OBJECTS	ACTIONS
remote control	smell
button	hear
computer	touch
phone	see
car	walk
sailboat	sing
camera	talk
television	dance
internet	vision
gps	laugh
mp3 player	magic
book	swim
	play
	tell a story

SEMANTIC INTUITION

WHAT IS IT?

Semantic intuition is a method of generating ideas based on word associations.

WHO INVENTED IT?

Warfield, Geschka, & Hamilton, 1975. Battelle Institute

WHY USE THIS METHOD?

1. To find new solutions to a problem.

WHEN TO USE THIS METHOD

1. Explore Concepts

RESOURCES

Pens
Paper
Post-it -notes
White board
Dry erase markers.

HOW TO USE THIS METHOD

1. Define the problem to be explored.
2. The team brainstorms two to four word lists that are related to the problem. They could be for example a list of nouns, a list of verbs and a list of adjectives.
3. The team makes a forth lists of associations of two or three words from the lists that can form the basis of new ideas.
4. Combine one word from one set with another word from the other set.
5. The team visualizes new products services or experiences based on the word associations.
6. Each team member produces five to ten ideas based on the word associations over a 30 minute period.
7. The ideas are prioritized by the group by voting.

STP METHOD

WHAT IS IT?
STP is a brainstorming method designed to help define ways of reaching a goal.

WHO INVENTED IT?
Ava S Butler 1996

WHY USE THIS METHOD?
1. To generate new ideas

CHALLENGES
1. Group-think
2. Not enough good ideas
3. Taking turns
4. Freeloading
5. Inhibition
6. Lack of critical thinking
7. A group that is too large competes for attention.

RESOURCES
1. Pens
2. Post-it-notes
3. A flip chart
4. White board or wall
5. Refreshments.

HOW TO USE THIS METHOD
1. The moderator writes three headings on a white board. Situation, target and proposal.
2. The moderator reviews the rules of brainstorming. Go for quantity.
3. The moderator asks the question "What do you see as the current situation?"
4. When all ideas have been recorded the moderator asks "Which comments need clarification?"
5. After team members provide clarification the moderator asks " What is our ideal goal?"
6. After all ideas have been recorded and clarifies the moderator asks" What is our preferred target?"
7. After the team votes and a preferred target is selected the moderator asks "How can we get from our current situation to our preferred target?"
8. After all ideas have been recorded and clarified the team selects a preferred way to get to the target by voting.

SIX THINKING HATS

WHAT IS IT?
Six thinking hats is a tool for thinking described in a book by the same name by Edward de Bono. It can help a design team understand the effects of decisions from different viewpoints.
1. White Hat thinking is information, numbers, data needs and gaps.
2. Red Hat thinking is intuition, desires and emotion.
3. Black Hat thinking is the hat of judgment and care.
4. Yellow Hat thinking is the logical positive.
5. Green Hat thinking is the hat of creativity, alternatives, proposals, provocations and change.
6. Blue Hat thinking is the overview or process control.

WHO INVENTED IT?
Edward de Bono 1985

CHALLENGES
1. When describing your concept, be specific about your goal.
2. Utilize your thinking for practical solutions.
3. Always think in the style of the hat you're wearing.
4. Stick to the rules.

WHY USE THIS METHOD?
The key theoretical reasons to use the Six Thinking Hats are to:
1. Encourage Parallel Thinking
2. Encourage full-spectrum thinking

3. Separate ego from performance
4. Encourage critical thinking.

WHEN TO USE THIS METHOD
1. Know Context
2. Know User
3. Frame insights
4. Generate Concepts
5. Create Solutions

HOW TO USE THIS METHOD
1. Optimum number of participants is 4 to 8.
2. Present the facts White Hat.
3. Generate ideas on how the issue should be handled Green Hat.
4. Evaluate the ideas. Yellow Hat.
5. List the drawbacks Black Hat.
6. Get the feelings about alternatives Red Hat.
7. Summarize and finish the meeting. Blue Hat.
8. Time required 90 minutes.

RESOURCES
Paper and
Pens,
Descriptions of different hats
Symbols of hats
Space to sit in the circle

SYNECTICS

WHAT IS IT?

Synectics is a structured creativity method that is based on analogy. Synectics is based on observations collected during thousands of hours of group process and group problem solving and decision making activities (Nolan 1989) The word synectics combines derives from Greek "the bringing together of diverse elements."

WHO INVENTED IT?

George Prince and William Gordon 1976

WHY USE THIS METHOD?

1. Use to stimulate creative thinking and generate new problem solving approaches.
2. Synectics provides an environment in which risk taking is validated.
3. Synectics can be fun and productive.

CHALLENGES

1. Synectics is more demanding than brainstorming,
2. If the analogy is too obvious, then it may not promote innovative thinking.
3. Synectics works best as a group process.

HOW TO USE THIS METHOD

1. Problem definition.
2. Create an analogy. Use ideas from the natural or man-made world, connections with historical events, your location, etc.
3. Use this Sentence Stem: An is a lot like a y because...
4. Use a syntectic trigger Mechanism like a picture, poem, song, drawing etc. to start your analogical reasoning.
5. The group generates as many solution approaches, called springboards, as possible.
6. Idea selection.
7. Excursions - Structured side trips.
8. Develop the selected ideas into concepts.
9. Analyze the connections in the analogy you have created.

RESOURCES

Paper
Pens
White board
Dry-erase markers

"

The models that ultimately endure are the ones you intuitively know to be true. No intellectualizing necessary they are as undeniable as gravity, and as easy as remembering to breathe. They don't repress thinking they foster it.

MIROSLAV AZIS
IBM Design Thinking

"

Make your ideas
tangible with a series
of fast, inexpensive
prototypes.

Ask people to give you
feedback and use it to
improve the designs.

PROTOTYPE

"

Learning and innovation go hand in hand. The arrogance of success is to think that what you did yesterday will be sufficient for tomorrow

WILLIAM POLLARD
Physicist

APPEARANCE PROTOTYPE

WHAT IS IT?

Appearance prototypes look like but do not work like the final product. The are often fabricated using a variety of rapid prototyping techniques from digital 3d models or by hand in materials such as hard foam, wood or plastics. Usually, appearance prototypes are "for show" and short term use and are not designed to be handled.

CHALLENGES

1. Designers can become too attached to their prototypes and allow them to become jewelry that stands in the way of further refinement.
2. Clients may believe that the design is finalized when more refinement is required.
3. They are expensive to produce,

WHY USE THIS METHOD?

May be used to get approval for a final design from a client or to create images for literature or a web site prior to the availability of manufactured products.

HOW TO USE THIS METHOD

1. They give non-designers a good idea of what the production object will look like and feel like.

DARK HORSE PROTOTYPE

WHAT IS IT?

A dark horse prototype is your most creative idea built as a fast prototype. The innovative approach serves as a focus for finding the optimum real solution to the design problem.

WHO INVENTED IT?

One of the methods taught at Stanford University.

WHY USE THIS METHOD?

1. This method is a way of breaking free of average solutions and exploring unknown territory
2. A way of challenging assumptions.

CHALLENGES

1. Fear of unexplored directions
2. Fear of change
1. Designers can become too attached to their prototypes and allow them to become jewelry that stands in the way of further refinement.
2. Client may believe that system is real.

HOW TO USE THIS METHOD

1. After initial brainstorming sessions select with your team the most challenging, interestingly or thought provoking idea.
2. Build also a prototype of your idea that best balances business, human needs with appropriate use of technology
3. Create a low resolution prototype of the two selected ideas
4. Test with end users
5. With your team analyze and discuss the prototype.
6. Brainstorm ways of bringing back the dark horse concept into a realizable solution.
7. Refine and implement.

"

A prototype is worth a
thousand meetings

IDEO

GENERATIVE PROTOTYPING

WHAT IS IT?

A method also called "Thinkering" where participants build simple prototypes from supplied materials to explore ideas.

WHO INVENTED IT?

Pioneered by Liz Sanders 2002 and Lego
Johan Roos and Bart Victor 1990s.

WHY USE THIS METHOD?

1. Creative way to generate ideas involving users
2. Discovering user needs
3. Developing concepts with users
4. Designing prototypes with users

CHALLENGES

1. Demanding of participants:
2. Good moderation needed
1. Designers can become too attached to their prototypes and allow them to become jewelry that stands in the way of further refinement.

HOW TO USE THIS METHOD

1. "In generative prototyping users are asked to together with designers built low-tech prototypes or products using a large set of materials during a workshop. For example, in creating ideas for a new playground, children were asked to built their favorite playground element using ice lolly sticks, foam balls, etc
2. The basic idea is that by building, you start thinking and new ideas are generated."

source: Geke Luken

RESOURCES

Toy construction kits such as lego
Pop sticks
String
Tape
Post-it-notes
Cardboard
Paper
Markers

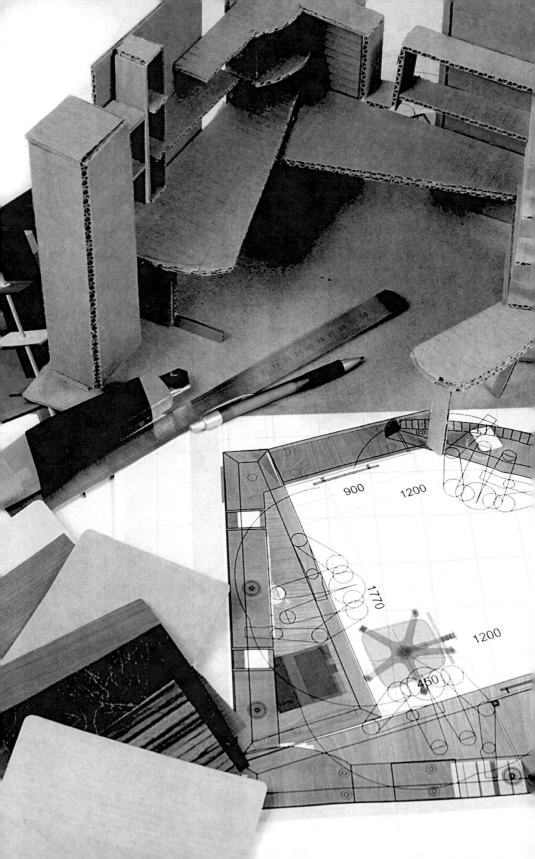

LOW FIDELITY PROTOTYPING

WHAT IS IT?

Low Fi prototyping is a quick and cheap way of gaining insight and informing decision-making without the need for costly investment. Simulates function but not aesthetics of proposed design. Prototypes help compare alternatives and help answer questions about interactions or experiences.

WHY USE THIS METHOD?

1. May provide the proof of concept
2. It is physical and visible
3. Inexpensive and fast.
4. Useful for refining functional and perceptual interactions.
5. Assists to identify any problems with the design.
6. Helps to reduce the risks
7. Helps members of team to be in alignment on an idea.
8. Helps make abstract ideas concrete.
9. Feedback can be gained from the user

CHALLENGES

1. A beautiful prototype completed too early can stand in the way of finding the best design solution.

HOW TO USE THIS METHOD

1. Construct models, not illustrations
2. Select the important tasks, interactions or experiences to be prototyped.
3. Build to understand problems.
4. If it is beautiful you have invested too much.
5. Make it simple
6. Assemble a kit of inexpensive materials
7. Preparing for a test
8. Select users
9. Conduct test
10. Record notes on the 8x5 cards.
11. Evaluate the results
12. Iterate

RESOURCES

Paper
Cardboard
Wire
Foam board,
Post-it-notes
Hot melt glue

LOW FIDELITY PROTOTYPE KIT

Here are some suggestions for
a kit of materials to help you
construct low fidelity prototypes

1. Copy paper
2. Magnets
3. Snaps
4. Masking tape
5. Duct tape (color would be ideal)
6. Tape
7. Post-it notes
8. Glue sticks
9. Paper clips, (asst colors ideal)
10. Decorative brads (square, crystal)
11. Hole punch
12. Scissors
13. Stapler (with staples)
14. Hot glue
15. Glue guns
16. Rulers
17. Pipe Cleaners
18. Colored card
19. Zip ties
20. Foam core sheets
21. Velcro
22. Rubber bands, multicolored
23. Assorted foam shapes
24. Markers
25. Scissors
26. Glue sticks
27. Tape
28. Glue guns
29. Straws
30. Paper Clips
31. Construction Paper
32. ABS sheets
33. Felt
34. Foam sheets
35. String
36. Foil
37. Butcher paper
38. Stickers
39. Pipe cleaners
40. Popsicle sticks
41. Multicolored card

PICTIVE

WHAT IS IT?

PICTIVE (Plastic Interface for Collaborative Technology Initiative through Video Exploration) is a low fidelity participatory design method used to develop graphical user interfaces. It allows users to participate in the development process. A pictive prototype gives a user a sense of what a system or a piece of software will look like and how it will behave when completed.

WHO INVENTED IT?

Developed by Michael J. Muller and others at Bell Communications Research around 1990

WHY USE THIS METHOD?

1. Less development time.
2. Less development costs.
3. Involves users.
4. Gives quantifiable user feedback.
5. Facilitates system implementation since users know what to expect.
6. Results user oriented solutions.
7. Gets users with diverse experience involved.

HOW TO USE THIS METHOD

1. A pictive is usually made from simple available tools and materials like pens, paper, Post-It stickers, paper clips and icons on cards.
2. Allow thirty minutes for initial design.
3. Allow ten minutes for user testing.
4. Ten minutes for modification.
5. Five minutes for user testing.
6. Create task scenario.
7. Anything that moves or changes should be a separate element.
8. The designer uses these materials to represent elements such as drop-down boxes, menu bars, and special icons. During a design session, users modify the mock up based on their own experience.
9. Take notes for later review.
10. Record the session with a video camera
11. The team then reviews the ideas and develops a strategy to apply them.
12. A pictive enables non technical people to participate in the design process.

ROLE PLAYING

WHAT IS IT

Role playing is a research method where the researcher physically acts out the interaction or experience of the user of a product, service or experience. It is a type of prototyping, a narrative or story about how people may experience a design in a particular future context. Role playing can be used to predict or explore future interactions with concept products or services.

WHY USE THIS METHOD

1. Role playing helps a designer gain empathy and insights into the experience of the user.
2. Useful for unfamiliar situations.
3. It is a physical activity so may uncover insights not apparent when using storyboarding
4. It helps designers empathize with the intended users and their context.
5. Is an inexpensive method requiring few resources.

CHALLENGES

1. It is difficult to envision all the ways a product or service could be misused.
2. Some people feel self conscious when asked to role play

RESOURCES

Note pad
Pens
Video camera
Empathy tools

HOW TO USE THIS METHOD

1. Identify the situation.
2. Identify scenarios and tasks users undertake.
3. Create storyboards.
4. Assign roles.
5. Isolate moments where the users interact with the product or service.
6. Use your own intuitive responses to iterate and refine the design.
7. This method can be used to test physical prototypes.
8. You can act out the tasks in the environments or context of use.
9. You can use empathy tools such as glasses to simulate the effects of age or a wheelchair.
10. Consider typical misuse cases.
11. Discuss insights.

STORYBOARD TEMPLATE

PROJECT   NAME   DATE   PAGE

DIALOGUE   DIALOGUE   DIALOGUE

ACTION   ACTION   ACTION

PROJECT   NAME   DATE   PAGE

DIALOGUE   DIALOGUE   DIALOGUE

ACTION   ACTION   ACTION

PROJECT   NAME   DATE   PAGE

DIALOGUE   DIALOGUE   DIALOGUE

ACTION   ACTION   ACTION

STORYBOARDS

WHAT IS IT?

The storyboard is a narrative tool derived from cinema. A storyboard is a form of prototyping which communicates each step of an activity, experience or interaction. Used in films and multimedia as well as product and UX design. Storyboards consists of a number of 'frames' that communicate a sequence of events in context.

WHO INVENTED IT?

Invented by Walt Disney in 1927. Disney credited animator Webb Smith with creating the first storyboard. By 1937-38 all studios were using storyboards.

WHY USE THIS METHOD?

1. Can help gain insightful user feedback.
2. Conveys an experience.
3. Can use a storyboard to communicate a complex task as a series of steps.
4. Allows the proposed activities to be discussed and refined.
5. Storyboards can be used to help designers identify opportunities or use problems.

HOW TO USE THIS METHOD

1. Decide what story you want to describe.
2. Choose a story and a message: what do you want the storyboard to express?
3. Create your characters
4. Think about the whole story first rather than one panel at a time.
5. Create the drafts and refine them through an iterative process. Refine.
6. Illustrations can be sketches or photographs.
7. Consider: Visual elements, level of detail, text, experiences and emotions, number of frames, and flow of time.
8. Keep text short and informative.
9. 6 to 12 frames.
10. Tell your story efficiently and effectively.
11. Brainstorm your ideas.

RESOURCES

Pens
Digital camera
Storyboard templates
Comic books for inspiration

VIDEO PROTOTYPING

WHAT IS IT?
Video prototypes use video to illustrate how users will interact with a new system. Video prototypes can be thought of as sketches that illustrate what the interaction with the new system will be like.

WHY USE THIS METHOD?
1. Capturing an experience over time requires a linear medium like video
2. Video prototypes are a good way of communicating a complex system of interactions in an easy to access way that can be shared with a large number of people.

RESOURCES
Video camera
Smart phone camera
Card for titles
Simple props
Actors
Lights
Post-it-notes

HOW TO USE THIS METHOD
1. Choose a director and a camera person.
2. Decide who the kactors are and who will create the storyboard and props.
3. Decide how you will communicate the story: title-cards only, an off-camera voice-over or through dialog.
4. Storyboard the sequence of shots.
5. Begin by shooting the initial title card 4 seconds with the name of the project, group, date, time and version number.
6. Shoot a title card 6 seconds that identifies the personas and the context.
7. Shoot an establishing shot that shows the user(s) in context.
8. Shoot the series of interaction points that tell the story and communicate the interaction.
9. Use mid shots to show conversation and close-ups to show devices.
10. "Editing-in-the-camera" involves shooting each sequence of the video prototype in the order that it will be viewed,so that it does not need to be edited afterwards.
11. Some video prototypes use a narrator or voice over, others use only title cards others rely on the actors to explain interactions.

WIREFRAMING

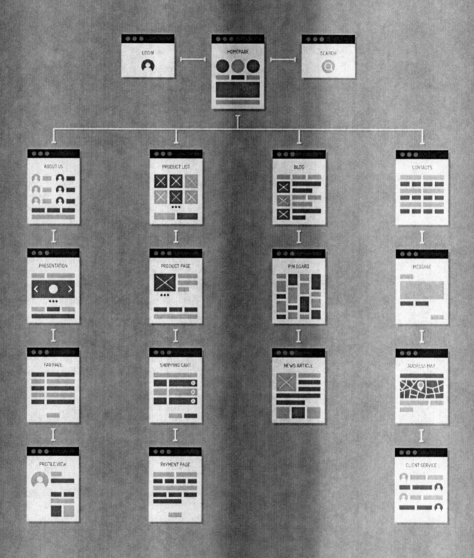

WIREFRAMING

WHAT IS IT?

Website wireframes are a simplified outline of the elements of a web page. They are useful for communicating the functionality of a website in order to get feedback on the design. The wireframe depicts the page layout, interface and navigation, and how these elements interact in use.

WHO INVENTED IT?

Matthew Van Horn claims to have invented the term around 1994 in New York.

WHY USE THIS METHOD?

1. Wireframes are useful for getting feedback on a design.
2. Wireframes can speed up the iteration process of a website design.
3. Enable on-line collaboration
4. Helps Identify needed changes early on in the development.
5. Wireframes are low cost

CHALLENGES

1. Notes to explain behavior are useful
2. Wireframes do not explain interactive details involving movement.

HOW TO USE THIS METHOD

1. There are a several ways to create wireframes. These include drawing by hand. Using Adobe Photoshop or Illustrator and using wireframe software.
2. Start by listing all of the elements that you want on your website.
3. Use simple boxes or outlines of the shape of elements, and name them. These elements can include: navigation: buttons, Company logo: can just be represented by a box, content areas and search box.
4. Review your design and adjust as necessary.
5. Make wireframe for each page in your site.

RESOURCES

Paper
Pens
Wireframe software
Computer

"You never learn by doing something right 'cause you already know how to do it. You only learn from making mistakes and correcting them."

RUSSELL AKOFF
Professor Emeritus of Management Science
at the Wharton School, University of Pennsylvania

TEST

Create a series of fast prototypes to test your design direction with end users

The Hasso Plattner Design School (d. school) at Stanford University propose three major reasons for testing.

1. To refine prototypes and solutions by informing the next iteration of a prototype even if it means going back to the drawing board
2. To accelerates the learning process by providing additional opportunities to learn about users often through deeper engagement and observation that yield totally unthought-of and unexpected insights.
3. To reveal instances when individuals and teams failed to frame problems correctly, which may invalidate favored solutions.

Source: Design without borders

OBTAIN FEEDBACK

Usability testing is a technique used in user-centered interaction design to evaluate a product by testing it on users. Usability testing focuses on measuring a designs fitness for an intended purpose. Usability testing involves observation under controlled conditions to determine how well people can use the design

1. Methods include:
2. Hallway testing five to six people are brought in to test the product, or service. The name of the technique refers to the fact that the testers should be random people who pass by in the hallway.

3. Remote usability Usability evaluators, developers and end users are located in different countries and time zones, .
4. Expert review. Involves bringing in experts with experience in the field to evaluate the usability of a product system or service.
5. Automated expert review Automated expert reviews provide usability testing but through the use of programs given rules for good design and heuristics. Though an automated review might not provide as much detail and insight as reviews from people, they can be finished more quickly and consistently.
6. A/B Testing. Two versions (A and B) are compared, which are identical except for one variation that might impact a user's behaviour.

DESIGN REVIEW QUESTIONS

1. Does the design conform to the design intent statement?
2. Is the design achievable?
3. Have the important risks been identified?
4. Is the design a solution to an identified need or problem?
5. What is the business case?
6. Is the design consistent?
7. Is the design as simple as possible?
8. Are the components recyclable?
9. Can the design be scaled?

10. Are all features necessary?
11. Is everything documented?
12. What are the risks associated with this design?
13. Are any new risks posed by the design that have not been identified?
14. Are the interfaces identified
15. Is the design consistent with the context?
16. Have critical features and interactions been prototyped and tested?
17. Is the cost of ownership reduced?
18. Is the design easy to maintain?
19. Have all legal requirements and regulations been addressed?
20. Have the key stakeholders been identified and involved?
21. What were the assumptions?
22. Is the design usable and accessible?
23. How will the design be implemented?
24. What is the scope of the design?
25. What design alternatives were considered?

TEST

The product, service or experience is tested, Improvements are made. The process is not over until the design works. The prototype may not work as well as expected, New ideas may need to be brainstormed and the prototype modified and retested

REFINE AND TEST AGAIN

Review you video of end users interacting with your prototype. Get feedback from as many stakeholders as possible including end users, and your design team. Brainstorm a list of insights generated. Brainstorm how the design could be improved to overcome any issues that you have seen. Refine your prototype build in the feedback and test it again. Go though this iterative process as many times as is necessary till your design works well for your intent.

HEURISTIC EVALUATION

Heuristic evaluation is an evaluation of by one or more experts. The experts measure the usability, efficiency, and effectiveness of the interface based on 10 usability heuristics defined by Jakob Nielsen in 1994.

Nielsen's Usability Heuristics, which have continued to evolve in response to user research and new devices, include:

1. Visibility of System Status
2. Match Between System and

the Real World
3. User Control and Freedom
4. Consistency and Standards
5. Error Prevention
6. Recognition Rather Than Recall
7. Flexibility and Efficiency of Use
8. Aesthetic and Minimalist Design
9. Help Users Recognize, Diagnose, and Recover from Errors
10. Help and Documentation

MAKE A VIDEO
Record the end user interacting with existing products and services as well as your prototypes. Recording the activity in it's natural setting will help you understand the subtle and complex nature of an activity and can be used for feedback from stakeholders to refine the design direction.

The first known ethnographic film was made by in 1895 by Felix-Louis Regnault who filmed a Senegalese woman making pots

Joseph Schaeffer suggested that there are at least four ways that video can be useful .
1. Videos allow for coverage of complex activities in their natural settings over an extended period of time.
2. Videos can increase quality and reliability of observations made regarding the activity.
3. Videos can be reviewed by researchers and participants which can help increase the scope and quality of understanding the activity.
4. Videos can be used to establish connections between understandings and the observed activities.

The sooner and more often you invite feedback, the better that your final design will be.
You do not discover the problems until you show your design to the stakeholders and ask for their feedback. Note the problems each time you get feedback and fix them. This is the process that Thomas Edison used to invent the first usable light bulb and that James Dyson used to invent the world's most successful vacuum cleaner. You can apply this iterative process to any type of design.

THINK OUT LOUD PROTOCOL

WHAT IS IT?

Think aloud or thinking out loud protocols involve participants verbalizing their thoughts while performing a set of tasks. Users are asked to say whatever they are looking at, thinking, doing, and feeling.

A related but method is the talk-aloud protocol. where participants describe their activities but do not give explanations. This method is thought to be more objective

WHO INVENTED IT?

Clayton Lewis IBM 1993

WHY USE THIS METHOD?

1. Helps a researcher understand interaction with a product or service,.
2. Enables observers to see first-hand the process of task completion
3. The terminology the user uses to express an idea or function the design or and documentation.
4. Allows testers to understand how the user approaches the system.

CHALLENGES

1. The design team needs to be composed of persons with a variety of skills.

2. Pick a diverse, cross disciplinary team.

WHEN TO USE THIS METHOD

1. Know Context
2. Know User
3. Frame insights
4. Explore Concepts

HOW TO USE THIS METHOD

1. Identify users.
2. Choose Representative Tasks.
3. Create a Mock-Up or Prototype.
4. Select Participants.
5. Provide the test users with the system or prototype to be tested and tasks.
6. Brief participants.
7. Take notes of everything that users say, without attempting to interpret their actions and words.
8. Iterate
9. Videotape the tests, then analyze the videotapes.

RESOURCES

Computer
Video camera
Note pad
Pens

"

Few ideas work
on the first try.
Iteration is key to
innovation

SEBASTIAN THRUN
Director of the Artificial Intelligence
Laboratory at Stanford University.

WIZARD OF OZ

WHAT IS IT?

Wizard of Oz method is a research method in which research participants interact with a computer interface that subjects believe to be responding to their input, but which is being operated by an unseen person. The unseen operator is sometimes called the "wizard"

WHO INVENTED IT?

John F. Kelley
Johns Hopkins University. 1980
USA
Nigel Cross

WHY USE THIS METHOD?

1. Wizard of Oz is good for the testing of preliminary interface prototypes.
2. A relatively inexpensive type of simulation
3. Identify problems with an interface concept
4. Investigate visual of an interface.

CHALLENGES

1. Requires training for the wizard.
2. It is difficult for wizards to provide consistent responses across sessions.
3. Computers respond differently than humans
4. It is difficult to evaluate systems with a complex interface using this method.

HOW TO USE THIS METHOD

1. The wizard sits in a place not visible to the research participant.
2. The wizard observes the user's actions, and initiates the system's responses.
3. The "wizard" watches live video from a camera focused on the participant's hands and simulate the effects of the participant's actions.
4. Users are unaware that the actions of the system are being produced by the wizard.

RESOURCES

Video camera
Software interface prototype
Computers

"

An architect's most useful tools are an eraser at the drafting board and a wrecking ball at the site

FRANK LLOYD WRIGHT
Architect

ITERATE

Modify the design prototype and test and refine until it works

DO A REALITY CHECK

At each milestone in a design development, the design team and important stakeholders such as customers, clients, manufacturers representatives can meet and review the design to see how real the solution is and refine the direction as necessary.

IDENTIFY STAKEHOLDERS FOR FEEDBACK

OBTAIN FEEDBACK

Usability testing is a technique used in user-centered interaction design to evaluate a product by testing it on users. Usability testing focuses on measuring a designs fitness for an intended purpose. Usability testing involves observation under controlled conditions to determine how well people can use the design

1. Methods include:
2. Hallway testing five to six people are brought in to test the product, or service. The name of the technique refers to the fact that the testers should be random people who pass by in the hallway.
3. Remote usability Usability evaluators, developers and end users are located in different countries and time zones, .
4. Expert review. Involves bringing in experts with experience in the field to evaluate the usability of a product system or service.
5. Automated expert review Automated expert reviews provide usability testing but through the use of programs given rules for good design and heuristics. Though an automated review might not provide as much detail and insight as reviews from people, they can be finished more quickly and consistently.
6. A/B Testing. Two versions (A and B) are compared, which are identical except for one variation that might impact a user's behaviour.

"

A designer is anyone
who plots change for the
better.

MARTIN NEULLER
Design Thinker

Manufacture your design. Distribute it and sell it.

IMPLEMENT & DELIVER

TEST AND EVALUATE

Testing is one of the core activities of Design Thinking The design team checks design capabilities, requirements by testing with end users and the ability to meet these, and epitomizing the design to combine these two. Testing is carried out with consumers through observation, focus groups and other methods. Testing and learning through feedback are activities in each design phase.

FINALIZE YOUR PRODUCTION DESIGN

The details of this phase will depend on the type of design area that you are working in.

BUILD EXTERNAL PARTNERSHIPS

Collaboration with other organizations and individuals is becoming an integral part of the design process. Organizations benefit from their partners' insights and expertise. Many of the best ideas have emerged not through the inspiration of a single mind, but through the exchange of ideas.

SIGN OFF FROM STAKEHOLDERS

When you believe that you have a design that can be distributed and sold, show it to all your stakeholders one last time before documenting the design for final manufacture.

MAKE YOUR PRODUCTION SAMPLES

AUTHORIZE VENDORS

Manufacture first samples Review first production with vendors.

LAUNCH

At this point in the design process the product or service is launched, and the process now includes liaison with appropriate internal teams in areas such as marketing, communications, packaging and brand.

1. How can you make it impossible for this to fail?
2. Decide on your goals.
3. Prepare.
4. Make it fun and interesting
5. Set a date.

PRE-LAUNCH

1. 3-4 weeks of pre-launch
2. Create the campaign.
3. Evoke emotion.
4. Create desire.
5. Prepare marketing materials.
6. Do something original.
7. Review what's working.
8. Create urgency.

MID-LAUNCH

1. Publish your blog post, send out your email announcement.
2. Post on social media and other various communication channels.
3. Listen and respond.

POST-LAUNCH

1. Have a party!
2. Ask for feedback from first buyers
3. Deliver a bonus that wasn't expected
4. Make it memorable.
5. Review and improve.

6. Plan ahead.

Source: Adapted from Jonathan Mead
"The 40 Step Checklist for a Highly Successful Launch"

DELIVER
Do final testing obtain sign off from stakeholders and launch. The design should successfully address the problem identified in the user research phase of the process.

Key activities and objectives during the Deliver stage are:

1. Final testing, approval and launch
2. Targets, evaluation and feedback loops.

DID THE DESIGN MEET IT'S GOALS?
Ideas that have emerged during the design process or in post-launch feedback may be put to one side but developed later, and will then go through the design process again on its own.

MEASURE SUCCESS
1. Determine how you will measure the success
2. 2 to 3 months after release measure the success
3. Measure the success and objectively evaluate.
4. Implement metrics and measurements

SOME WAYS TO MEASURE SUCCESS:
1. Customer satisfaction

2. ROI is standard business measure of project profitability, over the market life of the design expressed as a percentage of initial investment.
3. Increased usage
4. Increased revenue from existing customers
5. The ability of your product to solve the problem
6. New customer acquisition
7. Product margin
8. Cash flow
9. Product Team's satisfaction
10. Improved customer retention rate
11. Increased market share

WHAT COULD BE IMPROVED?
Invite customers to co-create, and integrate feedback.

DEFINE NEXT VISION
The design process is never complete. Now it is time to start planning the next product or service so that you can stay ahead of the many competitors.

Source: Adapted from Jonathan Mead
"The 40 Step Checklist for a Highly Successful Launch"

"

Design Thinking is a human-centered approach to innovation that draws from the designer's toolkit to integrate the needs of people, the possibilities of technology, and the requirements for business success

TIM BROWN
CEO IDEO

EXERCISES

DESIGN THINKING RESOURCES

1. Good size collaborative space
2. Large table
3. Chairs
4. Adhesive dots
5. Copy Paper
6. Markers and pens
7. Cutting mat
8. Scissors
9. Glue
10. Masking tape
11. Push pins
12. Printer
13. Projector
14. Video camera
15. Post-it-notes
16. Foam core boards
17. Cardboard
18. White-board
19. Large wall
20. Large Pin board
21. Prototyping kit

LOW FIDELITY PROTOTYPE KIT

1. Copy paper
2. Magnets
3. Snaps
4. Masking tape
5. Duct tape (color would be ideal)
6. Tape
7. Post-it notes
8. Glue sticks
9. Paper clips, (asst colors ideal)
10. Decorative brads (square, crystal)
11. Hole punch
12. Scissors
13. Stapler (with staples)
14. Hot glue
15. Glue guns
16. Rulers
17. Pipe Cleaners
18. Colored card
19. Zip ties
20. Foam core sheets
21. Velcro
22. Rubber bands, multicolored
23. Assorted foam shapes
24. Markers
25. Scissors
26. Glue sticks
27. Tape
28. Glue guns
29. Straws
30. Paper Clips
31. Construction Paper
32. ABS sheets
33. Felt
34. Foam sheets
35. String
36. Foil
37. Butcher paper
38. Stickers
39. Pipe cleaners
40. Popsicle sticks
41. Multicolored card

WARMING UP

Instructions

Break your team into groups of two people.
Each person should partner with someone they do not know if possible.
Warming up exercises help stimulate constructive interaction, help
people get to know each other and contribute effectively. Do one of the
following exercises:

Who am I?

Duration: 3 minutes
Draw or write a one sentence description of something that
represents yourself.
Duration 2 minutes per person
Each person introduces themselves to the group using their sketch or
description.

Common ground

Duration: 5 minutes
Each person should interview their partner and make a list of 3 things
that they have in common.

Desert Island

Duration: 3 minutes
Each person should list 3 things that they would take if that was all
they could take to a desert island.
Duration 2 minutes per person
Introduce yourself to the group using your list.

Outcomes

Duration: 5 minutes
Each person should sketch or write what they believe could be the best
possible outcome for the project.
Duration 2 minutes per person
Each person introduces themselves to the group using their sketch or
description.

Resources

Copy paper
Markers
White board

INTERVIEW

Instructions
Divide your team into groups of two. Each team member should interview their partner for 15 minutes to identify an unmet product or service need that they have. It should be something that can be actionable to design with available time and resources and that others also need.

Who is the audience?
Age, gender, geography culture

What is it?
Describe the unmet need

Why is it needed?

Where would it be used?

When would it be used?

How would it be used?

IDENTIFY KEY STAKEHOLDERS

Key stakeholders

Identify the stakeholders who may be affected by your design. They can be people or organizations. Stakeholders are those who can have a positive or negative effect the success of your design. They can be recruited to give you useful feedback.

End-users
1.
2.
3.
4.

Vendors
1.
2.
3.
4.

Community
1.
2.
3.
4.

Organizations
1.
2.
3.
4.

Employees
1.
2.
3.
4.

RESEARCH QUESTIONS

Instructions

Identify five people who may be prospective customers or end users related to the possible product or service that you identified in the previous stage. Interview each of the five people and when you are finished answer the following questions. Be prepared to change your targets based on what you discover.

Who are the competitors?

Name five products or services that compete in your target area.

What are the problems with the competitive designs?

Name one significant problem with each competitive design

What are the top 3 problems with the competitive designs?

List the 3 top problems in a hierarchy of importance

Ask why there is a need five times?
1.
2.
3.
4.
5.
Dig deeper until you understand the underlying need

What is the most significant underlying need for the design?

What insights did you discover?

SYNTHESIS QUESTIONS

Instructions
Explore the following questions in an interview with each participant.

Customer Segments
Identify three groups of customers who need this design

Value Proposition
What is the unique value proposition for each of 3 segments

Activities
What activities are needed to support the value propositions?
Name 3 activities

Channels
What channels could the design be distributed through? For example on-line or stores. Name 3 channels.

Revenue
What are customers willing to pay for? For example monthly fee or retail price. Name 3 revenue streams.

Resources
What resources would be needed to implement your business?
For example on-line storage. name three resources needed.

Partners
What partners would be needed to implement your business?
Name 3 partners.

Costs
Name your businesses 3 main costs?

Source: Adapted from Alexander Oswalder Business Model Canvas

YOUR ANSWERS

Customer Segments
1.
2.
3.

Value Proposition
1.
2.
3.

Activities
1.
2.
3.

Channels
1.
2.
3.

Revenue
1.
2.
3.

Resources
1.
2.
3.

Partners
1.
2.
3.

Main Costs
1.
2.
3.

SWOT TEMPLATE

Strengths

Weaknesses

Opportunities

Threats

POINT OF VIEW QUESTIONS

Instructions
What are your goals?
Answer the following questions

Specific
What will you design?

Measurable
How will you know when you have the best solution.
How will you measure progress toward your goal?

Attainable
Is your goal a possible to achieve with your time and resources?

Realistic
Is your goal realistic and within your reach? Are you willing to commit to your goal?

Relevant
Is your goal relevant to your long term needs?

Time
What is your target time-frame to reach the gaols?

IDEATION INSTRUCTIONS

Instructions

Generate 12 simple cartoon sketches that may be good design solutions for your user need.

Answer in one sentence each of the following questions for each design

For each design solution answer the following questions:

1. What unmet user needs does the design address?
2. How does the design utilize technology processes and materials to best advantage?
3. Why is the design a good business solution?
4. Who are the target audience for each design?
5. How is this design a better design than existing competitive designs?

PROTOTYPE

Create a low fidelity prototype of your favored design

Here are some suggestions for a kit of materials to help you construct low fidelity prototypes

Copy paper
Magnets
Snaps
Masking tape
Duct tape (color would be ideal)
Tape
Post-it notes
Glue sticks
Paper clips, (asst colors ideal)
Decorative brads (square, crystal)
Hole punch
Scissors
Stapler (with staples)
Hot glue
Glue guns
Pipe Cleaners
Colored card
Zip ties
Rubber bands, multicolored
Assorted foam shapes
Markers
Paper Clips
Construction Paper
ABS sheets
Felt
Foam sheets
String
Foil
Butcher paper
Popsicle sticks

TEST QUESTIONS

Instructions
Use some of the materials on the facing page to make a fast prototype of your design. Show the prototype to five people and ask them to answer the following questions.

What works in the design?

1.

2.

3.

4.

What doesn't work in the design?

1.

2.

3.

4.

What refinements need to be made?

1.

2.

3.

4.

ITERATION QUESTIONS

Instructions

Modify and improve your prototype based on your previous feedback. Show it to five people and answer the following questions.

What works in the design?

1.

2.

3

4.

What doesn't work in the design?

1.

2.

3.

4.

What refinements need to be made?

1.

2.

3.

4.

"

Are you a serial
idea-starting person?
The goal is to be an
idea-shipping person.

SETH GODIN
Author and entrepreneur

TEMPLATES

PERSONA TEMPLATE

PERSONA NAME

DEMOGRAPHICS
Age	Income
Occupation	Gender
Location	Education

CHARACTERISTIC S

GOALS

What does this person want to achieve in life?

MOTIVATIONS
Growth	Achievement
Incentives	Power
Fear	Social

FRUSTRATIONS

What experiences does this person wish to avoid?

QUOTE

Characteristic quote

BRANDS

What brands does this persona purchase or wish to purchase?

CHARACTERISTICS

EXTROVERT   **INTROVERT** **FREE TIME**

TRAVEL   **LUXURY GOODS**

TECHNICAL SAVVY   **SPORTS**

SOCIAL NETWORKING   **MOBILE APPS**

STORYBOARD TEMPLATE

PROJECT NAME DATE PAGE

DIALOGUE DIALOGUE DIALOGUE

ACTION ACTION ACTION

PROJECT NAME DATE PAGE

DIALOGUE DIALOGUE DIALOGUE

ACTION ACTION ACTION

PROJECT NAME DATE PAGE

DIALOGUE DIALOGUE DIALOGUE

ACTION ACTION ACTION

635 BRAINSTORM TEMPLATE

PROBLEM STATEMENT:		
	IDEA 1	**IDEA 2**	**IDEA 3**

	IDEA 1	IDEA 2	IDEA 3
1			
2			
3			
4			
5			
6			

CONTEXT MAP

TRENDS	POLITICAL	ECONOMIC	USER NEEDS	TECHNOLOGY	UNCERTAINTIES	TRENDS

COMPETITOR MATRIX

	BRAND A	BRAND B	BRAND C	BRAND D
BRAND				
BRAND STATEMENT				
VALUE PROPOSITION				
TARGET CUSTOMERS				
BUSINESS MODEL				
TECHNOLOGY				
ENVIRONMENTAL PERFORMANCE				
KEY DIFFERENTIATION				

EVALUATION MATRIX

CRITERIA	WEIGHT	DESIGN A		DESIGN B		DESIGN C		DESIGN D	
		SCORE	WEIGHTED	SCORE	WEIGHTED	SCORE	WEIGHTED	SCORE	WEIGHTED
TOTAL									

PERCEPTUAL MAP TEMPLATE

SPIDER DIAGRAM TEMPLATE

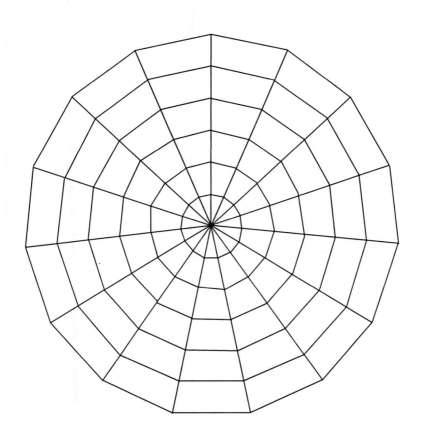

STAKEHOLDER POWER INFLUENCE MAP

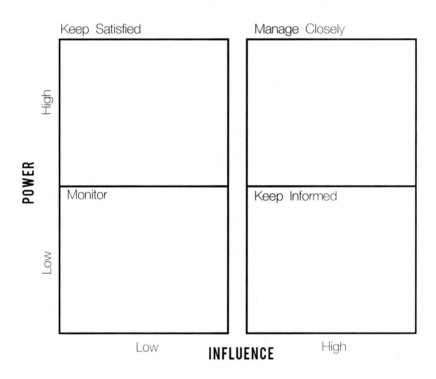

DESIGN THINKING RUBRIC

LEVEL	EXCEEDS EXPECTATIONS	STRONG	EFFECTIVE	DEVELOPING	EMERGING	NEEDS IMPROVEMENT
SCORE	6	5	4	3	2	1
AMBIGUITY	Comfortable when things are unclear	Comfortable when things are unclear	Limited comfort when things are unclear	Limited comfort when things are unclear	Uncomfortable when things are unclear	Uncomfortable when things are unclear
EMPATHY AND HUMAN VALUES	Sees and understands others point of view. Focuses on user needs	Sees and understands others point of view. Focuses on user needs	Has limited understanding of other points of view	Has limited understanding of other points of view	Sees only own point of view	Sees only own point of view
COLLABORATIVE	Collaborates effectively with people from other disciplines with different backgrounds and viewpoints	Collaborates effectively with people from other disciplines with different backgrounds and viewpoints	Collaborates with people from other disciplines with different backgrounds and viewpoints in a limited way	Collaborates with people from other disciplines with different backgrounds and viewpoints in a limited way	Cannot collaborate with other. Sees only own point of view.	Cannot collaborate with other. Sees only own point of view.
CURIOUS	Is interested in things that are not understood and seeing things with fresh eyes.	Is interested in things that are not understood and seeing things with fresh eyes.	Shows limited interest in things that are not understood and seeing things with fresh eyes.	Shows limited interest in things that are not understood and seeing things with fresh eyes.	Is not interested in things that are not understood and seeing things with fresh eyes.	Is not interested in things that are not understood and seeing things with fresh eyes.
HOLISTIC	Balances perspectives of business, human values, the environment and technology	Balances perspectives of business, human values, the environment and technology	Considers the perspectives of business, human values, the environment and technology in a limited way	Considers the perspectives of business, human values, the environment and technology in a limited way	Does not consider the bigger context focusses on only one aspect such as business profitability	Does not consider the bigger context focusses on only one aspect such as business profitability
NON JUDGMENTAL	Crafts ideas with no judgement of the idea or idea creator	Crafts ideas with no judgement of the idea or idea creator	Some judgement of ideas and other idea creators	Some judgement of ideas and other idea creators	Extensive judgement of ideas and other idea creators	Extensive judgement of ideas and other idea creators
OPEN MINDSET	Is able to tackle problems regardless of industry or scope. Out of the box thinker	Is able to tackle problems regardless of industry or scope. Out of the box thinker	Can address problems over a number of industries and a limited range of scope	Can address problems over a number of industries and a limited range of scope	Can only address problems in a single industry of limited scope	Can only address problems in a single industry of limited scope
BIAS TOWARD ACTION	Creates prototypes and physical embodiments of ideas and actions that effectively move project forward	Creates prototypes and physical embodiments of ideas and actions that effectively move project forward	Creates some prototypes and progress but in a limited way	Creates some prototypes and progress but in a limited way	Talks about ideas but does not create physical prototypes or move project forward through actions	Talks about ideas but does not create physical prototypes or move project forward through actions
EXPERIMENTAL	Embraces experiment as an integral part of work	Embraces experiment as an integral part of work	Experiments in a limited way	Experiments in a limited way	Does not experiment	Does not experiment
COMPLEXITY	Creates clarity from complexity	Creates clarity from complexity	Limited ability to address complex problems	Limited ability to address complex problems	Cannot address complex problems	Cannot address complex problems
PROCESS	Is mindful of process	Is mindful of process	Follows process in a limited way	Follows process in a limited way	Has no process	Has no process
SHOSHIN	An attitude of openness, eagerness, and lack of preconceptions even when at an advanced level.	An attitude of openness, eagerness, and lack of preconceptions even when at an advanced level.	Some openness, and eagerness. Some preconceptions	Some openness, and eagerness. Some preconceptions	Lack of openness, and eagerness. Many preconceptions	Lack of openness, and eagerness. Many preconceptions
ITERATIVE	Makes improvements with prototyping feedback loops and cycles regardless of design phase	Makes improvements with prototyping feedback loops and cycles regardless of design phase	Limited ability to refine or improve ideas through iterative user feedback and prototyping	Limited ability to refine or improve ideas through iterative user feedback and prototyping	No ability to refine or improve ideas through iterative user feedback and prototyping	No ability to refine or improve ideas through iterative user feedback and prototyping

DO AN ON-LINE PROGRAM
HTTPS://DCC-ONLINE.SELZ.COM

If you liked this book and want to learn more about Design Thinking we regularly offer on-line classes and courses presented by the author. They are held at different times of day to suit your schedule and time zone.

You can find more information and register at the URL below and order print copies of this book or on Amazon soon.

Half day introductory workshop
http://dccintrodesignthinking.eventbrite.com

Five week and 8 week on-line certificate programs
http://dcc-designthinking.eventbrite.com

We have presented many face to face in-house workshops in global locations. If you would like more information related to creating a custom workshop for your team contact us at
info@curedale.com

OTHER TITLES IN THE SERIES
HTTPS://DCC-ONLINE.SELZ.COM

DESIGN THINKING
PROCESS AND METHODS MANUAL
Author: Robert A Curedale
Published by:
Design Community College Inc.
Edition 1 January 2013
398 pages
ISBN-10:   0988236214
ISBN-13:   978-0-9882362-1-9

DESIGN THINKING POCKET GUIDE
EDITION 1
Author: Curedale, Robert A
Published by:
Design Community College, Inc
Jun 01 2013
198 pages
ISBN-10: 098924685X
ISBN-13: 9780989246859

50 BRAINSTORMING METHODS
FOR TEAM AND INDIVIDUAL IDEATION
Author: Robert A Curedale
Published by:
Design Community College Inc.
Edition 1 January 2013
184 pages
ISBN-10:   0988236230
ISBN-13:   978-0-9882362-3-3

CHINA DESIGN INDEX 2014
China Design Index 2014
Author: Curedale, Robert A
Published by:
Design Community
College, Inc.
Edition 1 Feb 01 2014
384 pages
ISBN-10:1940805090
ISBN-13: 9781940805092

INTERVIEWS OBSERVATION AND FOCUS
GROUPS
Author: Curedale, Robert A
Published by:
Design Community College, Inc.
Edition 1 Apr 01 2013
188 pages
ISBN-10:0989246833
ISBN-13: 9780989246835

MAPPING METHODS
Author: Curedale, Robert A
Published by:
Design Community College, Inc.
Edition 1 Apr 01 2013
136 pages
ISBN-10: 0989246825
ISBN-13: 9780989246828

SERVICE DESIGN

Author: Curedale, Robert A
Published by:
Design Community College, Inc.
Edition 1 Aug 01 2013
372 pages
ISBN-10:0989246868
ISBN-13: 9780989246866

SERVICE DESIGN POCKET GUIDE

Author: Curedale, Robert A
Published by:
Design Community College, Inc.
Edition 1 Sept 01 2013
206 pages
ISBN-10:0989246884
ISBN-13: 9780989246880

DESIGN RESEARCH METHODS
150 WAYS TO INFORM DESIGN

Author: Curedale, Robert A
Published by:
Design Community College, Inc.
Edition 1 January 2013
290 pages
ISBN-10: 0988236257
ISBN-13: 978-0-988-2362-5-7

50 SELECTED DESIGN METHODS

Author: Curedale, Robert A
Published by:
Design Community College, Inc.
Edition 1 Jan 17 2013
114 pages
ISBN-10:0988236265
ISBN-13: 9780988236264

DESIGN METHODS 1
200 WAYS TO APPLY DESIGN THINKING

Author: Robert A Curedale
Published by:
Design Community College Inc.
Edition 1 November 2013
396 pages
ISBN-10:0988236206
ISBN-13:978-0-9882362-0-2

DESIGN METHODS 2
200 MORE WAYS TO APPLY DESIGN THINKING

Author: Robert A Curedale
Published by:
Design Community College Inc.
Edition 1 January 2013
398 pages
ISBN-13: 978-0988236240
ISBN-10: 0988236249

30 GOOD WAYS TO INNOVATE

Author: Curedale, Robert A
Published by:
Design Community College, Inc.
Edition 1 November 2015
108 pages
ISBN-10: 1940805139
ISBN-13: 978-1940805139

DCC ONLINE DESIGN EDUCATION
HTTPS://DCC-ONLINE.SELZ.COM

Start today, DCC expert online programs for designers and managers. More accessible than traditional design education and better value. Classes for different world time zones. Connect to classes anywhere with an internet connection. Study from home or train your whole team in your office. Free textbook with most courses. Check links below for all scheduled dates and local time calculator. Contact us at info@curedale.com for current information.

30 GOOD WAYS TO INNOVATE
https://dcc-30waystoinnovate.eventbrite.com

DESIGNING WITH COLOR
http://dcc-designingwithcolor.eventbrite.com

INTRODUCTION TO DESIGN THINKING
http://dccintrodesignthinking.eventbrite.com

DESIGN THINKING ONLINE PROGRAMS
http://dcc-designthinking.eventbrite.com

CREATING EXPERIENCE MAPS, JOURNEY MAPS, AND SERVICE BLUEPRINTS
http://dcc-experiencemaps.eventbrite.com

INTRO TO SERVICE DESIGN
http://dcc-introservicedesign.eventbrite.com

SERVICE DESIGN ONLINE PROGRAMS
http://dcc-servicedesign.eventbrite.com

INTRODUCTION TO DESIGN RESEARCH
http://dcc-introdesignresearch.eventbrite.com

DESIGN RESEARCH ONLINE PROGRAMS
http://dcc-designresearch.eventbrite.com

INTRODUCTION TO INDUSTRIAL DESIGN
http://www.eventbrite.com/e/introduction-to-industrial-design-tickets-16591880762

INDUSTRIAL DESIGN ONLINE PROGRAMS
http://dcc--industrialdesign.eventbrite.com

DESIGN RESEARCH: INTERVIEWING & FOCUS GROUPS
https://dcc-interviewsandfocusgroups.eventbrite.com

CREATING A SUCCESSFUL DESIGN PORTFOLIO
http://dcc-portfolio.eventbrite.com

PRODUCT DESIGN PROPOSALS
https://dcc-designproposals.eventbrite.com

INTRODUCTION TO HUMAN FACTORS ONLINE
http://dcc-humanfactors.eventbrite.com

DESIGN SYNTHESIS
http://dcc-designsynthesis.eventbrite.com

DESIGN IDEATION METHODS
https://dcc-ideation.eventbrite.com

INDEX

Symbols

10 x 10 sketch method   287
635   37, 296, 297
635 Method   37
.x   108, 109, 179, 183, 191,
    192, 193, 194, 195, 197,
    199, 254, 256, 257, 287,
    307, 312, 314, 343

A

action plan   113
activities   263, 289, 351
Activity   175, 176, 190, 193,
    233, 243, 263, 349, 351
actors   289, 353
Actors   289, 326
adapt   325
affinities   141, 259
Affinity   141, 151
Affinity diagram   36, 141, 151
Affinity diagrams   141, 258
age   65
Aguiler, Francis J   37
Alexander   37, 41
Alexander, Ian   41
Allport, Gordon   36, 154, 159
Ambidextrous Thinking   40
ambiguity   55, 57
Analysis   165, 279
Analytical thinking   48
analyze   201, 303, 341
Analyze   141, 249, 289, 297,
    324
aoki method   298
appearance   325

Archer, Bruce   34, 38, 56
Archer, L. Bruce   36, 37
attributes of Design Thinking   57
audio   166, 245

B

Backcasting   231
Bagnall, Jim   39
bar chart   212, 213
Battelle Institute   331
Bavelas, Alex   36, 203
Bavelas, ALex   153, 164, 203
Becker, Ernest   147
behavior   144, 154, 159, 175,
    184, 190, 191, 192, 193,
    194, 195, 197, 198, 199,
    227, 257, 355, 358, 366
Behavior   154, 159, 175, 184,
    190, 191, 192, 193, 194,
    197, 198, 199, 355
Behavioral map   147
Behavioral Maps   37
Bell Communications   347
Benchmark   65
Benchmarking   119, 149
Benefits   233
Benefits map   233
Bernd Rohrbach   297
Blueprint   263
Bodystorm   299
bodystorming   41, 299
Bodystorming   299
Bonislaw Malinowski   35
Bossard   181
boundaries   219
Boundary   300

Boundary shifting   300
brainstorm   276, 303
Brainstorm   66, 205, 237, 305,
        323, 341, 351
brainstorming   312, 314, 320,
        323, 332, 341
Brainstorming   34, 37, 56, 237,
        251, 258, 259, 263, 279,
        295, 296, 297, 301, 309,
        313, 315, 318, 319, 322,
        324, 327, 334, 402
Brainstorming: brainwriting   301
Brainstorming: kj method   309,
        327
Brainstorming: method 635   296,
        297
Brainstorming: nhk method   313
brainstorming:
nominal group method   314
Brainstorming: nyaka   315
brainstorming: out of the box
        312
Brainstorming: personal   318
Brainstorming: personas   319
Brainstorming: resources   322
brainstorming: rolestorming   323
brainstorming: stp   332
brainstorms   113, 215, 253, 273,
        331
Brainwriting   301
Brandt   41, 160
Brown, Tim   34, 42, 55, 56, 68
Bruere, Robert   35
Buchanan, Richard   33, 34, 40,
        56
Buchenau   41, 299
Business   48, 96, 258, 281

Butler, Ava S   332

C

Camera   244, 263
Card   141, 172, 173
Cards   141, 150, 151, 157, 172,
        173, 205, 309, 313, 345
C-box   236, 237
challenge   43
change management   157
Charette   156
checklist: environmentally
responsible   design   271
choosing a technique   292
clarity   55
Cluster   205
co-creation   35
Collaboration   95, 355
collaborative   55, 57, 347
Collins, Allan   35, 259
Collins, J   269
color   320
communication   271
Communications   281
competitive products   65
Competitive strategy   233, 261,
        265
competitors   253
complex   96, 141, 351
complex problems   399, 419
Concept   152, 153, 177, 289,
        311, 326, 333, 345, 349,
        363
concepts   141, 237, 287, 289,
        311
Concepts   49, 108, 297

conflict 273
Conran, Terence 40
constraints 65, 139
constructive 57
consumption 271
context 48, 57, 65, 75, 95,
137, 149, 151, 153, 154,
155, 156, 159, 160, 164,
169, 171, 174, 177, 179,
182, 183, 184, 186, 187,
189, 190, 191, 192, 193,
194, 195, 197, 198, 199,
203, 276, 277, 299, 303,
321, 326, 333, 349, 359,
361, 399, 418, 419
Context 48, 75, 108, 151, 153,
164, 166, 169, 171, 174,
177, 182, 186, 187, 189,
190, 191, 192, 193, 197,
198, 201, 203, 239, 244,
249, 263, 289, 299, 321,
326, 349, 351
Contextual inquiry 166, 169
Contextual Inquiry 40
Contextual interviews 166, 169,
178
Contextual laddering 171
Conversation cards 172
covert 191
Cradle to Cradle 41
create a strategy 292
Creative class 34, 56
Creative Class 41
Creative Thinking 48
Creative toolkits 155
creativity 34, 39, 56
Creativity Methods 34, 56
critical design 41

critical thinking 312, 323, 332
Critics 303
Cross, Nigel 34, 39, 42, 56,
363
crowd sourcing 42
Cultural 150, 151, 173, 239
culture 65, 108, 181, 253
Curedale, Rob 327, 402, 403
curiosity 55, 57
customer 57, 201, 244, 245,
249, 262, 263, 303
customers 57, 111, 201, 244,
245, 249, 263, 275, 366

D

dark horse prototype 339, 341
data 141, 201, 281
David Kelley 33, 34, 40, 42, 56
de Bono, Edward 39, 333
De bono, Edward 270
De Bono, Edward 333
decision-making 35
defer judgment 294
Delft 237
deliverables 65
democratic 237
Democratic 297
Design charette 156
Designerly Ways of Knowing 39,
42
Design Methods 34, 36, 38, 56
design problem 139, 237, 311,
341
Design thinking 48, 65, 96, 114,
138, 374
Design Thinking 6, 30, 44, 48,

49, 57, 79, 91, 96, 258, 336, 402
Design thinking process   65
diagram   141, 205, 245, 259, 311
dialog.   353
Diary study   189
differentiation   66, 279
Dilts   303
director   353
disassembly   271
discussion   263, 287, 289, 297
Disney method   303
Disney, Walt   36, 351
disposable   271
divergent   237
diversity   81, 95
Document   65, 66, 166
doing   245
Doran, George   39
Dot voting   304, 305, 321
Dreamers   303
Dry-erase markers   141, 244, 259, 263, 279, 289, 311
d.school   33, 41, 55, 68
Dunne, Anthony   41

E

ecological   271
Edison   360
editing-in-the-camera   353
Einfühlungsvermögen   35, 75
Eisenhower   108
E-mail   174
Emotional   173, 243
Emotional journey map   243

Emotion cards   173
empathy   35, 41, 55, 57, 75, 137, 152, 160, 299, 318, 319, 322, 349
Empathy   48, 75, 95, 96, 152, 160, 201, 244, 299, 318, 319, 322, 349
Empathy map   244
Empathy maps   244
empathy tools   41
Empathy tools   349
employees   188
encourage wild ideas   294
end-of-life   271
energy   271
engagement   258
environmental   96, 271
Environmental   48, 96
ethnography   201
experience   65, 81, 89, 95, 137, 138, 139, 157, 160, 164, 165, 243, 244, 245, 246, 248, 249, 262, 263, 289, 299, 315, 321, 326, 327, 347, 349, 351, 358, 359, 366, 414, 418
Experience design   34, 56
experiences   245, 247, 249, 263, 289, 305, 324, 345, 351
Experiences in Visual Thinking   33, 38

F

facilitating   293
Fast Company   68
Faste, Rolf   33, 34, 38, 39, 40,

INDEX

41, 43, 56
feasibility 237
feedback 57, 66, 205, 347, 351
feeling 245
fieldwork 245
fish bone diagram 37
Five Whys 163
flexibility 95, 108
Florida, Richard L 41
focus groups 245
Focus groups 164, 165
Focus Groups 402
follow-up sessions 144
Fox, William 314
Frame 49, 108, 166, 201, 244, 263, 297
framework 289, 311
French, John R. P. 253
fresh eyes 57, 399, 419
Fulton 41, 299
functionality 237
future wheel 254, 255

G

Gaver, Bill 151
Gaze plots 161
Gaze replays 161
gender, 65
Generative 157
generative prototyping 343
Georg von Mayr 35
Gilbreth, Frank 219
Glenn, Jerome 255
global warming 271
Goal 149, 172, 173, 178, 333
goal grid 273

goal map 273
goals 194, 195, 253, 273
Goals 169, 201, 231, 289, 326
Google 269
Gordon, William 334
Graph 213
Gray, Dave 244
group 65, 141, 201, 205, 237, 244, 297, 303, 305, 324, 414
Groupthink 305
Grunnet 41, 160
guerilla ethnography 39

H

habitat 271
hallway testing 358, 366
Hartfield, Bradley 40
Harvard 33, 39, 42
Harvard Graduate School of Design 39
Hasso Plattner Institute of Design 33, 41, 293, 294
hear 75, 330
hearing 245
Heat maps 161
Helvetica 70, 71, 72, 73, 74
Herbert A. Simon 33
Hermagoras of Temnos 207
heuristic ideation 307
Hierarchy 205, 298, 309, 315
High fidelity prototype 86
holistic 55, 57
Holtzblatt 40, 169, 177
Hopes and hurdles 119
How Designers Think: The Design

Process Demystified   39
Howe, Jeff   42
HPI at Potsdam   42
human-centered   33, 38, 39
human-centered design   33, 38,
      39, 40
Human Centered Design   34, 56
Humphrey, Albert   37, 279

I

IBM   361
Icebreaker   114
idea   57, 66, 95, 237, 259, 305,
      311, 341, 345
idea advocate   308
ideas   57, 66, 95, 237, 259,
      279, 281, 287, 297, 303,
      305, 311, 324, 345, 351
ideation   245, 247
IDEO   33, 42, 67, 68
imitate   325
indirect observation   190
Inhibition   305
innovate   3, 108
innovation   42, 43, 81, 108, 109,
      111, 237, 258, 294, 414
Innovation   109, 110, 237, 258
innovation diagnostic   108
innovative   46, 48, 95, 111, 237,
      321, 323, 324, 334, 341
insight   201, 345
insights   49, 108, 119, 141, 147,
      149, 152, 153, 154, 155,
      156, 159, 160, 166, 169,
      175, 177, 182, 183, 187,
      190, 191, 192, 193, 194,
      195, 197, 198, 201, 202,
      203, 227, 243, 244, 263,
      289, 297, 299, 307, 314,
      321, 326, 333, 349, 359,
      361, 370
inspiration   68, 317, 370
integrative thinking   41, 42
intellectual property   66, 292
intent   49, 65
interact   164, 299, 349, 355,
      363
interaction   353
Interview   65, 120, 141, 154,
      159, 166, 169, 171, 172,
      174, 175, 176, 177, 178,
      182, 184, 185, 186
interviews   181
Interviews   258, 402
intuition   263
investment   111, 244, 281, 325,
      345
Ishikawa, Kaoru   37
Iteration   66, 355
iterative   57, 313, 359, 360, 399,
      419
iteratively   263

J

Jiro Kawaita   141
J. Muller, Michael   347
John Venn   35
Jones, John Chris   38
Jones, John Christopher   38
judgement   75, 399, 419

K

Kahn, Herman   36, 289, 326
Kaoru Ishikawa   251
Kawaita, Jiro   141
Kawakita, Jiro   36
Kelley, John F.   363
Kimbell, Lucy   34, 56
Kipling, Rudyard   162, 372, 388, 415
Kj method   309
Klein, Gary   277

L

Laddering   171
Lawson, Bryan   34, 39, 41, 56
leadership   181
Lego   188, 343
Leifer   33, 42
Leifer, Larry   33
Levinson, Jay Conrad   39
Lewis, Clayton   361
life cycle   271
linking diagram   215
Lockwood, Thomas   42
Lotus blossom   310, 311
Louis Emile Javal   35
Low fidelity prototyping   345

M

Magic thing   187
Malinowski, Bonislaw   35
Malinowski, Bronisław   192, 195, 197

Management   214
Manufacture   66
manufacturing   214
Manzini, Ezio   34, 56
Map   147, 205, 233, 235, 237, 239, 243, 244, 245, 248, 249, 259, 261, 263, 265
market   111, 214, 245, 271, 275, 281
marketing   257, 275
market opportunities   271
Martin, Roger   34, 41, 56
Martin, Roger L   42
maslow's hierarchy   256
Mason, Richard O   229
materials   66, 325, 345
Materials   251
matrix   229, 276
Matsumura, Yasuo   311
Matthews, Scott   244
McKim, Robert   33, 34, 38, 56
ME101: Visual Thinking   38
Mead, Margaret   35, 192, 195, 197
meaning   89, 183, 199, 202, 270, 309
Meinel   42
Meinel, Christoph   42
Merton, Robert   35
Merton, Robert K.   165
Meta Design   34, 56
method   57, 141, 163, 205, 237, 244, 245, 259, 287, 297, 303, 305, 311, 324, 341
method bank   188
Mind map   258, 259
mind maps   35, 36

mindset 55, 57
mission statement 269
Misuse 289, 299, 321, 326, 349
misuse scenario 41
Misuse scenarios 289, 299, 321, 326
Mitchell 205
Mobile 189
Mobile diary study 189
Moger, Susan 274
Monteiro, Robert A. 164, 203
Morgan, Michael 276

N

narrator 353
nature 271
need 139, 257, 332, 358
Need 65, 95, 159, 185, 201, 208, 235, 299, 345
needs 33, 47, 57, 89, 95, 114, 137, 139, 152, 153, 164, 202, 203, 227, 257, 269, 271, 333, 343, 361, 399, 419
Nelson, Doreen 202
Nhk method 313
Nokia 269
Nonaka, Ikujiro 40
non judgmental 57
Non verbal 75, 189
Norman, Don 34, 56
notes 141, 166, 205, 237, 244, 245, 247, 249, 263, 279, 311, 324, 345
Nussbaum, Bruce 34

Nyaka 315

O

objectives 66, 191, 192, 193, 197, 198, 273
objectstorming 317
observation 137, 153, 164, 190, 191, 192, 193, 194, 195, 197, 198, 199, 203
Observation 153, 190, 191, 192, 193, 197, 198, 201, 203
observation: structured 198
observe 67, 68, 75, 138, 153, 164, 169, 177, 182, 191, 192, 193, 194, 199, 203, 299
Observe 65, 164, 166, 169, 177, 182, 192, 193, 194, 299
observer 164, 190, 191, 192, 193, 194, 197, 198, 199
Offering 49
One-on-one 166, 169, 171, 177, 182
open mindset 55, 57
opposable nind 42
organization 108, 111, 244, 245, 259, 279
Organizational 108
Osborn, Alex 34, 56
Osborn, Alex F. 37
Osborn, Alex Faickney 36, 317, 318, 319, 322
outcomes 215, 255

P

pain   245, 247
participants   141, 297, 303, 305
Participatory   157
participatory design   347
Perceptual map   237
performance   65, 271
permission   194, 195
persona   201, 244, 245, 246, 247
Personal inventory   202
personas   201, 244, 245, 249, 303, 321, 326
Personas   147, 151, 201, 244, 245, 249, 289, 319
PEST Analysis   37
Peter Rowe   33, 34, 39, 56
phases   237, 263
Photograph   141
photographs   183
PICTIVE   347
pin cards   320
Plato   35
Plato's Republic   35
Plattner, Hasso   33, 41, 293, 294
Point of view   95, 153, 166, 169, 177, 182, 203, 243, 249
Polanyi, Michael   36, 40
pollution   271
Porphry of Tyros   35
Porras, J   269
Post-it-note   141
Post-it-notes   119, 141, 205, 239, 244, 263, 279, 311, 324, 345
Post-it voting   294
premortem   277
Prince, George   334
problem   48, 57, 65, 95, 237, 289, 303, 311, 324, 341
problems   57, 141, 244, 245, 247, 345, 351
problem solving   157
process   57, 65, 66, 95, 108, 111, 205, 245, 258, 263, 287, 289, 297, 305, 325, 351, 402
product   46, 66, 95, 111, 166, 201, 244, 271, 275, 279, 281, 289, 324, 325, 339, 351, 414
Product   66, 86, 89, 95, 139, 149, 157, 166, 169, 171, 175, 177, 182, 201, 203, 243, 261, 279, 281, 289, 324, 325, 326, 349, 351
profitable   303
props   353
prototype   47, 66, 67, 68, 95, 160, 187, 339, 341, 347, 359, 361, 363
Prototype   66, 86, 95, 160, 187, 361, 363
prototyped   359
prototypes   66, 95, 144, 339, 341, 343, 347

Q

quadrants   237
qualitative   65, 108
quantitative   65, 108

R

Radcliff-Brown   192, 195, 197
Rank   141
Rause, William   34, 56
Realists   303
recyclable   358
recycled   271
refine   66, 263, 289, 351
refinement   237, 341
reframing matrix   276
refreshments   293
Related contexts   321
relationship   166, 205
relationships   141, 205, 259
remote usability testing   358, 366
research goals   194, 195
resources   111, 281, 322, 325
responsible   271
Richard O. Mason   229
Rickards, Tudor   274
risks   65, 95, 195, 303, 358,
    359
Rittel, Horst   34, 56
Robert McKim   33, 34, 38, 56
Rohrbach, Bernd   37, 297
role playing   349
Role playing   160, 187
Rolf Faste   33, 34, 38, 39, 56
Roos, Johan   157, 343
Rotman School   33, 41, 42
Rowe, Peter   48
Royal College of Art   37, 151
rules for brainstorming   293
Runco, Mark A   274

S

Sachichi Toyoda Sakichi   163
Sanders, Liz   157, 343
SAP   33, 41, 55, 68
saying   245
Scamper   324
SCAMPER   324, 325
Scenario   177, 187, 289, 326
Scenarios   65, 187, 231, 289,
    299, 321, 326, 349
Schnelle, Wolfgang   320
Schon, Donal   34, 56
Schön, Donald   39
Scope   65, 289, 326
Secondary research   65
seeing   245
Segment   201, 245
sensorial method   327
sensory   245
sensory experience   245
service   66, 271, 275
Service   89, 139, 149, 175, 201,
    261, 263, 279, 289, 315,
    324, 326, 349
Service Design   34, 56
Services   95, 149, 157, 261,
    263, 265, 281, 289, 326,
    349
Shadowing   147
shoshin   293
Shoshin   78
Shostack, Lynn   263
Simon, Herbert   37
Simon, Herbet   34, 56
simple   95, 213, 287, 343, 347,
    358

Six thinking hats 333
sketch 287, 320
Smart phone 353
smell 327, 330
space 333
Spectators 303
Spradley, J. P. 132
stakeholder 87, 108, 163, 205
Stakeholder map 163, 205
stakeholders 65, 66, 87, 108,
        155, 156, 181, 205, 245,
        253, 263, 276, 359, 366
Stakeholders 65, 66, 119, 139,
        150, 155, 205, 231, 263
Stanford 33, 37, 38, 39, 41, 42
Stanford University 341
Steward, Julian Haynes 150
Story 89, 121, 139, 177, 207,
        243, 289, 326, 349, 351
storyboard 153
Storyboards 258, 289, 326,
        349, 350, 351, 391
Storytelling 121, 177
STP 332
Strategic 108, 119, 150, 155,
        235, 239
strategic thinking 157
strategies 271
strategy 65, 108, 253, 275,
        303, 347
Strickland, Rachel 202
structure 273
structured 198, 229
Structured 149, 166, 169, 177,
        182, 184, 297, 309, 334
style 181
substitute 95, 325
Survey 150

Sustainability 85, 265
swim lanes 263
Swot 279, 353
Swot analysis 279, 353
SWOT Analysis 37
sympathy 75
Synectics 334

T

Tacit knowledge 119, 166, 169,
        177, 178
task 351
Tasks 115, 116, 117, 118, 120,
        122, 129, 132, 133, 166,
        169, 171, 172, 173, 174,
        175, 176, 177, 178, 179,
        182, 183, 184, 185, 207,
        233, 289, 326, 345, 349,
        361
Tassoul, Marc 237
taste 245, 327
team 65, 95, 141, 205, 237,
        244, 245, 249, 287, 289,
        297, 303, 305, 324, 341,
        345
Team alignment 265
team building 138
team members 113, 307, 323,
        332
teams 57, 96, 110, 414
Technologies 108, 281
Telephone 186
test 66, 95, 104, 191, 192,
        193, 197, 198
testing 299, 347, 358, 363,
        366, 371

The All New Universal Traveler 39
The Deep Dive 41
the environment 294
think aloud 361
Thinkering 343
thinking out loud 361
Titchener, E.B. 35, 75
title card 353
Tolman, Edward 36
Toolkits 155
touch 154, 159, 327, 330
Touchpoints 263
toxic 271
Toyota 163

U

Unstructured 185
User 108, 166, 201, 244, 258, 263
user-centered 358, 366
User Centered Design 34, 56
user experience 137, 299
user needs 343

V

Van Gundy 307
Van Horn, Matthew 355
Venn Diagrams 35
Venn, John 223
Vernile, Lucy 164, 203
Victor, Bart 157, 343
video 166, 244, 245, 279, 289
video prototype 353
Video prototypes 353

vision 65, 66, 289, 414
voice over 353
Voting 157, 304, 305, 321

W

Walt Disney 36
web analytics 245
web site 339
Weinberg 42
white board 205, 237, 246, 263, 279
White board 141, 244, 259, 263, 279, 289, 297, 311, 324
Whiteside, Bennet 169, 177
wicked Problems 33, 40
Wicked Problems in Design Thinking 33, 40
Winograd, Terry 33
Wireframe 355
wizard 363
Wizard of Oz 363
workarounds 138
Workshops 157
Wurman, Richard Saul 129
Wwwwwh 207

ABOUT THE AUTHOR

Rob Curedale was born in Australia and worked as a designer, director and educator in leading design offices in London, Sydney, Switzerland, Portugal, Los Angeles, Silicon Valley, Detroit, and Hong Kong. He designed or managed the design of over 1,000 products as a consultant and in-house design leader for the world's most respected brands. Rob has three decades experience in every aspect of product development and design research, leading design teams to achieve transformational improvements in operating and financial results. Rob's design scan be found in millions of homes and workplaces around the world and have generated billions of dollars in corporate revenues.

Design practice experience
HP, Philips, GEC, Nokia, Sun, Apple, Canon, Motorola, Nissan, Audi VW, Disney, RTKL, Governments of the UAE,UK, Australia, Steelcase, Hon, Castelli, Hamilton Medical, Zyliss, Belkin, Gensler, Haworth, Honeywell, NEC, Hoover, Packard Bell, Dell, Black & Decker, Coleman and Harmon Kardon. Categories including furniture, healthcare, consumer electronics, sporting, housewares, military, exhibits, and packaging.

Teaching experience
Rob has taught as a full time professor, adjunct professor and visiting instructor at institutions including the following: Art Center Pasadena, Art Center Europe, Yale School of Architecture, Pepperdine University, Loyola University, Cranbrook Academy of Art, Pratt, Otis, a faculty member at SCA and UTS Sydney, Chair of Product Design and Furniture Design at the College for Creative Studies in Detroit, then the largest product design school in North America, Cal State San Jose, Escola De Artes e Design in Oporto Portugal, Instituto De Artes Visuals, Design e Marketing, Lisbon, Southern Yangtze University, Jiao Tong University in Shanghai and Nanjing Arts Institute in China.

Awards
Products that Rob has designed and managed the design of have been recognized with IDSA IDEA Awards, Good Design Awards UK, Australian Design Awards, and a number of best of show innovation Awards at CES Consumer Electronics Show. His designs are in the permanent collections of a number of museums including the Powerhouse Design Museum. In 2013 Rob was nominated for the Advanced Australia Award. The Awards celebrate Australians living internationally who exhibit "remarkable talent, exceptional vision, and ambition." In 2015 Rob was selected with a group of leading international industrial designers to provide opening comments for the international congress of societies of industrial design conference ICSID in Gwangju, South Korea.

"

Around here, we do not look backwards for very long. We keep moving forward, opening up new doors and doing new things, because we're curious and curiosity keeps leading us down new paths."

WALT DISNEY
American entrepreneur, cartoonist, animator, voice actor, film producer and Design Thinker

APPENDIX A
CRITICAL THINKING SCORING RUBRIC

LEVEL	EXCEEDS EXPECTATIONS	STRONG	EFFECTIVE	DEVELOPING	EMERGING	NEEDS IMPROVEMENT
SCORE	6	5	4	3	2	1
SUMMARIZES THE PROBLEM	Clearly identifies the challenge and relationships of the design problem	Clearly identifies the challenge and relationships of the design problem	Summarizes the issue. Some aspects are incorrect or confused	Summarizes the issue. Some aspects are incorrect or confused	Summarizes the issue. Some aspects are incorrect or confused	Fails to identify the challenges and relationships of the design problem
CONSIDERS CONTEXT	Analyzes the design problem with sense of scope. Identifies the influence of context.	Analyzes the design problem with sense of scope. Identifies the influence of context.	Explores context in a limited way. Relies on authorities.	Explores context in a limited way. Relies on authorities.	Explores context in a limited way. Relies on authorities.	Analyzes the problem with bias of own context. Fails to justify opinion
COMMUNICATES ORIGINAL PERSPECTIVE	Demonstrates own perspective supported by experience and unassigned sources. Integrates contrary interpretations	Demonstrates own perspective supported by experience and unassigned sources. Integrates contrary interpretations	Presents own perspective . Addresses other views inconsistently	Presents own perspective without addressing other views	Single view simplistic position adopted with little consideration. Fails to justify opinion	Single view simplistic position adopted with little consideration. Fails to justify opinion
ANALYZES SUPPORTING EVIDENCE	Examines evidence and questions bias accuracy and relevance	Examines evidence and questions bias accuracy and relevance	Selective use of evidence. Discerns fact from opinion. May not recognize bias.	Selective use of evidence. Discerns fact from opinion. May not recognize bias.	Repeats information without question. Does not distinguish between fact and opinion	Repeats information without question. Does not distinguish between fact and opinion
ASSESS CONCLUSIONS CONSEQUENCES	Considers context, assumptions and evidence. Ideas are qualifies. Considers ambiguities	Considers context, assumptions and evidence. Ideas are qualifies. Considers ambiguities	Conclusions consider evidence. Present implications that may impact other people.	Conclusions consider evidence. Present implications that may impact other people.	Fails to identify conclusions. Conclusions are absolute and from an external source.	Fails to identify conclusions. Conclusions are absolute and from an external source.
USES OTHER PERSPECTIVES	Addresses divers perspectives to inform analysis. Justifies own view while respecting views of others	Addresses divers perspectives to inform analysis. Justifies own view while respecting views of others	Integrates multiple viewpoints in a limited way. Some evidence of self assessment	Integrates multiple viewpoints in a limited way. Some evidence of self assessment	Presents single perspective. Fails to recognize other perspectives	Presents single perspective. Fails to recognize other perspectives

APPENDIX B
DESIGN THINKING SCORING RUBRIC

LEVEL	EXCEEDS EXPECTATIONS	STRONG	EFFECTIVE	DEVELOPING	EMERGING	NEEDS IMPROVEMENT
SCORE	6	5	4	3	2	1
AMBIGUITY	Comfortable when things are unclear	Comfortable when things are unclear	Limited comfort when things are unclear	Limited comfort when things are unclear	Uncomfortable when things are unclear	Uncomfortable when things are unclear
EMPATHY AND HUMAN VALUES	Sees and understands others point of view. Focuses on user needs	Sees and understands others point of view. Focuses on user needs	Has limited understanding of other points of view	Has limited understanding of other points of view	Sees only own point of view	Sees only own point of view
COLLABORATIVE	Collaborates effectively with people from other disciplines with different backgrounds and viewpoints	Collaborates effectively with people from other disciplines with different backgrounds and viewpoints	Collaborates with people from other disciplines with different backgrounds and viewpoints in a limited way	Collaborates with people from other disciplines with different backgrounds and viewpoints in a limited way	Cannot collaborate with other. Sees only own point of view.	Cannot collaborate with other. Sees only own point of view.
CURIOUS	Is interested in things that are not understood and seeing things with fresh eyes.	Is interested in things that are not understood and seeing things with fresh eyes.	Shows limited interest in things that are not understood and seeing things with fresh eyes.	Shows limited interest in things that are not understood and seeing things with fresh eyes.	Is not interested in things that are not understood and seeing things with fresh eyes.	Is not interested in things that are not understood and seeing things with fresh eyes.
HOLISTIC	Balances perspectives of business, human values, the environment and technology	Balances perspectives of business, human values, the environment and technology	Considers the perspectives of business, human values, the environment and technology in a limited way	Considers the perspectives of business, human values, the environment and technology in a limited way	Does not consider the bigger context focusses on only one aspect such as business profitability	Does not consider the bigger context focusses on only one aspect such as business profitability
NON JUDGMENTAL	Crafts ideas with no judgement of the idea or idea creator	Crafts ideas with no judgement of the idea or idea creator	Some judgement of ideas and other idea creators	Some judgement of ideas and other idea creators	Extensive judgement of ideas and other idea creators	Extensive judgement of ideas and other idea creators
OPEN MINDSET	Is able to tackle problems regardless of industry or scope. Out of the box thinker	Is able to tackle problems regardless of industry or scope. Out of the box thinker	Can address problems over a number of industries and a limited range of scope	Can address problems over a number of industries and a limited range of scope	Can only address problems in a single industry of limited scope	Can only address problems in a single industry of limited scope
BIAS TOWARD ACTION	Creates prototypes and physical embodiments of ideas and actions that effectively move project forward	Creates prototypes and physical embodiments of ideas and actions that effectively move project forward	Creates some prototypes and progress but in a limited way	Creates some prototypes and progress but in a limited way	Talks about ideas but does not create physical prototypes or move project forward through actions	Talks about ideas but does not create physical prototypes or move project forward through actions
EXPERIMENTAL	Embraces experiment as an integral part of work	Embraces experiment as an integral part of work	Experiments in a limited way	Experiments in a limited way	Does not experiment	Does not experiment
COMPLEXITY	Creates clarity from complexity	Creates clarity from complexity	Limited ability to address complex problems	Limited ability to address complex problems	Cannot address complex problems	Cannot address complex problems
PROCESS	Is mindful of process	Is mindful of process	Follows process in a limited way	Follows process in a limited way	Has no process	Has no process
SHOSHIN	An attitude of openness, eagerness, and lack of preconceptions even when at an advanced level.	An attitude of openness, eagerness, and lack of preconceptions even when at an advanced level.	Some openness, and eagerness. Some preconceptions	Some openness, and eagerness. Some preconceptions	Lack of openness, and eagerness. Many preconceptions	Lack of openness, and eagerness. Many preconceptions
ITERATIVE	Makes improvements with prototyping feedback loops and cycles regardless of design phase	Makes improvements with prototyping feedback loops and cycles regardless of design phase	Limited ability to refine or improve ideas through iterative user feedback and prototyping	Limited ability to refine or improve ideas through iterative user feedback and prototyping	No ability to refine or improve ideas through iterative user feedback and prototyping	No ability to refine or improve ideas through iterative user feedback and prototyping